# CHAOTIC COGNITION
## Principles and Applications

This

C

# CHAOTIC COGNITION
## Principles and Applications

Ronald A. Finke
*Texas A&M University*

Jonathan Bettle
*Southwest Texas State University*

**LEA** LAWRENCE ERLBAUM ASSOCIATES, PUBLISHERS
1996    Mahwah, New Jersey

Lawrence Erlbaum Associates, Inc., Publishers
10 Industrial Avenue
Mahwah, New Jersey 07430

Cover designed by Gail Silverman

Library of Congress Cataloging-in-Publication Data

Finke, Ronald A.
Chaotic Cognition : principles and applications / Ronald A. Finke and Jonathan Bettle.
p. cm.
Includes bibliographical references and indexes.
ISBN 0-8058-1739-5.—ISBN 0-8058-1740-9 (pbk.)
1. Cognitive styles. 2. Thought and thinking. 3. Human information processing. I. Bettle, Jonathan. II. Title.
BF311.F474 1996
153.4—dc20
95-41907
CIP

Books published by Lawrence Erlbaum Associates are printed on acid-free paper, and their bindings are chosen for strength and durability.

Printed in the United States of America
10 9 8 7 6 5 4 3 2

# Contents

# Preface

This book was originally conceived as a result of many spirited discussions between the two authors, one of whom is a cognitive scientist and ordered thinker, and the other a counselor and chaotic thinker. From the outset, it was obvious that we had markedly different views on human nature and life in general. Arguments for the importance of organizing and structuring one's life, planning for the future, and expressing ideas simply and directly were met with equally compelling, chaotic arguments for the importance of allowing structures to emerge naturally, living for the moment, and expressing ideas metaphorically.

Gradually, however, each of us began to move toward the other's perspective and to see the virtues of the other's thinking style. It was not that ordered thinking was inherently better or worse than chaotic thinking, but that both styles had their strengths and weaknesses. We also realized that both types of thinkers could benefit by learning about the other style. Ordered thinkers, for example, could make their plans less rigid by becoming more aware of immediate conditions and exigencies. Chaotic thinkers could temper their impulsiveness by thinking more about the consequences of their actions. Ideally, ordered and chaotic thinkers could mutually benefit one another.

Once we had explored the contrasting features of our own thinking styles, we began to notice similar contrasts in others. Although they might vary in extremes, most people could be seen as being predominantly ordered or chaotic in the way they conducted their lives. We also noticed that these same two styles were often depicted in novels and movies, with ordered and chaotic thinkers frequently misunderstanding one another. Eventually, we realized that one could make a general distinction between ordered and chaotic approaches to many things, such as generating ideas, developing relationships, managing employees, and running governments. It thus became apparent that this was a broad, general distinction that could be applied throughout modern society.

We also noted how the differences in our thinking styles reflected differences in our backgrounds. The ordered-thinking author had worked for many years in pursuit of career goals and carefully structured writing projects, and he identified with other ordered thinkers. The chaotic-thinking author had concentrated on personal goals, enjoyed improvising creative solutions in response to the needs of the moment, and identified with other chaotic thinkers.

This book is intended for both ordered and chaotic thinkers, with the hope that it will encourage greater harmony and understanding between the two types. Ordered thinkers could become more aware of the value of chaotic thinking and learn to accept chaos in their lives rather than fight against it. Chaotic thinkers could begin to see the value of their special talents in dealing with chaotic situations and the contributions they can make to society. The book will also help to demystify chaotic thinking for many ordered thinkers, who have tended to regard it as something deviant, undesirable, or even threatening.

One of the reasons we felt it was important to articulate the principles and benefits of chaotic thinking is that modern society has become excessively ordered and structured, with the result that chaotic thinkers have become increasingly undervalued and underappreciated. They are commonly regarded as being lazy or scatterbrained, or a burden to society. This reflects a widespread misunderstanding of the true nature of chaotic thinking. A second reason for wanting to produce this book is that chaotic thinkers themselves are often not strongly motivated to write down their ideas or methods.

We therefore felt that it was time for chaotic thinking to be reevaluated. This is not only because it has often been neglected and misunderstood, but also because of the recent interest in applying formal chaos theory to many fields, including psychology and human cognition. Given that the importance of chaotic processes is now being recognized, it seemed that the value of chaotic thinking could now be better appreciated.

We should emphasize that this is not a traditional scientific book, in that it is not based on an explicit set of empirical research studies or the development of formal models. Rather, the book attempts to open up an entirely new field of inquiry, by taking a chaotic approach. The general principles and techniques of chaotic thinking emerge by combining insights from traditional areas within psychology and related fields with those gained from observation and everyday examples.

This departs from the usual practice of restricting an investigation to a specific set of methods and analyses. It is hard to capture the essence of chaotic thinking using only standard, empirical approaches, because that essence is multifaceted and touches on many things. To try to examine each piece of chaotic thinking in isolation is to miss its whole point. By its very nature, chaotic thinking is a Gestalt process, requiring that one examine its workings and manifestations within a much broader context.

Many readers, particularly those who are ordered thinkers, may find parts of this book unconventional or even disturbing. This reaction probably reflects a general unfamiliarity and discomfort with the chaotic thinker's perspective, which may seem foreign, unnatural, or excessively frivolous. This is especially true if chaotic thinking is seen within a narrow context or from a single point of view. We therefore recommend that one consider the entire spectrum of ideas presented in this book before attempting to evaluate the concepts or apply the methods of chaotic thinking.

The notion of chaotic thinking is not new, and previous approaches have touched on many of its important features. Our intention is to seek a more explicit expression of the basic principles of chaotic thinking, and how they can best be applied. We begin by examining the major characteristics and benefits of chaotic thinking. This is followed by a description of various practical techniques that can be used to deal with many types of chaotic situations. We then discuss some important limitations of chaotic thinking, and consider some implications of bringing the two types of thinking closer together.

Specifically, in chapter 2, we describe the major characteristics of chaotic thinking, identifying its reactive, adaptive, impulsive, and metaphorical qualities, and its tendency to increase complexity, eschew pride, and allow structures to emerge naturally. In chapter 3, we describe the primary benefits of chaotic thinking, including its usefulness in assisting survival, enhancing creativity, encouraging irrational people to behave rationally, revealing the true intentions of others, creating favorable illusions, and helping to unravel mysteries. Chapter 4 introduces the basic techniques that chaotic thinkers typically employ, such as utilizing natural events, avoiding repetition, increasing purposeful clutter, making rapid decisions, and creating useful symbolism.

The next three chapters describe specific applications of these techniques in various contexts. In chapter 5, we discuss chaotic strategies for playing games, solving problems, marketing new products, conducting legal battles and political campaigns, and dealing effectively with pranks and other forms of harassment. Chapter 6 considers the uses of chaotic thinking in various types of interpersonal situations, such as how to avoid overstructuring relationships, how to improve communication, how to deal with irresponsible or irrational people, how to interact effectively with children, and how to apply chaotic techniques in therapeutic contexts. Chapter 7 concentrates on survival applications, such as how to deal with emergency situations, how to survive hard economic times, how to deal with career and marital changes, how to survive dangerous encounters or being confined, and how to survive psychological attacks.

The final three chapters address more general issues. Chapter 8 considers some of the limitations of chaotic thinking, putting these various principles and techniques into perspective. In spite of its many advantages, chaotic thinking can sometimes create problems, especially when it becomes excessively impulsive, inconsistent, or fatalistic. Chapter 9 considers how ordered and chaotic thinking might assist one another, while emphasizing the key point that one style is not necessarily better or worse than the other. Rather, by incorporating elements from the opposite style, one is often better equipped to use one's own natural strengths. There are, however, some potential risks in combining the two styles, and these are also discussed. In chapter 10, we consider the potential role that chaotic thinking could play in predominantly ordered institutions such as science, business, government, and education, as well as some of its implications for cognitive science, personality theory, and traditional sex roles.

Many of the ideas we propose in this book might be regarded as speculative, for as we have said, they are not based on direct, empirical research. Our hope, however, is that by calling attention to the contrasts between ordered and chaotic thinking, and by considering the many implications of these contrasts, we will lay a foundation for future, empirical studies on chaotic thinking.

## ACKNOWLEDGMENTS

The authors would like to express their appreciation to the following people for their helpful insights, suggestions, and support: Judi Amsel, Carol Bettle, John Bowerman, Judy Collins, Jennifer Freyd, Richard Held, Jerilyn Higa, Lorrie Irish, Joel Johnson, Marvin Levine, Donna McKeown, Chad Neff, Larry Parsons, Nancy Rosen, Jonathan Schooler, Jay Schumacher, Jeff Simpson, Steven Smith, Thomas Ward, Marie Wasson, and David Woehr.

# 1

## Introduction

*Chaotic cognition* refers to a way of thinking about and viewing the world that has become increasingly neglected in modern times. The primary assumption underlying chaotic thinking is that the world is essentially a chaotic, unpredictable place where things simply happen. From a chaotic perspective, there is little point in trying to impose structure, plan for the future, or exert control. Among the advantages of chaotic thinking is that it is often sensitive to immediate conditions and impending changes, and is effective in dealing with sudden, unexpected problems, especially those that arise in a crisis. It is in marked contrast to ordered thinking, which is based on the premise that the world is an ordered, predictable place where one can make long-range plans for the future and structure one's life in anticipation of future rewards.

The general theme of this book is that there are two opposing forces that exist in the physical world, those that promote order and structure, and those that promote disorder and chaos. To survive, living things must therefore adopt either an ordered strategy or a chaotic strategy. For most people, this choice is derived from how they perceive the world, whether they focus primarily on its ordered or chaotic aspects. This results in two general cognitive styles, ordered and chaotic thinking. The former has advantages when life is stable and predictable, whereas the latter has advantages when life becomes chaotic and the future becomes uncertain.

Ordered thinking has predominated throughout modern society. Most scientific fields, for example, have embraced the notion that new findings should follow predictably from highly structured theories (e.g., Popper, 1959; Van Doren, 1991). Our educational system is highly structured as well, and has been governed by the philosophy that learning needs to be scheduled (e.g., J. A. Johnson, 1994; Rich, 1981). In business and industry, hierarchical organizations and bureaucracies have flourished; these are seen as necessary structures for maintaining order and controlling progress (e.g., Bryans, 1984; University Associates, 1980). In psychology and counseling, formal models and therapeutic systems have attempted to provide new insights by imposing structure and predictability (e.g., Egan, 1986; Falwell, 1974). Even in sports and games, there has been a strong emphasis on developing specific plans and making detailed preparations (e.g., Fuoss & Troppmann, 1981).

Naturally, ordered thinking has many advantages. It provides a sense of continuity, not only in many professional fields, but also in one's personal and social life. It allows one to exert control over, and take pride in, one's accomplishments. It offers the comfort of believing that the future can always be anticipated. But it also has serious drawbacks, especially in times of rapid change, when things are no longer predictable and ordered structures can no longer be counted upon. At such times, one may be forced to abandon long-range plans and deal with the exigencies of the moment. This is when chaotic thinking is often most useful.

The term *chaotic* is somewhat pejorative; it might imply that a person is flaky or scatterbrained. However, this is not its intended meaning here. Far from being random or meaningless, chaotic thinking often leads to new and meaningful understandings that transcend traditional assumptions and conceptual boundaries. It encourages the natural emergence of order and structure in chaotic situations. It resembles the kind of thinking that often occurs in dreams, where one encounters unpredictable or seemingly bizarre events that can eventually lead to meaningful insights and discoveries. Chaotic thinking is symbolic, impulsive, and free-flowing, but it is also practical and highly adaptive.

Chaotic thinking also refers to more than just flexible or creative thinking; it reflects an entirely different way of viewing the world. Chaotic thinking is flexible, not by choice or intention, but because the world is seen as continually changing. It inspires creativity, not because one merely chooses to think of novel ideas, but because one embraces a situation, sees multiple perspectives on it, and rapidly infers their implications. Although ordered thinking can often display some flexibility over extended periods of time, chaotic thinking usually exhibits this flexibility spontaneously and over a much shorter time frame, to the extent that it might seem disconnected, incoherent, or even irrational.

The ideas behind chaotic cognition have been around for quite some time. They have shown up, for example, in various literary works that have depicted the chaotic lifestyle as rather wild and existing on the fringes of ordered society (e.g., Kerouac, 1957; H. S. Thompson, 1982; Wolfe, 1968). The spirit of chaotic thinking has also been expressed in the surrealist movement in art (e.g., Sandrow, 1972), and more recently, in the deconstruction movement in philosophy and literature (e.g., Lehman, 1991). Our intention is to clarify and distill many of these ideas, and to provide a more explicit delineation and analysis of the contrast between chaotic and ordered thinking.

There are three main goals of this book. The first is to provide a strong theoretical statement concerning the nature and significance of chaotic thinking. The second is to provide a social critique of the predominance of ordered thinking and the relative neglect of chaotic thinking in modern society. The third is to illustrate how the principles of chaotic thinking can be applied to a variety of contemporary issues and problems.

Our study of chaotic cognition draws on a diverse range of areas within psychology, such as human cognition, perception, personality theory, and counseling. It also touches on many fields outside psychology, including education, government, business, and sociology. We are thus treating chaotic thinking not as an isolated psychological topic, but as a more general topic with broad practical and sociological implications. In addition, although we consider many applied aspects of chaotic thinking, our primary concern is to analyze the differences between ordered and chaotic thinking and to explore how those differences might best be resolved.

This book also describes differences between ordered and chaotic thinkers. Chaotic thinkers are those who employ chaotic thinking as a way of life. They are typically reactive, impulsive, spontaneous, playful, metaphorical, fatalistic, and often brilliantly creative and innovative in response to unexpected or unusual problems. Ordered thinkers are those who generally rely on ordered thinking. They are typically proactive, controlled, deliberate, serious, literal, idealistic, and usually do better in structured and repetitive tasks. Whereas ordered thinkers often try to impose order on chaos in an effort to minimize it or remove it entirely, most chaotic thinkers regard chaos, uncertainty, and unpredictability as natural aspects of an inherently chaotic world.

Again, to say that one relies on chaotic thinking is not to imply that one's thinking is irrational or arbitrary. Rather, as we will attempt to show, chaotic thinking is a rational, coherent style of thinking that is ideally suited for responding to and dealing with a variety of unexpected, unpredictable, or undesirable situations. Contrary to popular misconceptions, chaotic thinkers are not typically illogical or irresponsible. They are simply employing a different style of thinking, which has its own set of strengths and weaknesses.

## CRISIS AND CHAOS

Whenever a crisis arises, most people find it difficult to react appropriately, especially if they have become accustomed to responding only in highly structured and organized ways. This can result in a wide range of problems, from major dilemmas in professional fields to everyday conflicts in human relations. Chaotic thinking can help to address these problems at many levels. For instance, consider the following examples, which depict different types of crisis situations in which chaotic thinking might be useful.

1. The wife of a business executive comes home one day and announces that she has felt stifled for years and is leaving her husband to pursue her own life. The husband is shocked. This was not part of the plan; up to that point, their relationship had always unfolded in just the way he had expected. His initial reaction is anger, but it is not anger directed at her. Rather, he is angry because the plan has come to an end, and he does not know how to deal with the emotional chaos and uncertainty that he must now confront. This is a common problem in ordered thinking, and results from the tendency to overplan for the future.

2. One day the president of a major corporation announces a plan to lay off several hundred workers so that the business can run more efficiently. The plan wreaks havoc on working relationships and personal agendas, and many of the remaining employees threaten to quit. In frustration, the president becomes more determined than ever to enforce the plan, and tells the workers, defiantly, "This is the way it's going to be, and you'll just have to get used it." Confrontation is a common byproduct of ordered thinking, and it often backfires. In chaotic thinking, nonconfrontational approaches are usually preferred, and often lead to more sensible and productive results.

3. The manager of a major-league baseball team has carefully prepared for a big game, and has determined the best strategy for defeating the opposing team. But suddenly his star pitcher strains his arm and has to leave the game. The shortstop makes a stupid error that further complicates the situation. The umpire makes a bad call. The manager is now in an frenzy, because the game did not go as planned. Much of this frustration could be avoided by using chaotic thinking, where these unexpected events could be seen as opportunities for improvising alternative strategies.

4. A group of medical researchers who have been working for many months to develop a new vaccine are suddenly taken by surprise when their latest test results are completely at odds with what they expected to find. Unable to make sense out of the results, they completely abandon the entire project and start over, believing that they have now reached a dead end. Because the results have also been abandoned, however, there is an unnecessary delay in the development of the vaccine. From the perspective of chaotic thinking, failure does not necessarily mean having to start over; it can also represent an opportunity to utilize the failure and possibly discover a new breakthrough.

People who think in ordered ways often have trouble adapting when such crises occur. When their plans suddenly go awry, when things do not work out as they expected, they often respond by doing inappropriate things. By employing chaotic thinking, one is better able to deal with these types of situations. This is because the essential nature of chaotic thinking encourages a person to avoid making or adhering to specific plans, to react to the needs of the moment, and to accept the complexity and unpredictability of life.

An additional virtue of chaotic thinking is that it can discourage people from always trying to structure the lives of others. For example, suppose you had to deal with someone who had a certain agenda in mind and was intent on imposing that agenda upon you, no matter what. This could be your boss trying to make you work on projects you hated, or your mother trying to tell you the type of person you should be dating. Using ordered thinking, one would normally try to confront the person directly, perhaps by providing rational arguments for why one should not have to work on hated projects, or why one's mother has no right to meddle in one's affairs. This usually encourages angry reactions, turns the situation into a contest of wills, and leads to further confrontation.

Most chaotic thinkers would try to avoid confronting the person directly in these situations. Instead, they would encourage chaos. They might create the impression of going along with the person's plans and intentions, but then complicate them in creative and unexpected ways. For example, they might agree to follow the mother's recommendations for dating a certain type of person, but then raise irrelevant issues that complicated matters, such as whether or not the date had exactly the right height, hair color, shoes, hobbies, or eating preferences. Eventually, the mother would be forced to modify or abandon her efforts to regulate the person's dating preferences, realizing the futility of those efforts.

## STRUCTURING TENDENCIES IN MODERN SOCIETY

As everyone knows, the world is becoming less and less predictable every day. Jobs are less secure, relationships are changing without warning, cherished principles and values are vanishing. As we have stated, chaotic thinking is ideally suited for dealing with these types of uncertainties and for finding creative ways to adapt when unexpected events occur. Ordered thinking, in contrast, is usually less effective in dealing with unexpected changes, and often makes the situation worse. Yet there continue to be strong biases in favor of ordered thinking in our society, and continued misunderstandings and misgivings about chaotic thinking.

As a rule, ordered thinking predominates in societies that have achieved major technological advances. Such advances encourage thinking that is highly structured, anticipatory, and future-oriented (Boyer, 1984; Mesthene, 1970). We are taught, for instance, that it is important to plan ahead, to pursue specialized careers, and to develop our lives along narrowly defined and clearly visible paths. We are then rewarded for these efforts. Chaotic thinking, which emphasizes living for the moment and avoiding long-range plans, is thus discouraged or suppressed.

This bias towards ordered thinking can be seen, for example, in the common tendency for parents to over-structure the lives of their children. Parents now schedule a seemingly endless array of activities for the child—Little League, soccer, football, gymnastics, Girl Scouts, Boy Scouts, orchestrated field trips, dance, ballet—and other organized events that completely fill in the day. It used to be that children could improvise a baseball game, picking teams and making up their own rules. Now it has to be formally sanctioned by an official league, with uniforms and trophies. Even our parks and playgrounds have become highly structured, with exercise programs and workout routines, as if having free, open space in which to play and to explore were no longer permitted.

This structuring process begins early. Many parents, for example, have become obsessed with having their children enrolled in the right preschool, believing that otherwise they will not get into the right college, which will then prevent them from having a successful career. This obsession with properly structuring a child's education almost inevitably causes problems. If the child is naturally a chaotic thinker, it will result in enormous frustration, and the child is likely to develop a negative self-image. If the child is naturally an ordered thinker, these structuring tendencies will be strongly reinforced, and the child will then become even more anxious and upset when chaotic situations arise.

Our colleges and universities have also contributed to this bias towards ordered thinking. Students are taught that mental discipline and planning are essential for later success in life. Their formal training consists largely of prearranged courses that are taken in a predetermined sequence. They are channeled towards finding particular types of jobs when they graduate. Many professors are now promoted largely on the basis of having a consistent rate of productivity over time, successfully attacking opposing points of view, and displaying a serious, professional work ethic. Scholars who display sporadic brilliance, who avoid developing formal theories, or who are generally unconcerned with achieving professional rank or status have a much harder time succeeding in modern university life. We discuss other implications of chaotic thinking for education in the final chapter.

Consider, also, how these structuring tendencies have affected the medical profession. Most modern hospitals have become highly ordered institutions that are poorly suited for dealing with the chaotic needs and emotional reactions of their patients. Physicians have grown detached, not only because they have become increasingly busy, but also because they have come to rely on their own preconceived plans and diagnoses, for which the patient's input is minimal (e.g., Cousins, 1979). Many hospitals and medical schools have begun to recognize this problem, and have initiated sensitivity training courses so that doctors can learn how to listen to their patients.

Even the study of the human mind itself has been strongly influenced by ordered thinking. In the field of cognitive psychology, for instance, the mind has often been regarded as a highly organized structure, consisting of executive controls, plans, and hierarchies (Anderson, 1983; Miller, Galanter, & Pribram, 1960; Neisser, 1967). More recent approaches, however, have begun to consider the role that chaotic processes might also play in human cognition (e.g., Abraham & Gilgen, 1995). This is seen, for example, in the advent of models proposing that the mind processes information using parallel, distributed processing units within complex, interactive networks (e.g., McClelland & Rumelhart, 1986). Additional implications of chaotic thinking for the study of human cognition will be considered in later chapters and at the end of the book.

In the cultural revolution of the 1960s, chaotic thinking enjoyed a temporary resurgence, despite fears that radicals would take over society. By the end of that decade, however, the movement had become more structured, and began to impose order onto its original chaotic qualities. This was unfortunate, because chaotic thinking is needed now more than ever. We are not, however, advocating that chaotic thinking replace ordered thinking, which was the spirit of the cultural revolution. Rather, our interest is in exploring how chaotic and ordered thinking can coexist in a mutually beneficial, interactive manner.

## THE FUTURE BECOMES THE PRESENT

The future used to be far ahead; now it comes to us immediately. We are experiencing what Toeffler (1970) called "future shock" in almost every aspect of modern life. People who rely on ordered thinking would generally prefer to keep the future well out in front, so that they could anticipate it and make it conform with their plans. When the future is suddenly thrust upon them, however, and they discover that their plans are falling apart, they are often devastated.

The future has begun to merge with the present, due in part to the information age. Television has provided us with an essentially chaotic medium, in which we receive instant news and experience instant reactions. If we hear about the possibility of a milk shortage, the next day milk prices have already increased. There may be no actual shortage, but just the news that cows are dying causes the price of milk to go up. If we learn that a riot has broken out in some far-away place, we might immediately begin to worry about it. In the past, by the time news about the riot had arrived, it would have already been quelled. Now, news that the riot is underway causes similar riots to spring up in other places almost instantaneously.

We are now able to ponder the meaning of an event while the event is still occurring. Most people who depend on ordered thinking need time to anticipate what will happen next, and television has taken away that time. To plan for the future, they usually need to be shielded from it, at least temporarily, and the information age has made this difficult, at best. In contrast, when rapidly changing events are pushed into the present, it usually works to the advantage of chaotic thinking.

Chaotic thinkers are usually at their best under conditions that scientists call "bifurcation points," where reality is up for grabs and one cannot predict what will happen next (Gleick, 1987). A crisis situation is a common example, where future events can unfold along many unpredictable paths. In every crisis, there comes a point where the previous structures break down, the old plans no longer work, and almost anything can occur. In such situations chaotic thinkers are often able to seize the moment and provide the inspiration and guidance that puts the future back on track. Ordered thinkers, in contrast, are usually at their best when the crisis is over, and things are once again predictable.

## DISTINGUISHING ORDERED AND CHAOTIC THINKERS

Although we explore more fully the characteristics of ordered and chaotic thinkers in chapter 2, it will be helpful to provide some general criteria at this time for distinguishing the two types of thinkers. As a rule, ordered thinkers are highly structured in the way they approach most situations. They like to be in control, so that events will proceed in orderly and predictable ways. They generally avoid excessive stimulation, intensity, or complexity. They are often able to hold their impulses in check, not wanting to jeopardize their plans. They usually adopt a particular point of view, and like things to be direct and precise. They typically regard hard work and successful planning as essential human endeavors, and often take considerable pride in their accomplishments.

Most chaotic thinkers are drawn to intense and uncertain situations, where things can become delightfully complex and where the future can go in many possible directions. They rarely try to impose order or control situations, but prefer to let structures emerge from the totality of life's complexities. They are often passive, reactive, playful, and adaptable. They tend to act on their impulses, often without regard to the long-term consequences of doing so. They often prefer metaphorical, rather than direct expressions. They normally place personal needs above professional achievements, and often display a distinct lack of pride in what they might accomplish.

Another contrast between the two types of thinkers is that ordered thinkers usually act according to principle. Something is fair because a law or principle supports it. Most chaotic thinkers assess fairness according to the situation or circumstance. Street justice, not formal law, defines their ethics. For this reason most chaotic thinkers are less likely to be concerned with rules and regulations and generally respond as the situation demands. They are thus less likely to apply a general principle when it is inappropriate or unreasonable to do so, as in the case of the self-righteous citizen who stops every pedestrian on the street and lectures them on the evils of jaywalking.

Many of these contrasts are illustrated by the so-called "yuppie" versus "hippie" lifestyles. The former is characterized by dedication to one's career, having everything planned in advance, working towards the future, and putting life's rewards, including personal relationships, on a schedule. The latter is characterized by avoiding traditional careers, planning nothing very far in advance, living for the present, and taking advantage of opportunities when they arise. Whereas the hippie's activities are determined largely by situational factors, such as the day's events or the weather conditions, the yuppie's activities are internally controlled, and often proceed as planned in spite of unexpected changes in the weather or the current situation.

As another example, consider differences in driving habits that ordered and chaotic thinkers are likely to exhibit. Ordered thinkers usually plan their routes in advance, carefully record their gas mileage, and try to anticipate any mechanical problems that might arise. Most chaotic thinkers would seldom plan their routes, care little about their gas mileage, and add oil whenever the warning light comes on. They would rarely display the ordered thinker's preparedness or punctuality, yet they would usually be better at dealing with unexpected breakdowns or emergencies.

One can also point to a contrast between the writing styles of most ordered and chaotic thinkers. Ordered thinkers usually prefer to state their ideas directly, to get to the point of what they want to convey as logically and efficiently as possible. In this regard, they tend to do more telling than showing. Most chaotic thinkers prefer to be less direct and more metaphorical in their writing, to allow new insights and interpretations to emerge. They tend to do more showing than telling. Typically, ordered thinkers would first conceive of an idea and then craft sentences to express it. In fact, they would often make outlines and lists of topics before beginning to write. Chaotic thinkers would be more likely to allow their ideas to emerge from the very act of writing itself, implicitly assuming that important points would develop and change as the writing progressed (e.g., Elbow, 1981).

There are several helpful indicators when trying to decide whether a person is more likely to be an ordered, as opposed to a chaotic, thinker. The first is the determined adherence to a plan, even when it has become impractical or unrealistic. The second is pride. The third indicator is idealism, as opposed to fatalism. The fourth indicator is having a strong work ethic, rather than a play ethic. Fifth, the overall style of an ordered thinker tends to be proactive, rather than reactive. Finally, most chaotic thinkers tend to be easily approachable, whereas most ordered thinkers tend to be rather guarded when approached by someone, especially a perfect stranger.

For purposes of classification, we propose that a person can be considered as one type of thinker or the other if they exhibit most of the characteristics pertaining to that type. For instance, a person who is generally goal-directed, is concerned about the future, is well organized, takes work seriously, and avoids excessive stimulation is likely to be an ordered thinker. Someone who seems to lack long-term goals, is relatively unconcerned about the future, takes an unstructured approach to life, is seldom serious about work, and frequently seeks out stimulation is likely to be a chaotic thinker. As we emphasize in chapter 2, however, there are degrees to which a person might rely on ordered and chaotic thinking, and not every ordered or chaotic thinker will exhibit all of the proposed characteristics.

## CONTRASTING STYLES IN LITERATURE AND FILM

Contrasts between ordered and chaotic thinkers have often been depicted in novels, narratives, and films. Popular books that have described how chaotic thinkers attempt to survive in an ordered world include *On the Road, The Electric Kool-Aid Acid Test, Catcher in the Rye, Catch 22,* and *Fear and Loathing in Las Vegas.* Examples of books that have explored ordered thinking and its implications include *The Mosquito Coast, The Fountainhead, The Prisoner,* and classics such as *Les Miserables* and *Moby Dick.* In *Moby Dick,* for example, Captain Ahab's obsession with hunting down and destroying the white whale exemplifies the tendency in ordered thinking to try to fulfill one's plans at all costs. In *Les Miserables,* the hero steals bread to feed his children, and is pursued relentlessly by an official who insists that justice must be served. In the end, however, the official cannot bring himself to arrest the hero, and then commits suicide, having failed his own principles.

Some examples of popular movies that have depicted conflicts or misunderstandings between ordered and chaotic thinkers include *Shane, Cool Hand Luke, Rebel Without a Cause, Easy Rider, Lawrence of Arabia, My Fair Lady, Animal House, My Dinner With Andre,* and more recently, *Unforgiven, Tombstone, Forrest Gump, Pulp Fiction,* and *Reality Bites.* For instance, in *Cool Hand Luke,* after being complimented on the success of his brilliant escape plan, Luke replies, almost as a creed for chaotic thinkers, "I never planned anything in my life." The movie also contains one of the classic statements of ordered–chaotic conflicts: "What we have here is a failure to communicate!"

## NOTABLE ORDERED AND CHAOTIC THINKERS

The distinction between the two styles can be further illustrated by considering some differences between notable ordered and chaotic thinkers. Consider, first of all, the contrast between Freud and Jung. Freud was very likely an ordered thinker. His ideas were highly structured, and he felt that they should be the basis for all psychoanalysis. He saw the world as determined and predictable, and believed that future actions are largely governed by past events and conflicts (Babcock, 1988; Ellenberger, 1970). Jung, on the other hand, was very likely a chaotic thinker. His work was not unified in the sense that Freud's was; whereas Freud left behind an organized school of thought, Jung's work consisted largely of unstructured insights and metaphors (e.g., Brome, 1978; Jung, 1964). His concept of synchronicity was strongly chaotic—the notion that all things are connected in the moment, without causal antecedents. Whereas Freud believed that the world could be improved by applying certain methods and analyses, Jung believed that one should be concerned not with changing the world but with trying to understanding it. Whereas Freud's ideas were grounded in Western positivism, Jung's ideas were grounded in Eastern transcendentalism.

Consider Plato versus Socrates. Plato was very likely an ordered thinker. He expressed a strong idealism, his concepts were highly ordered, and he was very much concerned with writing down and preserving his ideas (e.g., McKirahan,

1978). Socrates, the founder of the dialectic approach, was very likely a chaotic thinker. He liked to question ideas, and encouraged new insights to emerge by exposing the limitations of accepted notions. Also, like most chaotic thinkers, he preferred conversation. Having to write down ideas is usually frustrating to chaotic thinkers, for their thoughts are constantly changing with the moment. It was thus left to Plato to record Socrates's insights. Moreover, Socrates did not attribute any importance to his death, which is characteristic of the fatalism of many chaotic thinkers.

A more recent example is Nixon versus Reagan. Nixon was almost certainly an ordered thinker. He had enormous pride in his accomplishments, and wanted full control over everything that happened in his administration. When his plans backfired, he tried to cover them up, as ordered thinkers will sometimes do. Reagan, on the other hand, was probably a chaotic thinker. He had little pride and much personal warmth, he usually took advantage of the moment, he adopted a hands-off approach to the presidency, and he adored conversation.

One can also distinguish between ordered and chaotic thinking in the works of noted writers. The writings of Kafka, for example, dealt with subject matter that was highly ordered and structured but with little meaning or essence, as in his descriptions of senseless bureaucracies that kept grinding the individual down (Kafka, 1937, 1954). In contrast, the writings of Joyce expressed meaning and essence, but with little order or structure, as represented by the "stream of consciousness" style, which flows on without organization or explicit points of reference (Joyce, 1939).

Or consider Dickens, the timeless novelist, versus Keats, the poet. Dickens viewed writing as a profession, a way of ensuring that he would never be poor. His novels were highly organized and structured. He often marketed them by selling them to magazines as serials. Keats regarded his works as momentary, having little significance over time. His epitaph, "Here lies one whose name was writ in water," are the classic words of a chaotic thinker.

A more contemporary example is Stephen King versus Ken Kesey. King has turned out profitable books on a regular basis, year after year, whereas Kesey has written books sporadically and mainly as a form of expression, as opposed to a regular source of income. Whereas Kesey's style is largely metaphorical, King's style is more direct and literal. King will do commercials to promote his books or a product; Kesey would never do this, except perhaps as a joke.

One could include many other contrasts between notable people who are likely to have been chaotic thinkers, such as Hannibal, Joan of Arc, Lawrence of Arabia, Alexander Graham Bell, Charles Lindbergh, Will Rogers, and Marshal McLuhan, and those who are likely to have been ordered thinkers, such as Julius Caesar, Alexander the Great, Rene Descartes, John Stuart Mill, Richard Wagner, Joseph Stalin, and George Patton. In drawing these contrasts, however, it should be emphasized that these represent opposite ends of the spectrum, and that most people will fall somewhere in between. In general, there will be some ordered tendencies in most chaotic thinkers and some chaotic tendencies in most ordered thinkers.

It is not always easy to identify ordered and chaotic thinkers, because each can exhibit certain mannerisms that mask their natural thinking style. For instance, ordered thinkers who are highly extraverted and who display an enormous amount of pride may appear to be chaotic. A good example is Custer—a man whose ostentatious mannerisms might lead one to think that he was a wildly chaotic thinker, yet he exhibited most of the major characteristics of ordered thinking. He carefully planned his attacks, and remained committed to those attacks even when they became unnecessary. He thrived on victory, glory, and ego gratification (e.g., Monaghan, 1959). Had he existed in modern times, he might have become a yuppie who wore defiant clothing and pursued an exuberant lifestyle. We will have more to say about Custer later in the chapter.

Another example is Beethoven, who exhibited personal habits of the most chaotic sort. His rooms were in amazing disarray, with clothing and manuscripts mixed together and scattered about, food and wine spilled here and there. Then there were his remarkable mood swings—euphoric one minute, outraged or depressed the next; one moment singing in the streets, the next, screaming at his servants. And yet Beethoven was almost certainly an ordered thinker. The structured nature of his music, the long-range plans for composition, the preoccupation with success and recognition, the romantic idealism, the commitment to principles and justice—not to mention one of the grandest egos in the history of mankind—all indicate that he was an ordered thinker, rather than a chaotic thinker (e.g., Forbes, 1967).

On the other hand, chaotic thinkers who are soft-mannered and introverted may appear to be ordered thinkers. Einstein, for example, was probably a chaotic thinker, despite his structured habits. His thinking was playful, he enjoyed exploring multiple realities, and he was unconcerned with professional competition or personal glory (Clark, 1971; Frank, 1947; French, 1979). In fact, Einstein seemed to have had little pride whatsoever.

In distinguishing ordered and chaotic thinkers, it is therefore important to separate thinking style from personal habits. An ordered thinker can have seemingly chaotic mannerisms, and a chaotic thinker can have seemingly ordered mannerisms. A lack of concern for neatness or social graces may simply result from an overwhelming commitment to perfecting the structure of a plan or an idea. Similarly, regular habits and routines can belie the impulsive, chaotic nature of one's thinking.

## MISUNDERSTANDING THE OPPOSITE STYLE

Not surprisingly, ordered and chaotic thinkers often misunderstand one another, and each can seem irrational from the other's perspective. Ordered thinkers sometimes accuse chaotic thinkers of being undisciplined, unreliable, frivolous, unstable, and disorganized. They might regard the rapid shifts in chaotic thinking as a sign that the person has a wavering, capricious disposition. Chaotic thinkers will sometimes accuse ordered thinkers of being rigid, authoritarian, uncaring, negative, and detached. They might regard an ordered thinker's resistance to change as a sign that the person has lost touch with reality. But neither style of thinking is inherently more rational or superior than the other. Both have their advantages and disadvantages, their strengths and weaknesses.

From their point of view, most chaotic thinkers do not see themselves as actually creating chaos. Rather, they are merely reacting to an inherently chaotic world. Ordered thinkers, however, often see them as creating chaos and disrupting the natural order of things. They sometimes perceive chaotic thinkers as threatening and accuse them of subverting the ordered way. To most ordered thinkers, their own way of thinking has a certain purity; their plans are beautifully organized and deeply satisfying. But because chaotic thinkers usually try to see things in a multiplicity of ways, they are frequently adding new and unexpected complications. As a result, ordered thinkers might begin to feel that their plans are no longer pure and unified, and they might come to think that chaotic thinkers are just ruining their world.

When this happens, ordered thinkers may go on the warpath, trying to rid their lives of any chaos whatsoever. They might begin imposing order and structure with even greater determination, in an effort to shield themselves. The president of a company, for example, might begin eliminating all chaotic thinkers from the organization. A husband or wife might begin structuring his or her marriage so rigidly that no distractions or uncertainties are permitted. These efforts to remove or suppress chaotic thinking are almost always self-destructive.

And yet, ordered thinkers are sometimes fascinated by chaotic thinking and can become irresistibly drawn to it. There are at least three reasons why this attraction occurs. First, they are often surprised to discover that there are multiple perspectives on an issue or problem, having been accustomed to seeing things in only one way. Second, they are often intrigued by the sensitivity of chaotic thinkers to personal needs and feelings. Third, they are often struck by the spontaneity and creativity of chaotic thinkers. Ordered thinkers might have one idea that they focus on and develop for many years; chaotic thinkers can have twenty new ideas in the course of a single conversation. But although these features might start out being very attractive, they can also become increasingly irritating as time progresses, and might eventually be seen as distracting and inconsequential. This can lead ordered thinkers to conclude that chaotic thinkers, though interesting and creative, are simply not great achievers, which is often their bottom-line judgment.

## THE MAJOR DISADVANTAGE OF ORDERED THINKING

In this section, we examine in more detail the main disadvantage of ordered thinking, which is that it often leads to an overreliance on preconceived plans.

Suppose, for example, that a football team was about to play against a vastly superior opponent, and had little chance of winning. A coach who was an ordered thinker might develop a game plan that represented the most logical strategy for directly countering the opponent's strengths, and then stick to that plan throughout the game. This strategy would almost certainly fail.

Instead of developing and relying on such plans, a chaotic coach might simply try to create unexpected complications for the opposing team. The players might be told to try to make the game as confusing as possible, and take advantage of any momentary opportunities that this confusion created. From a chaotic perspective, this would offer the best chance for success against a superior opponent, especially if the opponent was relying on a careful, well-planned strategy.

Ordered thinkers often make the mistake of imposing their plans or strategies prematurely, and not taking into account the current situation. A football coach who is committed to a game plan and sticks to it, no matter what, invites defeat if the game does not progress as expected or if the information on which the plans were based was incorrect. For example, thinking that the opposing team will rely on a passing game might be based on erroneous scouting reports or incomplete knowledge about the health of the quarterback. These problems can often be avoided in ordered thinking by not relying too heavily on preconceived plans or expectations.

A common situation in which ordered thinkers might over-plan for something is when they prepare to go out on a date. They will often imagine how the date is supposed to unfold, and decide exactly what they will do and in what sequence. This takes away from the spontaneity of the date. It also leads to fear and apprehension, as one begins to imagine ways in which the date might not succeed as planned. An ordered thinker might make plans to go dancing, but upon finding out that the person is on crutches, might not escape the feeling that the date is now ruined. A chaotic response would simply be to accept the situation as it is and then to try to find some other, more appropriate activity.

When a blunder occurs, ordered thinkers will often try to repair the plan, which then carries the blunder into the future. This encourages later denials and rationalizations. As a result, ordered thinkers tend to learn the wrong lessons from their mistakes, such as "Don't get caught." From the perspective of chaotic thinking, once an error occurs, it belongs in the past, and is no longer important. This frees one to move on.

There is also a tendency for many ordered thinkers to regard their plans as perfect creations, and thus to try to get others to appreciate and believe in them. Yet they often resist having people get too close to their plans, for fear that the plans might then be contaminated or disrupted. It is like building a beautiful tower that you want people to enter and appreciate, but then keeping the people away because you do not want the tower to be messed up. This can result in a person's plans becoming shielded from healthy scrutiny and feedback.

This particular limitation of ordered thinking has been depicted in several popular novels. For instance, in *The Fountainhead,* Rand (1968) describes an architect who designs a building, but his ideas are stolen and are then modified by others. The building is then constructed using the modified plans, and he blows it up. Because his ideas have been altered, and therefore contaminated, he feels that he must now destroy them.

Another example comes from Theroux's *The Mosquito Coast* (1982), in which the main character takes his family from New England to South America, where they settle on a jungle island. In the middle of the jungle, he builds a gigantic icehouse, and gives out blocks of ice to the natives. He thinks this icehouse is a truly great achievement, even though the natives do not really need the ice. Having become so caught up in the pride of his accomplishment, he does not realize its folly or see what it has done to his family.

Ordered thinkers are often seemingly prepared for catastrophes, but only until they actually strike. Having made extensive plans to deal with a catastrophe, they often mislead themselves into believing that they have anticipated all possible consequences of it. As a result, they can have trouble handling unexpected developments and complications. In particular, they often cannot deal effectively with the emotional consequences of catastrophes, which are almost always spontaneous and unpredictable.

Similarly, in their personal relationships, ordered thinkers will often try to plan ahead to anticipate possible problems. They might sign prenuptial agreements, talk with their attorneys, or make financial plans, but they are usually unprepared for the chaotic complexities and emotional traumas of actual breakups. In fact, they might even avoid emotional involvements for just this reason, especially if they have previously had a traumatic experience.

Of course, it is important to anticipate at least some of the consequences of future events, and this is what most ordered thinkers are usually very good at. Indeed, they are often capable of preparing impressive and detailed contingency plans for handling almost any situation. Yet these preparations often create the illusion that one will be protected from any and all consequences. This can blind one to real dangers that suddenly arise.

As these examples illustrate, a major drawback of ordered thinking is that it often leads one to adhere to plans and their expected rewards regardless of what is happening in the moment. In extreme cases, ordered thinkers might go jogging in the middle of a blizzard because the plan to go jogging has already been made, or become furious in a restaurant if they cannot order their favorite dessert. This tendency to push a plan to its limits can create serious problems, but these problems can often be avoided by employing the principles of chaotic thinking.

## THE NEED FOR BOTH STYLES

We emphasize that, in considering the disadvantages of ordered thinking, we do not mean to imply that it should be abandoned or replaced by chaotic thinking. Even though much of this book is devoted to describing the less-familiar chaotic style, and calling attention to its virtues, both styles are needed, and each can benefit the other.

As we try to show, both ordered and chaotic thinking play important roles in modern society. One cannot simply rely on plans for the distant future, nor can one simply ignore the future and live for the moment. Ordered and chaotic thinking need to coexist and work cooperatively; both structure and adaptability have their place.

As a general rule, if ordered thinkers do not accept change, change will eventually be forced upon them. An example would be a corporate executive who refuses to adapt to changes in the market, and who then faces bankruptcy. On the other hand, if chaotic thinkers do not accept order, then order will eventually be forced upon them. An example would be a free spirit who runs afoul of the law, having never learned to temper his or her impulses, and who then ends up in prison, where order is provided by the system. Denying chaos completely promotes self-destruction through excessive idealism, whereas denying order completely promotes self-destruction through excessive impulsiveness.

Relying entirely upon one style of thinking, to the exclusion of the other, eventually leads one to feel that something is missing. Recall the earlier example of the yuppie versus the hippie. At first, hippies are often denigrated by yuppies for their unconditional niceness and warmth, whereas yuppies are often denigrated by hippies for their rigid idealism and preoccupation with the future. Yet sooner or later each begins to wonder about the other style. At some point, the yuppie yearns to be free, to escape all of the structure and planning, whereas the hippie laments the absence of order and accomplishment. Over time, each is drawn more and more to the qualities of the other.

Although we argue that it is important to learn about and eventually experience both styles of thinking, there are certain risks in doing so, which we address in chapter 9. For instance, ordered thinkers might be corrupted by the freedom and impulsiveness exemplified by chaotic thinkers, whereas chaotic thinkers might be corrupted by the ambition and drive exemplified by ordered thinkers. Nevertheless, we believe that the many advantages of bringing the two styles together usually outweigh such risks.

## RELATION TO FORMAL CHAOS THEORY

Although there has been considerable interest in extending the mathematical formalism of chaos theory to psychology and social problems (e.g., McCown, Johnson, & Shure, in press; Prigogine & Stengers, 1984), we do not adopt a formal, mathematical approach to chaotic cognition in this book. The primary reason is that it is not clear that such formalisms could be directly transferred into psychological insights about chaotic thinking. For example, there are many characteristics of chaotic thinking that would not be captured merely through a scientific analysis of chaotic processes. For this reason, we prefer a comparative analysis of chaotic and ordered thinking that is based on broader cognitive and psychological perspectives.

Chaotic cognition is therefore only tangentially related to "chaos" in the scientific sense, which has been the subject of many recent, popular books (e.g., Gleick, 1987; Lewin, 1992; Waldrop, 1992). These books have called attention, for example, to the emergence of unpredictable structures in various chaotic situations, such as in weather patterns, chemical reactions, and certain mathematical processes. Although emergent structure is an important feature of chaotic thinking, our primary interest is in exploring what is essentially a cognitive style, rather than the scientific or formal aspects of chaotic processes themselves.

## RELATION TO OTHER APPROACHES

Chaotic thinking is related in certain respects to Eastern thinking, right-hemisphere thinking, Gestalt thinking, and divergent thinking, all of which have become popular terms in the creativity and psychological literature. None of these concepts, however, fully capture the essence of chaotic thinking and its relation to contemporary issues and problems. For example, many books have drawn a contrast between Eastern and Western philosophies and have touched upon some of the distinctions we make in this book (e.g., Pirsig, 1974), but they do not explain how the ordered and chaotic aspects of these philosophies affect human cognition in general, nor do they discuss their practical implications. Our intention is to provide both a detailed, comparative analysis of ordered and chaotic thinking and a practical discussion of the specific ways in which chaotic thinking can be applied.

Eastern thinking is related to chaotic thinking in that it emphasizes the importance of letting go of goals and ambition, of focusing on the present rather than the future, of considering a multiplicity of viewpoints, of accepting the world as it is, and of achieving harmony with nature rather than dominance over it. Like chaotic thinking, Eastern thinking is reactive and encourages the passive integration of knowledge (e.g., Bolen, 1979). Yet someone who reads a manual on Eastern philosophy would have a difficult time seeing how these concepts relate to surviving in specific, chaotic situations. We are thus concerned with making the principles of chaotic thinking more explicit and more directly connected to modern issues and problems.

Right-hemisphere thinking emphasizes global thought processes that take into account many possibilities at once, and that facilitate the rapid detection of complex relations (e.g., Edwards, 1986; Springer & Deutsch, 1981). These are both important characteristics of chaotic thinking. There is also a strong integrative quality to chaotic thinking, which is related to the basic principles of Gestalt psychology (e.g., Kohler, 1947; Perls, 1969). In trying to understand the world, chaotic thinkers usually try to see things from many different perspectives, and then attempt to discover how those perspectives are connected.

Divergent thinking emphasizes the exploration of unusual or remote associations among ideas, which promotes novel insights (e.g., Guilford, 1968; McLeod & Cropley, 1989). This relates to the spontaneity, interconnectedness, and creativity of chaotic thinking. Chaotic thinkers are often adept at intensifying the moment and exploring multiple connections to every thought, which enables them to raise a surprising number of alternative possibilities and considerations.

Chaotic thinkers are naturally drawn to books on Eastern philosophy, Gestalt psychology, right-hemisphere thinking, and divergent thinking, because they identify with many aspects of these approaches. None of these approaches, however, provide both the scope and analytical depth that we are attempting in this book. In addition, our distinction between ordered and chaotic thinking reflects an important cultural split in modern society. There is the very real danger that chaotic thinking will continue to be misunderstood and neglected, at a time when it is needed more than ever.

Several popular books on personality types have described contrasting styles that resemble our distinction between ordered and chaotic thinking. For example, Jung (1971) proposed general personality types based on the dimensions of introversion–extraversion, intuition–sensation, thinking–feeling, and judging–perceiving, which have led to the development of formal personality scales such as the Myers–Briggs Inventory (Keirsey & Bates, 1984; Myers, 1962). These dimensions are related to ordered and chaotic thinking in that ordered thinkers tend to be more idealistic, impersonal, and judgmental, whereas chaotic thinkers tend to be more pragmatic, sensitive, and perceptive. However, such characterizations are sometimes misleading. As discussed previously, it is important to distinguish one's thinking style from one's personal qualities and habits.

Other books have drawn distinctions between time-dependent people and those who live in the moment (Malone, 1977), between territorial people and those who have open boundaries (Malone, 1977), and between idealistic, principled people and those who are fatalistic and empirical (James, 1907). These distinctions also touch upon contrasting aspects of ordered and chaotic thinking. Most ordered thinkers focus on the past or future, develop strong plans, and commit themselves to ideals and principles. Most chaotic thinkers live for the moment, adopt a fatalistic approach to life, and generally avoid commitments to principles or ideals. In chapter 10, we consider other implications of ordered and chaotic thinking for personality types and cognitive styles.

We should also mention that there are many "self-help" books that provide practical techniques for how to deal with specific crisis situations, and which bear on some of the applied aspects of chaotic thinking that we consider. However, these books seldom provide an extensive analysis of why the techniques work, or a theoretical perspective that allows the techniques to be extended to a wide range of chaotic situations. Our interest is in developing very broad applications of the principles of chaotic thinking, while at the same time providing a general, theoretical foundation for these principles.

## ARGUMENTS FOR THE PROPOSED DICHOTOMY

In view of the many different thinking styles and personality types that have been proposed, we wish to anticipate the criticism that our distinction between ordered and chaotic thinking is too simplistic. After all, the human mind is remarkably complex, and there are an enormous number of ways in which individual thinking patterns might differ. It might seem, therefore, that we are oversimplifying matters by dividing people into ordered and chaotic thinkers. We offer several responses to this criticism.

First, in proposing these two general categories, we acknowledge that there are no doubt many other useful distinctions among people or styles of thinking that could be made. For example, one could subdivide ordered and chaotic thinkers into additional categories in an effort to better capture the various ways in which these thinking styles might be expressed. But it is not our intention to provide a complete description of all possible individual variations in these styles. Rather, we prefer to focus on the general distinctions and their implications.

Second, even general categorical distinctions can often lead to complex analyses and useful insights. For example, consider plants versus animals. This is a broad distinction, yet it results in many useful comparisons. By thinking in general terms of plants and animals, one can explore the many common characteristics that the members of each group share, as well as important differences between the groups, without having to distinguish among every possible type of plant or animal. Similarly, our purpose in distinguishing ordered and chaotic thinking is to explore their general characteristics, and not to try to delineate everyone's thinking style to the nth degree. Nor are we claiming that this particular distinction is the only useful way to divide up the world.

Third, we feel there is a danger in overstratifying people through the use of multiple categories, personality types, or cognitive styles. For example, multiple-trait theories often fail to take into account the interaction between certain traits and the effects of situational context (Mischel, 1986). In this book, we explicitly consider how ordered and chaotic thinking are manifested across many different types of situations.

One can also raise the issue of whether our proposed dichotomy reflects the way people actually do think and interact, or is merely an arbitrary distinction. We propose that the various contrasts and examples presented throughout this book touch upon things that most readers have already experienced in many real-life situations. They are thus likely to see themselves or people they know as belonging more to one style of thinking or the other. Our distinction between ordered and chaotic thinking is not merely something we invented; it already existed in nature. We are simply putting a name to it.

As a final point, in making a general distinction between these contrasting styles, we do not mean to imply that they are mutually exclusive. Nearly everyone will exhibit some characteristics of both ordered and chaotic thinking. Also, sometimes a person will appear to have mastered both styles, and can employ either one as the situation demands. We believe, however, that most people prefer to adopt one style or the other as their dominant way of thinking. As an analogy, one can draw a general distinction between people who are introverted and those who are extraverted, although most will exhibit some qualities of both introversion and extraversion (e.g., Eysenck & Eysenck, 1985). Similarly, although ordered versus chaotic thinking represents a continuous dimension, we believe that most people can be classified as predominantly ordered or chaotic thinkers.

# 2

## Major Characteristics of Chaotic Cognition

At first, chaotic thinking might appear strange and incomprehensible. Yet to chaotic thinkers, it is a perfectly natural way to think about the world. It is a style of thinking, however, that most ordered thinkers have trouble understanding and appreciating.

This chapter explores the major characteristics of chaotic thinking, provides examples that illustrate them, and shows how they contrast with those of ordered thinking. In describing these characteristics, we consider not only those that appear central to the nature of chaotic thinking, such as its unstructured, reactive, and impulsive qualities, but also those that are often associated with it, such as the relative lack of pride or ambition.

We stress that not every chaotic thinker exhibits all of these characteristics. Rather, we propose that most chaotic thinkers exhibit most of them, in the same way that the defining characteristics for most natural categories exhibit a "family resemblance" quality (e.g., Rosch & Mervis, 1975). The same is true of the proposed, contrasting characteristics of ordered thinkers. We also stress that most ordered thinkers exhibit at least some of the characteristics of chaotic thinkers, and vice versa, because few people are perfectly ordered or chaotic. Rather, both ordered and chaotic tendencies exist to some degree in virtually everyone.

This point can be illustrated by an analogy. Consider how dogs and cats could still be distinguished even if they were physically identical. They would still show distinct behavioral patterns that would indicate the existence of two separate categories, even though not every dog or cat would act in exactly the same way. Further, some dogs would show some cat-like qualities, and some cats would show some dog-like qualities. But it would be apparent that dogs and cats were fundamentally different, and could be distinguished in terms of general characteristics.

Essentially the same argument can be made for distinguishing ordered and chaotic thinkers.

## UNSTRUCTURED RATIONALITY

As mentioned in the previous chapter, chaotic thinking is not typically irrational, contrary to what one might suppose. Rather, it is normally a rational form of thinking that is relatively transient and unstructured. Chaotic thinkers usually focus on the exigencies of the moment, without employing preconceived plans or anticipating the long-range consequences of their actions. They often quickly assess the necessary priorities in a situation and respond accordingly. Instead of doing this randomly or arbitrarily, however, most chaotic thinkers evaluate what needs to be done and then coordinate their responses in the most effective way. Whenever they need to organize something, it is usually done only as a temporary convenience. In general, they create few enduring structures.

In contrast, ordered thinking is generally highly structured and extends linearly into the future. Most ordered thinkers see the world in terms of a simple chain of events, which can be anticipated and controlled. The structured nature of ordered thinking usually leads one to assume stability, reliability, and predictability. Most chaotic thinkers, in contrast, see the world in terms of a multiple set of connections, for which the underlying structures are yet to emerge or be discovered. This usually enables them to have much greater flexibility in dealing with unexpected events. By not committing themselves to specific plans, structures, and anticipations, chaotic thinkers are often better able to respond naturally and realistically to whatever might occur.

Ordered and chaotic thinkers tend to regard each other as irrational, but this is because each is judging rationality from his or her own perspective. Most chaotic thinkers see all external structures and organizations as ephemeral and constantly evolving over time into new and unexpected forms. When confronted with an ordered thinker's more linear, time-oriented style, the content of a chaotic thinker's ideas can thus seem like a hodgepodge of unimportant irrelevancies. To many ordered thinkers, it therefore seems as if random chance were occurring in the minds of chaotic thinkers, who are continually seeing new connections and possibilities.

Chaotic thinkers, in turn, tend to regard ordered thinkers as irrational and unrealistic. Although they can often see the logical points ordered thinkers are trying to make, they usually think that ordered thinkers are only seeing a small part of the overall picture, and are not using all of the information that is relevant to what they are doing. They tend to see them as plodding along, always missing the point, and seldom aware of the total context of the situation at any given moment.

The rationality of chaotic thinking is often manifested by an immediate acceptance of the situation at hand and the ability to quickly discover appropriate responses to it. For example, if a hurricane suddenly struck, most chaotic thinkers would probably respond to the destructive forces by creating makeshift repairs, without concern for whether or not the repairs were done in a proper or professional manner. If a screen door blew out, they might try to fix it using rope, tape, or whatever might be available, improvising as necessary.

Most ordered thinkers would usually need time to assess the situation and develop a specific plan of action, such as deciding how many nails were needed to repair the door, or what type of hammer to use. The problem with these excess concerns is that they lead to many other unnecessary problems while the emergency is still occurring. Although there is much to be said for wanting to do a job correctly, in a crisis situation many things need to be taken care of right away, and there is little time to develop careful plans. Chaotic situations usually require immediate, chaotic responses.

Because ordered thinkers tend to idealize situations, they often lose perspective on the immediate consequences of a crisis. For instance, faced with a sudden job loss, an ordered thinker might imagine other people eagerly wanting to hire him or her, and might simply wait by the phone. Most chaotic thinkers would regard this as irrational, because the simple fact is that once you are fired you usually need to find another job as soon as possible.

When forced to take action, most chaotic thinkers would rely on an intuitive sense for how to react in that moment. They would seldom stop and think, or try to formulate plans. If they were being harassed by someone, for example, they would normally not waste time plotting revenge against the person. Instead, they would probably do something impulsive, unexpected, and unstructured, which seemed to fit the moment and would render the person's antagonisms ineffective or inappropriate.

Another aspect of the unstructured nature of chaotic thinking is that it is often nonhierarchical. Authority figures might be acknowledged, but they are seldom truly respected. For instance, when chaotic thinkers have an idea or a complaint at work, they may be just as likely to go to the president of the company as to their immediate superior. There is little consideration of hierarchical rank or chain of command. Most chaotic thinkers would respond to a policeman as a person with a gun who can arrest you, not as an authority figure per se.

Chaotic thinking also tends to be unscheduled. Chaotic thinkers generally avoid imposing any kind of regular structure upon their daily existence. Unlike most ordered thinkers, they rarely make outlines or create mental lists of things to do at the beginning of the day. They usually prefer to take every day as it comes, and seldom perform routine tasks in exactly the same manner.

Ordered thinking, in contrast, is much more deliberate and controlled. An ordered thinker might plan to sit down and work through a problem at a particular time, using an established analytical approach to arrive at a conclusion. Chaotic thinkers, on the other hand, are often struck by interesting thoughts at the oddest moments. They might awaken out of a deep sleep, and have a fascinating thought. They might go out for a walk, and have another fascinating thought. The spontaneous, unscheduled quality of chaotic thinking can make these ideas seem almost magical at times. Because they are seldom tied to a specific plan or purpose, the ideas may appear to simply emerge from out of the blue. They may then be quickly forgotten, however, especially if there is no one around to record them.

These characteristics help to define the unstructured rationality of chaotic thinking, which strikes most ordered thinkers as foreign and strange. Yet it is often remarkably sensible, especially in response to a crisis, or when unexpected problems arise. Those situations that demand immediate responses, that are changing rapidly, that have unpondered variables, or that have a strong sense of urgency, all play to the strengths of chaotic thinking.

In speaking of the rationality of chaotic and ordered thinking, we should clarify that there are actually two senses in which a person's thinking can be considered rational. It can mean that the thinking is logical, or that it is realistic (e.g., Stebbing, 1959). Ordered thinkers tend to display rational thinking that is logical, whereas chaotic thinkers tend to display rational thinking that is realistic. When ordered thinkers become irrational, it is often because their logic defies realistic considerations. When chaotic thinkers become irrational, it is often because their focus on immediate concerns overlooks long-term consequences.

## INTENSIFYING THE MOMENT

We have previously mentioned that chaotic thinkers usually respond to what is happening in the moment. In fact, they often *intensify* the moment—a principle that is at the heart of many of the chaotic techniques we describe in later chapters. Because they normally have little concern for what has happened in the past or might happen in the future, most chaotic thinkers strive to achieve the maximum intensity they can in each and every moment. From the perspective of ordered thinking, a person might decide, "I can wait to get married or travel; I've got another 20 years to live." That future reality, however, does not exist for most chaotic thinkers, who might behave as if they only had a few hours left to live.

The notion of intensifying the moment requires some clarification. It is not that chaotic thinkers are unable to think about the future. Instead, most of them regard the future as inherently unpredictable, and thus believe that thinking about it precludes their ability to deal with the moment. Because they prefer to deal with things as they are happening, they generally do not see the point of thinking about the future and its consequences.

One advantage of intensifying the moment is that it helps a person to avoid dwelling on the mistakes of the past. For example, people often mentally replay their past mistakes as a way of trying to understand what went wrong, so that they can rectify the mistakes and erase the past. If a person's marriage breaks up, for instance, he or she might dwell on who was at fault and what could have been done to save it. Most chaotic thinkers would simply accept the fact that the marriage is over and move on to something else.

## REACTIVE QUALITIES

Much of chaotic thinking is, by its very nature, reactive. Accordingly, most chaotic thinkers see themselves as playing an essentially passive role within the environment. When chaotic thinking produces new insights or adaptations, it is usually in response to something that is occuring in the immediate present. Whereas ordered thinkers tend to initiate actions as a consequence of their plans, chaotic thinkers seldom initiate actions apart from the situation at hand.

When stimulated or provoked, chaotic thinkers often respond quickly and decisively, and their ideas can then seem like counterpunches. For instance, when insulted, they usually respond to the insult right away, often turning it into something harmless or fatuous, whereas ordered thinkers might simply get angry, not knowing exactly what to say, and then dwell on the insult and think of a good comeback later on.

Chaotic thinkers usually do their best work when interacting with other people, where they can react immediately to their actions and ideas. They usually prefer to have someone to bounce ideas off of, which intensifies the moment and opens up new possibilities. When talking with chaotic thinkers, it is often quite common for them to suddenly take a conversation down new and interesting paths, in response to what one has just said. Even when they are thinking to themselves, there is an almost didactic quality to their thoughts. In ordered thinking, there is a tendency to communicate though monologues, to talk *at* people rather than talking *with* them.

In keeping with their reactive nature, most chaotic thinkers are supreme opportunists, and adopt a utilitarian approach to life in general. They normally try to utilize whatever comes their way. This contributes to their often striking ability to improvise, especially in a crisis. For instance, as we have mentioned, many chaotic thinkers have a remarkable talent for finding clever uses for everyday things. They might use a coat hanger and a plastic bag to make an emergency umbrella, or a dollar bill and some masking tape to repair a tear on a bicycle tire. Or they might use a refrigerator to help dry their clothes, by putting the clothes in the freezer and then shaking the ice out of them. In general, they tend to be less fixated on conventional ways of doing things (e.g., S. M. Smith, 1995; S. M. Smith, Ward, & Schumacher, 1993).

In order to be successful at utilizing whatever happens in a situation, one needs to have a fairly extensive, interconnected knowledge about a great many facts and subjects. The chaotic thinker's mind is thus like a super spider web, where every strand ties into something else. This interconnectedness of diverse sources of knowledge and experience facilitates the rapid utilization of naturally occurring events. In contrast, an ordered thinker's mind is more like a desk that has many separate drawers, into which most knowledge is compartmentalized. This is usually more efficient when events are predictable, because the knowledge can then be accessed in a direct and organized way, but it can create problems when the unexpected occurs.

## PASSIVE RESISTANCE

Another characteristic of chaotic thinking is that active resistance and confrontation are avoided whenever possible. Instead of directly challenging a person's plans, chaotic thinkers often try to utilize those plans within the current context, complicating or frustrating them if necessary. In general, when inconvenienced or threatened, they usually resort to passive resistance.

Suppose, for example, that someone wanted to see a particular movie and insisted that you come along. Instead of arguing with the person, you could use passive resistance by initially agreeing to go, but then take too long in the bathroom getting ready, mention that your car was not running quite right, and then complain that your back was aching, all of which would create unanticipated delays and complications. At some point, you could then simply say, "We're going to be 5 minutes late for the movie; I don't think we should spend the money unless we can see all of it."

When employing passive resistance, most chaotic thinkers try to make it appear as if they were supporting the person's plans. People who rely heavily on ordered thinking can become quite upset when their plans suddenly fail, and might assume that someone else was responsible, unless it seems as if they failed accidentally. In such cases, they might still be upset, but they are less likely to apply blame, which relieves others of personal responsibility for the failure.

Sometimes chaotic thinkers use passive resistance to play off the prejudices of others. For instance, if your boss was determined to think of you as lazy, you might accept this impression and try to utilize it. Instead of confronting or challenging the prejudice, you could begin to do your job in a slow or frivolous manner, and would thus become a genuinely lazy person, if that is how you are going to be viewed anyway. This then frees you to do whatever you want while still fulfilling your boss's expectations.

The method of using passive resistance was advocated by Ghandi as a way to effect change through nonviolent means (Brown, 1977; Ghandi, 1951). Ghandi himself was very likely a chaotic thinker; he taught that refusal to cooperate was preferable to violence as a way of dealing with oppression. In general, in response to oppressive people or systems, chaotic thinkers tend to be subversive rather than revolutionary. They do not want to replace one structure with another; rather, they simply resist having too much structure. They express their resistance by refusing to cooperate, often down to the smallest levels of the system.

Chaotic thinkers also commonly employ "passive-aggressive" behavior (Parsons & Wicks, 1983), though generally not to a self-destructive extent, as when a person simply refuses to cooperate with anything or anyone. Rather, as mentioned, their lack of cooperation usually functions to encourage change in systems or situations that have become excessively rigid and unyielding. By the same token, ordered thinkers often exhibit obsessive-compulsive behavior when forming and imposing their plans (Rachman, 1980), but usually not to the point where it becomes pathological.

## SEEKING OUT STIMULATION

Most chaotic thinkers have a constant need to be stimulated, to seek out new and interesting things. Most ordered thinkers, in contrast, tend to be more concerned with structuring and organizing things. They thus avoid excessive stimulation, which they usually perceive as a distraction. For example, they will often avoid listening to music or the television when trying to work or study. Such distractions, however, often enhance chaotic thinking.

This need for stimulation contributes to the ability of many chaotic thinkers to intensify the moment, which we mentioned earlier. The immediate effect of intensifying the moment is to encourage rapid change within that moment. As a rule, the more the moment becomes the focus, the more chaotic thinkers are able to control or change things. When the moment gives way to past or future considerations, the more ordered thinkers can control or change things.

We need to clarify the notion that chaotic thinkers gain control in the moment, given their reactive nature. They generally see themselves as *agents* for change. They can often take a situation and transform it into something entirely new. Their control of the moment is thus a passive control, in analogy to the way a catalyst can help to bring about a change but is not the direct cause of it.

There are various things that chaotic thinkers typically do to increase stimulation and intensify the moment. They might suddenly decide to drive fast, which strengthens their need for excitement and adventure. If they were high up on a mountain or a building, they might sit on or walk along a ledge. If they were with someone on a date, they might suddenly suggest silly activities such as playing a game of tag. If they were at work, they might try transforming their tasks into contests or games. In fact, most chaotic thinkers are constantly looking for new ways of changing ordinary routines into interesting and stimulating activities.

Given their need for stimulation, one might think that chaotic thinkers would make good daredevils. However, professional daredevils are more likely to be ordered thinkers, for they tend to be very structured in their approach to stunts and challenges. For instance, most daredevils do carefully planned test runs, study mechanics and physics, and develop detailed contingency plans. Seldom do chaotic thinkers become professional thrill seekers; they would do such things merely for fun, and without preparation.

Chaotic thinkers are generally fun-loving. They like to play games and seek out new adventures. Yet they usually do not have what could be regarded as a traditional sense of humor, in comparison with the satire, irony, and enjoyment of pranks that is often derived from ordered thinking. Typically, ordered thinkers like to play pranks that are thoroughly planned, or tell jokes that are carefully rehearsed.

Most chaotic thinkers have a broader, unstructured conception of humor. They like word play that is spontaneous and opens up metaphorical possibilities. They like humor that is directed not at individual people, but at human nature in general, as in the humor of Mark Twain or Will Rogers. Few chaotic thinkers would deliberately try to mock or put others down, merely to establish their superiority.

When playing games, chaotic thinkers can become deeply absorbed for hours, as long as the game continues to provide stimulation. For instance, they can become so involved in skipping rope that they might keep on doing it for the rest of the day. They can become entranced by the sheer momentum of an activity, even with such simple things like bouncing a ball off the side of a wall. Whereas ordered thinkers usually want activities that have a specific goal, chaotic thinkers usually want activities that are stimulating.

Because of their seemingly carefree attitude, chaotic thinkers often appear frivolous to ordered thinkers, who might think that they are not taking a task seriously enough. This often causes ordered thinkers to underestimate them. For example, a chaotic thinker working on an assembly line might regard every bolt that comes by as having a different personality, or talk about screwing "Mr. Bolt" into "Mr. Hole," or hum a little tune. This might make it seem that chaotic thinkers are not doing their job properly, but it often enhances their productivity. Ordered thinkers often end up working against themselves, as when they pick up a bolt and say, "This is work. I hate doing this." In contrast, chaotic thinkers usually find some way of turning the work into fun and making it stimulating.

Although most chaotic thinkers prefer to be in stimulating situations, their inherent passiveness makes this more of a reactive need. They thus tend to let these situations be thrust upon them, as with the surfer who swims out and waits patiently for the big wave, the "bungee diver" who walks up to the platform and jumps off, or the fireman who is called upon to suddenly go into a burning building. These types of situations irresistibly attract most chaotic thinkers, because they make them feel alive and allow them to use their reactive skills to the fullest extent.

## INCREASING COMPLEXITY

In reacting to most situations, chaotic thinkers normally try to increase complexity as much as possible. They might take something that appears simple and ordered, like a rule prohibiting people from walking on the grass, and begin to see it in increasingly complex and multifaceted ways. Would this mean, for example, that people could skip or run on the grass, or could wear special shoes with elevated spikes? Chaotic thinkers would consider such possibilities not merely for the sake of complicating matters, but to discover new insights, connections, and ideas, which often then emerge from the complexity. Also, the uncertainty that complex situations create helps to satisfy their need for stimulation.

This aspect of chaotic thinking promotes openness and creative exploration. It may be contrasted with the more destructive tendency to increase complexity merely to disrupt things, which would be more characteristic of a gremlin. While it is true that chaotic thinkers will often increase complexity in order to frustrate a person's plans, this is not the primary reason they do so. Rather, it is usually done to raise new possibilities and to keep their options open, which enables most chaotic thinkers to do their best work.

Ordered thinkers, by contrast, can have trouble handling complexity, and thus they tend to oversimplify things. They are usually at their best when they have simple yes–no choices, which provide a greater sense of predictability and control. It is difficult to predict the future when every single choice has a multitude of possible options. From an ordered thinker's perspective, the future should consist of limited choices, so that plans can be made and expectations fulfilled. Thus, ordered thinkers generally strive to remove complexity and uncertainty from most situations in their lives.

By increasing the complexity of a situation, chaotic thinkers can deal with potentially unpleasant encounters stemming from a person's desire to impose an ordered plan. For example, suppose a friend insisted on coming over and convincing you of the relative merits of local political candidates. A chaotic response might be to agree to talk with the person, but then to introduce various complications into the conversation. For instance, you might suddenly mention that you heard that one of the candidates raises German shepherds, which you think are fascinating animals. You could then elaborate on the merits of German shepherds, which would steer the conversation away from its original, intended path.

These complications need not be tied directly to the topic of the conversation. For instance, other chaotic responses that you might use in this situation would be to mention that you were just getting over the flu and cough repeatedly, or to wear a pair of unusually dark glasses, explaining that you have recently had an eye infection. These incidental distractions would make it increasingly more difficult for the person to continue the intended conversation, while avoiding any direct confrontation.

Sometimes chaotic thinkers try to increase complexity by asking a series of seemingly relevant questions, but which merely serve to slow down a person's plan. For instance, if they were called in to talk with their boss about something they had apparently done wrong, they might listen patiently to the boss's lecture, but then ask various distracting questions, such as whether this kind of thing has happened to other employees, whether their boss's friends were upset by this, or whether this was affecting their boss's health. Usually, this will cause the person to give up on continuing the lecture, for it has now lost its momentum.

Increasing complexity is also accomplished in chaotic thinking by providing much more information than is actually needed. If chaotic thinkers were being cross-examined by an attorney, for example, instead of avoiding the questions or refusing to respond, they might provide details that were mostly irrelevant, with the intention of trying to be as complete as possible. For instance, if they were being accused of causing a car accident, they might try to recount the totality of events in their life that led up to their being in that particular situation at that particular time. They might explain that they felt the person needed to know all of these multiple details and connections in order to fully understand how they got there and how they were affected. These distant events, however, would not really be germane to the issue, and would merely serve to shut down any further inquiry.

## CONSIDERING MULTIPLE REALITIES

Chaotic thinking can be further distinguished by its natural acceptance of multiple realities. This is another reason that most chaotic thinkers are fascinated by complexity. They tend to see life as an enormous ambiguous figure with an infinite number of equally valid and meaningful interpretations. In chaotic thinking, the concept of a single, universal truth is generally rejected. There are multiple truths in any situation.

Whereas chaotic thinkers usually respond according to the principle that there are multiple truths and realities, ordered thinkers usually have a hard time not taking the first possibility they encounter and turning it into a single truth or reality. This helps to keep things simple, so that they can pick out the information that is most important and discard the rest. Accordingly, to the ordered thinker there is usually a best explanation for something, a best way of doing a task, a best interpretation of the facts. The problem that this often creates, however, is that once one comes to believe that one is in possession of the truth, there is no longer any reason to consider matters further. One is then more likely to become defensive or even angry if that truth is questioned.

Their belief in multiple realities enables chaotic thinkers to keep all possibilities open, and thus to avoid the single-mindedness that often plagues ordered thinking. It also contributes to their creativity and imagination. In a sense, they are continually creating new realities and perspectives, whereas ordered thinkers usually attach themselves to a single reality or point of view and may not want to think any more about it.

Because chaotic thinkers are usually more aware of alternative perspectives, they can often help people to break out of rigid patterns. For example, if someone were facing the possibility of losing his or her job as a teacher, a chaotic thinker might point out how having many years of experience in teaching can help one to move into management positions in many businesses. This provides an alternative reality to the belief that a teacher would have trouble finding work outside the world of education.

In exploring alternative realities, most chaotic thinkers continually seek out unusual connections and associations. They often exhibit *remote association* in their thinking, which refers to the search for unconventional relations among words and ideas (e.g., Mednick, 1962). This contributes to their ability to consider alternative possibilities and discover creative links. They also tend to exhibit what Langer (1989) referred to as *mindfulness,* an openness to alternatives and a willingness to accept uncertainty. Ordered thinkers, on the other hand, often exhibit *mindlessness,* and react according to habit, without stopping to think about whether or not other responses might be more appropriate. They thus tend to get locked into rigid patterns and avoid reflecting on alternative possibilities.

As an example, when ordered thinkers set up their plans, they often expect them to work out automatically. They might expect that the plans will simply unfold in a sequence of stages, like knocking down a string of dominos. From a chaotic perspective, however, a string of dominos has multiple chances to fail. All it takes is one of the dominos not falling as planned. Ordered thinkers generally do not like to think about these prospects, and may simply assume that all of their plans are going to succeed.

Many chaotic thinkers are voracious readers, which enables them to draw on a wealth of diverse knowledge in coming up with different perspectives on things. They can be veritable storehouses of interesting facts and viewpoints. This reflects their continual interest in finding alternative realities and tying everything to everything else. As a result, there is very little that most chaotic thinkers do not find interesting or potentially significant. In contrast, ordered thinkers generally draw a hard line between things they consider important and things they do not.

This contrast often shows up in their writing styles. Ordered thinkers tend to write in a style that says, in effect, "Here is the right way to think about this, and I'm explaining it to you as simply and directly as possible." Chaotic thinkers are more likely to consider alternative possibilities and interpretations as they write. This tends to make their writing style less definitive, and at times more confusing, but it also allows for greater imagination, symbolism, and diversity. Chaotic thinkers also tend to prefer free-form poetry, which lends itself to multiple inter-pretations, whereas ordered thinkers tend to prefer poetry that is carefully structured and has less ambiguous meanings.

These differences can be expressed by the following analogy: A typical ordered thinker is like a person who meticulously cultivates a garden, turning the soil and carefully planting a particular type of seed. A typical chaotic thinker goes out, scratches around in a square mile of open space, scatters various types of seeds here and there, and takes whatever comes up. The chaotic thinker thus gets a field covered with things of many varieties, whereas the ordered thinker gets one specific, predictable crop. Because of its diversity, chaotic thinking tends to fertilize itself.

## LETTING THE STRUCTURE EMERGE

Chaotic thinkers generally do not deny the existence or importance of structure. Rather, they normally assume that meaningful structures and concepts will gradu-ally emerge out of life's complexities, and thus see little need to impose structure.

As a consequence, they are often better able to discover the deeper, underlying principles that naturally connect ideas and events.

Consider, for example, how one typically comes to learn about and appreciate an ancient culture. If one reads about the myths of a culture, its people, its philosophy, and its literature, at some point one begins to get a feel for the culture and can then describe it in general terms. Eventually, one acquires a deep, emergent understanding of what the culture was truly like. This is how most chaotic thinkers approach the world in general.

A chaotic thinker might walk into an individual's room, and by noticing how the person organizes his or her desk, or what type of furniture the person prefers, can quickly get a feel for what the person is like. When traveling to a new place, chaotic thinkers can often tell, by simply observing the surroundings, how people are likely to act in that environment. They often acquire these understandings by immersing themselves in the situation, noticing various details and complexities, and then letting the structures emerge.

Instead of allowing structures to emerge naturally, ordered thinking usually imposes structures artificially and according to plans. For instance, when having to give a talk, an ordered speaker might try to structure the talk in advance and then tell the audience exactly what the main points are going to be. A chaotic speaker would probably not reveal the main points at the beginning, but would allow them to emerge and be discovered in the course of the talk. In fact, the speaker might even seem to be avoiding the key issues, by allowing the audience to infer them.

Similarly, in conversations, chaotic thinkers often start talking about something without knowing where it will lead. They normally see conversations as voyages of discovery, in which new insights and understandings will emerge in the natural course of exchanging ideas. Ordered thinkers often want to know exactly where a conversation is going and how it is likely to turn out, and thus try to steer it along a given path.

By imposing structures prematurely, ordered thinking is more susceptible to certain conceptual and perceptual illusions. For example, it often encourages false attributions, where one might conclude that a person has many ideal qualities just because the person happens to fit into one's immediate plans (Fiske & Taylor, 1984; Nisbett & Ross, 1980). It contributes to self-fulfilling prophesy, where one selects evidence to confirm one's expectations, and overlooks conflicting evidence (Curtis, 1989). It can even lead one to see flying saucers when looking at lights in the sky, or monsters in the shadows, if one organizes or interprets ambiguous patterns according to misguided perceptual hypotheses (e.g., Rock, 1983). Chaotic thinking avoids many of these illusions by allowing the structures and insights to emerge on their own—by encouraging one to stand back, defocus, and see the situation it in a much broader and often more realistic context.

The notion of letting the structure emerge is related to the concept of "direct" perception, which was proposed by Gibson (1966, 1979). According to Gibson, perceiving the underlying, invariant structure is a natural, reactive process, which results from careful observation and exploration. It seldom results from imposing specific plans or expectations. For example, consider how the underlying structure of a painting often seems to emerge naturally as you spend more time looking at it. It is not necessary that you know, in advance, what the underlying structure of the painting is supposed to be.

The commitment to multiple realities in chaotic thinking encourages the discovery of these underlying, emergent structures. By considering many different perspectives on a problem or situation, its essence often becomes clearer. Imagine, for example, making videotapes of a crime using a set of cameras that were spread out in a circle surrounding it, where each camera would provide a different perspective. By taking into account all of the perspectives, you would begin to see the true nature of the crime more clearly than if you had simply relied on only a single perspective.

Chaotic thinkers often try to encourage the emergence of underlying structures by letting others see a situation from many different perspectives at once. When presented with alternative possibilities in a gradual manner, people are usually able to formulate rebuttals or rationalizations for each of them. However, when suddenly bombarded with a multiple set of alternatives, they cannot dismiss them so easily, and they often begin to realize that there are other ways of seeing things. By getting them to consider multiple options and interpretations, chaotic thinkers can often help ordered thinkers to see more clearly the essence of what is happening in the moment.

This ability to consider multiple possibilities is related to the apparently disconnected quality of much of chaotic thinking. Often, chaotic thinking seems unrestrained or even contradictory. For instance, some of the alternatives a chaotic thinker might propose can appear totally inconsistent, especially at first. This is easy to misinterpret as irrational thinking if one does not realize that the ideas are coming from different perspectives. These apparent inconsistencies often then disappear once the underlying structure has emerged.

The chaotic thinker's penchant for letting the structure emerge is also related to the concept of *incubation,* in which one sets aside a problem temporarily in order to gain new insights into how to solve it (e.g., S. M. Smith & Blankenship, 1991). Their omnivorous reading habits and continual fascination with new facts and ideas provide many chaotic thinkers with an enormous amount of information, which seems to percolate in their minds. When confronted with a sudden problem, they are often then able to draw on these connections and associations and allow new and creative insights to emerge.

## PLAYFULNESS AND ADAPTABILITY

Chaotic thinking allows for considerable flexibility in responding to many types of unexpected problems and situations. This flexibility arises not only from its emphasis on considering multiple possibilities, but also from its inherent playfulness. Chaotic thinkers seldom take life as seriously as ordered thinkers, for they are usually intent on living within and appreciating the moment.

Ordered thinking often leads one to get locked into long-term commitments, and to expect others to respect those commitments. One can then become deeply irritated when things change and the commitments no longer hold. Chaotic thinkers either tend to avoid such commitments or fail to take them seriously. They thus tend to have fewer problems adapting to crises and other disruptions in their lives.

Typically, ordered thinkers feel the need to organize their activities, even those that are supposed to be fun. They often invent games having specific rules, or plan outings with specific agendas. Most chaotic thinkers would argue that you cannot put fun on a schedule, that it simply happens. They therefore try to keep their lives as unstructured as possible, which increases their freedom and flexibility.

At times, ordered thinking can become so rigid that it causes one to take even trivial inconveniences much too seriously. A familiar example is when people focus on and wait indefinitely for a certain parking space, even when there are other parking spaces nearby. Most chaotic thinkers would probably just park wherever they could, and not care if a certain space were already taken. In fact, they might even prefer to park farther away, which would help to keep their options open. Ordered thinkers usually want to park as close as possible to wherever they are going, whereas chaotic thinkers usually prefer to park where nobody is surrounding them, so they can easily pull out.

As we pointed out previously, chaotic thinking normally operates from a play ethic, whereas ordered thinking normally operates from a work ethic. This work ethic involves a commitment toward achieving specific rewards. If these efforts fail, and the rewards cannot be achieved, the result can be considerable anger and frustration. With a play ethic, failure is no big deal; one simply moves on to something else.

If they were to receive a bit of information that completely challenged their whole way of thinking, most chaotic thinkers would likely accommodate their thinking in response to it. Most ordered thinkers, in contrast, would have a tendency to reject that information. For example, suppose you suddenly found out that you belonged to another family because of a mix-up at the hospital where you were born. To many ordered thinkers, this would be so unbearable that they would probably completely deny it. At the very least, they would probably fight the idea for years before finally accepting it. Most chaotic thinkers, however, could adjust to the knowledge rather easily and would begin redefining themselves.

As part of their adaptive nature, chaotic thinkers are usually quick to pick up on new skills. It often takes ordered thinkers longer, although once they become committed to learning a skill they can often develop careful plans for doing so. When chaotic thinkers begin to play a new game, for instance, they tend to quickly pick up on the rules of the game, without having to formally learn them. Ordered thinkers, in contrast, may devote considerable time to reading about the principles of the game, and might even put themselves on a schedule for mastering it.

Chaotic thinkers will usually learn to play a game because it sounds like fun. Before ordered thinkers get involved in games, they usually want to know about all the best strategies and their consequences. They will often try to study everything they can about the game so that they can completely understand it. Most chaotic thinkers would totally reject that philosophy, and just learn what they needed to know at the appropriate moment. As a result, their performance in games and other activities tends to be much more flexible and unpredictable.

The relative lack of flexibility in ordered thinking is sometimes expressed by regarding one's career, ideas, or relationships as one's whole life. For instance, ordered thinkers might conclude that their life is now over because their husband or wife left them, or because they just lost their job. Chaotic thinkers usually avoid confusing thoughts and reality in this way. Instead of dwelling on the loss, they would tend to accept what has happened and then respond to the situation in ways that maximized their adaptability.

When confronted with a sudden loss, however, chaotic thinkers can be very intensely affected by it in that moment. The loss can be extremely painful, because of their immediate awareness of it. Ordered thinkers may not feel the full impact of a sudden loss right away; their pain may extend over prolonged periods, as they reflect upon the loss and what might have been. For most chaotic thinkers, there is extreme pain and extreme sadness when the loss occurs, but then the next day there are other things happening and they are once again drawn into the flow of life.

This might help to explain why some ordered thinkers have trouble mourning a loss, and why it might continue to affect them for a long time. From the standpoint of ordered thinking, the process of mourning is disturbingly chaotic. The pain and sadness are unpredictable, and take away from whatever plans were in progress. Ordered thinkers therefore often try to avoid the pain of mourning, and this merely intensifies the pain. From a chaotic thinker's perspective, it is better to accept and experience the pain and then let it pass.

## IMPULSIVENESS AND SPONTANEITY

One of the most salient characteristics of chaotic thinking is that it is highly impulsive. Ideas and cravings can appear suddenly and are often acted upon precipitously. If chaotic thinkers wake up in the middle of the night and want a candy bar, or a specific brand of ice cream, they might walk across town to get them. If they suddenly decide to visit an old girlfriend or boyfriend, they might drive all night to do so, without ever announcing their intentions. But then, once they arrive, they may not even act on their impulse, especially if other thoughts and distractions have intervened.

This is very different from the careful, logical style of thinking displayed by most ordered thinkers. They might want a certain candy bar, but then decide that it is too late to get one. They might consider visiting old girlfriends or boyfriends, but then decide that they probably now have a life of their own, and reject the idea.

They would normally strive to control their impulses, or in certain cases deny that those impulses even existed.

The spontaneity of chaotic thinking often strikes ordered thinkers as too intense and capricious. In ordered thinking, energy is usually directed towards achieving specific goals, and every task is allocated the necessary time and effort. Chaotic thinkers rarely pace themselves in this careful, controlled way. If they suddenly became interested in an activity, even something minor, they might throw themselves totally into it. That kind of passionate involvement would be regarded by most ordered thinkers as completely unrelated or nonessential to a plan. Chaotic thinkers may get terribly excited about some incidental aspect of a task, such as purchasing seeds for a garden, which ordered thinkers might regard as silly, perplexing, or even insane.

Because of their impulsiveness, chaotic thinkers often have moments of brilliance, but the intensity seldom lasts. Their energy is concentrated but temporary. Most ordered thinkers prefer to distribute their energy over time, which enables them to perform at a more consistent level. As an analogy, a chaotic thinker is like a magnifying glass on a sunny day, which can focus all of the sun's energy and can burst something into flames. An ordered thinker, however, is more like a pane of glass, which just lets the sun come through. Everything is warm, but there is no flame.

By following their impulses, chaotic thinkers often go farther than many ordered thinkers. Because they tend not to limit themselves, they can sometimes accomplish things that appear almost miraculous. For instance, they can often work effectively under conditions of extreme pain. Most ordered thinkers have a hard time enduring pain, because they tend to wonder, "How much longer will the pain continue?" The ability of most chaotic thinkers to work under pain is considerably greater, because they only have to endure each moment.

For this reason, chaotic thinkers are often the first to overcome established barriers in human performance. These barriers, like the 4-minute mile or the mountain that cannot be climbed, become almost like laws for many ordered thinkers, and they cannot overcome them. For most chaotic thinkers, such laws do not exist. Similarly, chaotic thinkers are usually the first to break social taboos, bringing previously unacceptable behaviors or attitudes into acceptance.

## METAPHORICAL QUALITIES

Much of chaotic thinking is highly metaphorical, and draws on abstract symbolism and association. This symbolism often enhances the openness and meaningfulness of a chaotic thinker's ideas. For example, chaotic thinkers might take something that seems relatively meaningless, like a lone pebble lying in the middle of a sidewalk, and make it symbolic, and thereby give it meaning. In a sense, they try to create the gold that lies at the end of the rainbow, which then gives meaning to the rainbow.

Most chaotic thinkers like to use metaphors for three reasons. First, metaphors enable one to take a nonconfrontational, indirect approach to communication. Second, they intensify the moment, by opening up unexpected possibilities. Third, they allow one to explore multiple meanings and interpretations, which increases the diversity and flexibility of human cognition (e.g., Glucksberg & Keyser, 1990; Ortony, 1979; Tourangeau & Rips, 1991).

It is often difficult for chaotic thinkers to convey the total complexity of what they want to say using simply declarative sentences. A story or metaphor allows them to deliver a message in a more complete way and to express its many subtle nuances. Declarative statements are the hallmark of ordered thinking, for they are simple and direct. They are poorly suited, however, to express the multiple realities of chaotic thinking.

Frequently, chaotic thinkers simply play with metaphors. They often consider open-ended statements such as "Life is like a record," and then try to interpret them in various ways. Such explorations can help one to discover multiple realities and alternative meanings. For instance, one might realize that life is like a record because it is a winding, circuitous thing that finally comes to an end. Or, that life is fragile, and can shatter at any moment. Chaotic thinkers often play these metaphorical games as a way of seeing new connections and achieving new insights.

Sometimes chaotic thinkers use familiar fables or stories to convey their ideas. For example, if someone were denigrating a former lover, a chaotic thinker might mention the fable about the fox and the sour grapes: Being unable to reach the grapes, the fox concluded that they must be unpalatable. As a way of communicating that gentle persuasion is often better than blustering attempts to force somebody to do something, a chaotic thinker might recount the story of the contest between the sun and the wind, to see who could get the man to take off his coat: The wind blows and blows at the man, and the man just clings more tightly to his coat, whereas the sun gracefully smiles at the man, and the man removes it.

At other times, chaotic thinkers might use particularly obscure metaphors, to frustrate those who are demanding simple, direct responses. For example, if told by someone that they needed to have more hope or optimism in their lives, chaotic thinkers might respond by saying, "Hope is the lily to the dragonfly." This abstract symbolism increases complexity, reduces confrontation, and avoids a straightforward debate. We consider further the more tactical uses of chaotic symbolism in chapter 4.

In general, chaotic thinkers prefer language that keeps their options open. They often like drifting away from their subject, finding remote connections to things, and discovering new territories. In a sense, a chaotic thinker's whole life is a digression. Their language usually reflects their multiple views of the world and their vast collection of information. Their metaphors often touch on many subjects, and can be surprisingly insightful, especially upon reflection. If one goes back over and ponders what a chaotic thinker has just said, one can often find multiple meanings and implications in their symbolism.

At the same time, chaotic thinkers generally avoid abstract, philosophical discussions, and prefer to focus on particular examples, incidents, or ideas. They usually like to start with something concrete and flow metaphorically outward from it, as opposed to starting out at an abstract level, with no clear reference point. Most chaotic thinkers would prefer to experience something in the moment than to talk about it in abstract terms. They would rather intensify ideas, whereas philosophical discussion usually comes across as too impersonal and places them at a distance.

The frequent use of free-flowing, abstract symbolism in chaotic thinking often causes ordered thinkers to accuse chaotic thinkers of avoiding issues and playing semantic games. They often do not realize that chaotic thinkers are simply exploring alternative realities. At times, this can make them seem frivolous or even evasive. Their digressions, however, rarely function to deliberately avoid an issue, and usually serve to stimulate other ways of seeing something.

Ordered and chaotic thinking also differ in the use of mental imagery. Most ordered thinkers use images to plan, anticipate, or control things, whereas most chaotic thinkers use them to create metaphors and explore alternative realities. The rich, symbolic imagery of chaotic thinking helps to intensify the moment, as when chaotic thinkers tell vividly detailed stories or metaphors. Ordered thinkers tend to focus more on concrete imagery, because they generally see the world in a more direct and literal way.

Concrete visualization often contributes to the compelling nature of an ordered thinker's plans. For example, when ordered thinkers visualize the anticipated results of their plans, those results often become more vivid and seem more attainable. It also contributes to the structured quality of ordered thinking, insofar as concrete images tend to be highly structured and organized (Finke, 1989; Kosslyn, 1980; Pylyshyn, 1973; Ward, in press). In contrast, the preference for symbolic imagery and metaphors in chaotic thinking encourages a less structured style, with loose and flexible associations.

Because they tend to arrive at fairly literal interpretations of most symbolic works, ordered thinkers sometimes have difficulty interpreting poems, novels, or movies. Yet many ordered thinkers believe strongly in certain types of symbolism, such as trophies, flags, or logos. The difference is that these are symbolic objects, as opposed to symbolic concepts, and thus tend to be interpreted rather narrowly, as in regarding the flag as a symbol of our country, and nothing else.

## DESIRE TO BE INVISIBLE

In keeping with their passive, reactive nature, most chaotic thinkers prefer to remain "invisible" and blend into their surroundings. In a moment of crisis, attention is often suddenly drawn to them, but once the crisis is over they usually fade like the Cheshire Cat, who leaves only his smile. If they become too visible, they might become highly vulnerable, as in the case of celebrities like Marilyn Monroe, James Dean, and Charles Lindbergh. If they become sufficiently fascinating to others, excessive demands might be made on them, and they can lose touch with who they are. In fact, chaotic thinkers often fail to recognize their own celebrity status, which would require stepping back from the moment.

Many ordered thinkers, on the other hand, prefer to be seen and recognized, which helps to define their identity and makes them feel important. They often need to have other people around to acknowledge and validate their existence. But for most chaotic thinkers, constantly being seen would be like becoming trapped in amber.

The presence of others can sometimes take away the chaotic thinker's spontaneity and restrict what they naturally do. They can then become overwhelmed by what others want and need. In particular, if someone were trying to get them to lead a more structured and predictable life, and kept imposing these demands upon them, most chaotic thinkers would simply want to disappear.

To increase their visibility, ordered thinkers often try to create positive images for themselves. For example, they might become highly concerned with wearing the right clothes and looking neat, in order to make the right impressions, as when going on a job interview. This allows them to feel that they have more control over the uncertainties of a situation, such as the possibility of being rejected. Chaotic thinkers generally care less about things like neatness and proper dress, and are thus less likely to make a good first impression.

Although there are certainly merits to appearing attractive, ordered thinkers sometimes carry this too far. By placing too much emphasis on selling themselves, they often fail to properly express themselves. Chaotic thinkers, in contrast, usually wear clothes that they feel good about and express who they are, and are generally unconcerned with whether or not others might be offended by it. They seldom look neat, but their lack of neatness appears natural.

By the same token, most chaotic thinkers tend to judge others by their underlying character, and not their appearances. They are seldom impressed by fancy clothes or graceful manners. Also, fulfilling certain social obligations, such as holding a steady job or going to church regularly usually matter very little when chaotic thinkers evaluate a person. How the person expressed his or her feelings or treated others would be much more important considerations.

## THE UNNECESSITY OF PRIDE

In chaotic thinking, pride is seen as an obstacle to adaptability and growth. Chaotic thinkers seldom see the purpose of pride, because in their view of the world things simply happen. An ordered thinker might typically say, "I caused this to happen," and feel proud about it. In response, a chaotic thinker might point out that meteors often fall from the sky. Something causes this to happen, but is there any pride?

For that matter, why should anyone be proud of any accomplishment, since interesting and remarkable things happen all the time?

Similarly, most chaotic thinkers are reluctant to take any credit for their ideas. Their philosophy is that things just happen, even one's thoughts. Ordered thinkers might contemplate a particular problem, figure it out, and then take pride in having solved it. Chaotic thinkers might read a variety of things, come up with a wealth of interesting ideas, and then wonder why anyone should be proud of them.

One of the major drawbacks of pride is that it can cause a person to stick too rigidly to courses of action that are no longer appropriate. This is a common problem in ordered thinking, where one might become so proud of a plan that one refuses to let go of it. For instance, a person might plan on arriving at a destination by a certain time, and if the traffic caused a delay, might then take unnecessary chances on the road just to salvage the plan.

Because of pride, people can sometimes be threatened with the destruction of their reputation. They might then expend considerable energy defending principles or ideals that have little relevance to the issue or situation at hand. For instance, consider what happened at Custer's Last Stand: Custer fought a battle he did not need to fight, merely to save his reputation. He began to believe in his own greatness, instead of carefully planning and thinking about his next achievement. He ceased to validate his pride with realistic accomplishments, and this led to his ultimate destruction (e.g., Monaghan, 1959).

Pride can also compel one to devote considerable time and effort to justify one's past behavior. For instance, years after a relationship has ended, a prideful person might still feel the need to explain why it ended, why it was not really their fault, or why they were justified in doing what they did. If caught doing something wrong, they might carry on a court battle for years, trying to defend their actions even though there was little chance of winning.

Why does ordered thinking promote excessive pride? There are at least three reasons. First, ordered thinkers usually acquire a sense of mastery and control whenever their plans are successful. The ensuing pride then inspires them to create further plans and push them to completion. Second, as mentioned previously, ordered thinkers often need to be acknowledged for their accomplishments, and to know that they have succeeded. Third, the plans of most ordered thinkers have an inherent strength or momentum such that, once engaged, they are often hard to disengage. This perceived strength of a plan contributes to an ordered thinker's pride, especially if the plan works out as expected.

Pride does have certain virtues. For instance, it helps one to avoid becoming discouraged when momentary setbacks occur, and to feel better about oneself. However, like any virtue, pride can become a liability, especially if it grows unbounded or leads to pointless behaviors. Chaotic thinking avoids many of the problems associated with pride, but it also lacks the strength of purpose that pride often creates.

As we discuss in later chapters, knowing when to lower pride is important when relying on ordered thinking. This is especially true whenever one is caught doing something wrong or illegal, where the tendency is to try to give rational justifications for one's actions or to simply express defiance, as when a person says to a judge, "There's no way you can convict me," or "There's no prison that is too tough for me." In such cases, it is usually better to swallow one's pride and appear victimized or contrite.

## SENSITIVITY TO PERSONAL NEEDS

Chaotic thinking tends to be highly sensitive to the needs and feelings of others. Most chaotic thinkers show considerable empathy and sympathy, even for strangers. They might spend all day talking to someone who seems to be having a problem, or drive hundreds of miles to help a friend. This sensitivity comes from their awareness of what is happening in the moment, and their ability to see things from another person's perspective.

Chaotic thinkers usually welcome unexpected visitors, and are seldom offended when people show up unannounced. This relates to their basic belief that things simply happen, and that the future is unpredictable. Moreover, when chaotic thinkers visit other people, they are generally aware of how disruptive a visit can be, and may even avoid visiting someone if they perceive that it might cause an inconvenience.

Ordered thinkers tend to be somewhat less sensitive to the needs and feelings of others. They are more likely to be annoyed when people show up unexpectedly at their homes, especially if this interrupts a planned activity, yet they are also more likely to do this to others. For instance, if they decided that they wanted to visit somebody, they might just figure that the person would be happy to see them, in spite of the actual circumstances or how the person might be feeling.

Because of their sensitivity to personal needs, most chaotic thinkers show commitment to individuals, as opposed to principles or organizations. For instance, they might quit a job rather than fire or betray a friend. They are generally loyal to people, even when situations change, whereas ordered thinkers tend to remain loyal to rules and principles. Having fired a friend, for example, an ordered thinker might feel sorry for the person, and might offer to help or have a going-away party, but will usually regard the act as part of his or her job.

With ordered thinking, people are sometimes regarded as expendable, or at least, secondary to plans. If one wanted to talk to a highly ordered thinker about some pressing personal matter, one would often have to wait (and might even be asked to make an appointment), because the plans that the person had made previously would usually take precedence. For this reason, chaotic thinkers are usually sought out as "friends in need"; they are more likely to respond immediately to a person's problems and concerns.

Adhering to plans, but without really caring for individuals, often results in a distorted sense of personal responsibility in ordered thinking. For instance, ordered thinkers might take great pride in being "good providers," without having any real personal commitment to or involvement with their family. Consider, for example, the husband who pursues his career by working 60 hours per week, and has no time for his wife or children. When his wife complains, and his children become alienated, he might become angry and claim that he is doing it all for them. Ordered thinkers typically assume there is an implicit contract; that if they provide and succeed at their careers, they will then be loved and appreciated.

Differences between ordered and chaotic thinkers in their sensitivity to individual needs are also reflected in their contrasting attitudes toward personal possessions. Ordered thinkers usually become attached to their possessions and try to take good care of them. They usually keep things well oiled, to make them last. Sometimes, however, they come to think that this also applies to people, believing, in effect, that if they keep their spouse "well oiled," then the relationship will last, too. They thus tend to allow materialism to substitute for genuine warmth.

Chaotic thinkers, in contrast, tend to neglect their possessions, for several reasons. First, they usually attach no permanence to them. Like everything else, possessions exist only in the moment. Second, whereas ordered thinkers might like to be defined by their possessions, especially those that conveyed a sense of status or accomplishment, most chaotic thinkers would want to avoid being defined in this way. Third, by getting rid of their possessions, chaotic thinkers usually acquire a greater sense of freedom. They are therefore willing to give away even valuable possessions, especially if they sense that others have a greater need for the possession than they do.

In fact, chaotic thinkers often discard books after reading them. Once they discover the essence of a book, and absorb its ideas, the book is merely a shell. When ordered thinkers read books, it is often to discover specific techniques that will fit into their plans. They therefore tend to see books as a means to an end, and are more likely to hold onto them. As a general rule, possessiveness is more characteristic of ordered thinking, for it contributes to the structured qualities of the ordered mind and provides visible proof of successful accomplishment.

Most chaotic thinkers adopt a selfless approach to life. By denying themselves, they are then free to explore and discover new things, and to become more attuned to the needs and feelings of others. For this reason, they are often more approachable than ordered thinkers, and display a greater amount of personal warmth. One often gets the sense that one can go right up to most chaotic thinkers and talk with them about anything. Ordered thinkers tend to be more suspicious and guarded if you approach them suddenly, and might suspect ulterior motives. Chaotic thinkers are generally more approachable because they usually feel connected to all living things.

Many chaotic thinkers, in fact, can still be compassionate even when they do not like somebody, knowing that an enemy today may not be an enemy tomorrow.

In general, they do not see people as inherently bad or evil; rather, people do evil things because of circumstance, and are not truly responsible for their actions. In ordered thinking, enemies can last for a lifetime, because people are generally seen as being responsible for whatever they think or do.

# 3

## Primary Benefits of Chaotic Cognition

The main value of chaotic thinking is that it helps to keep structuring forces in perspective, and to prevent ordered systems and the plans supporting them from operating so efficiently that they ignore the needs of the moment or the actual complexity of a situation. Its primary purpose is not to eliminate ordered thinking, but to keep it from trying to control nature to an irrational degree. To this end, chaotic thinking has a number of specific benefits.

We consider these benefits in this chapter; they include improving the chances for surviving a crisis, enhancing creative insight and discovery, and promoting adaptive changes in one's personal and professional life. Chaotic thinking can also help to encourage rational behavior, reveal a person's true intentions, create favorable illusions, frustrate narrow-minded thinking, reverse preconceived notions, unravel complex mysteries, and improve a person's sensitivity to meaningful details. These benefits follow from the various characteristics of chaotic thinking that were considered in the preceding chapter.

In describing these benefits, we do not mean to imply that all chaotic thinkers are equally skilled at dealing with crises and other chaotic situations. There are skilled and unskilled chaotic thinkers, just as ordered thinkers can vary in their ability to plan and organize things. Also, we do not mean to imply that these benefits are exclusive to chaotic thinking.

We acknowledge, in addition, that the benefits of chaotic thinking are generally two-sided. A benefit in one context can often be a liability in other contexts, and this is true of both ordered and chaotic thinking. For instance, the relative insensitivity of ordered thinking to things that are happening in the moment can be an advantage when it is important to block out everyday distractions and plan ahead, which chaotic thinkers often have difficulty doing. There are times, therefore, when ordered thinkers can benefit from not taking in all the information, or not dealing with the total complexity of a situation. Similarly, chaotic thinkers may be at a disadvantage in those situations where it might be necessary to impose order and structure, or reduce the amount of uncertainty.

## ASSISTING SURVIVAL

In chapter 1, we proposed that chaotic thinking is especially useful whenever unexpected events occur and one needs to quickly find some way to survive or adapt. In such cases, chaotic thinkers are often able to focus on the crisis at hand and do whatever the moment calls for. By dealing with the crisis as it is happening, they generally avoid worrying about future problems or contingencies, and can focus on immediate survival.

Some of the characteristics that help chaotic thinkers to survive a crisis include having a heightened sense for the exigencies of the moment, considering multiple realities and possibilities, and reacting to the total context of the situation. They tend not to get frozen in one particular view of a crisis, which might end up trapping them. In ordered thinking, one often perceives a crisis in terms of past or future plans, and then considers only one path of action. This greatly limits one's options, and often reduces the appropriateness of one's responses.

Consider, for example, the sort of crisis in which a person suddenly loses his or her job. Those who always rely on ordered thinking might waste time trying to reformulate their original plans for the future, or considering logical arguments for why other companies would want to hire them. Most chaotic thinkers in this situation would probably assess their various skills and abilities and begin preparing broadly targeted resumes. They would generally avoid making long-range plans or worrying about what might have been. Instead, they would probably consider as many other options as possible, knowing that the type of job they just had may no longer exist.

Ordered thinkers often feel threatened in times of rapid change and uncertainty. Their life's plans are normally geared towards long-term survivability, not short-term, adaptive responding. Therefore, when a crisis strikes, many ordered thinkers can become temporarily paralyzed. They tend to stop and worry about why the crisis is happening or what went wrong, instead of reacting immediately to it. An extreme example would be the man who remained in his car following a serious automobile accident, as the gasoline tank was ready to explode, thinking about how the accident would now disrupt his plans for the rest of the week.

One of the trademarks of ordered thinkers is that they normally have their emotions under control. In a crisis, however, they tend to lose this control, and their emotions can overwhelm them. Chaotic thinkers are usually more open and free with their emotions, but in a crisis they tend to focus their emotions on the situation and keep them under control. Similarly, ordered thinkers tend to become more distracted in a crisis and allow their thoughts to diverge, whereas chaotic thinkers tend to become less distracted in a crisis and focus their thoughts on what needs to be done.

Chaotic thinking is also useful in dealing with sudden changes in health. When ordered thinkers come down with a serious illness, they tend to worry about all of the plans that might never be completed. In chaotic thinking, the completion of such future plans would be seen as irrelevant. Most chaotic thinkers would simply assess the illness and act in such a way as to minimize its disruption. If the illness prevented them from doing one thing, they would do something else. If their recovery required major changes or treatments, then so be it.

In fact, chaotic thinkers often look forward to crisis situations, because they intensify the moment and provide them with opportunities for having new insights. These conditions of heightened stimulation and uncertainty are when chaotic thinking can be most effective. Much of the time, a chaotic thinker might be bored by life, especially when it offers little excitement or intensity. In a crisis, however, most chaotic thinkers become immediately involved, because the level of stimulation is suddenly increased. Even if they were to discover that they were about to die, many chaotic thinkers would find the situation appealing in some sense, for it would then liberate them to do whatever they wanted, without a future to limit them.

To avoid having to deal with unpleasant people or unstimulating situations, chaotic thinkers often create their own "mini-crises." These might include running out of money, experiencing a sudden allergy attack, needing to fix a broken car, or having to help a friend with an unexpected problem. These self-generated crises often provide convenient excuses for side-stepping confrontations, particularly with ordered thinkers. Chaotic thinkers often like to push things to a crisis, especially when dealing with highly ordered situations, because they are then in their element, and usually have the advantage.

In chapter 7, we consider more specific types of survival situations and various techniques of chaotic thinking that can be effective in dealing with them.


## ENHANCING CREATIVITY

Creative ideas often come at unexpected moments and in unexpected ways, creating a kind of mental chaos. In general, chaotic thinking is ideally suited for utilizing these creative moments. Chaotic thinkers can usually draw upon vast sources of knowledge that cut across many different subjects and categories, to explore the multiple implications of a new idea. This helps to break up conventional mental sets, which typically limit creativity (e.g., S. M. Smith, 1995), and enables one to discover emergent, meaningful patterns (e.g., Finke, 1990; Perkins, 1981).

As a result, one can often experience a flood of new, creative insights after talking with chaotic thinkers. These insights, moreover, often come from unexpected sources, which one might never have considered. Suppose, for example, that a scientist became stuck while working on a difficult problem. A chaotic thinker might mention something he or she had read in the newspaper, such as a story about a new product on the market, which might suddenly stimulate an insight into how to solve the problem.

As discussed in chapter 2, chaotic thinkers often serve as catalysts for creative insight by calling attention to unexpected associations that can suddenly become relevant and meaningful. They typically violate the implicit constraints and limitations that most people are taught to accept, which then opens up new possibilities for insight and discovery. By exploring some of the consequences of having broken the rules, one often begins to see the value of alternative approaches and perspectives (e.g., Sternberg & Davidson, 1995).

Another reason that chaotic thinkers can often inspire creative insights is that they tend to think metaphorically, as discussed previously. Metaphors are powerful vehicles for opening up creative explorations, as has long been known (e.g., Gordon, 1961; Holyoak & Thagard, 1995). In fact, it is often possible to reconceptualize an entire problem simply by putting it in terms of a metaphor (Gentner & Stevens, 1983; Gick & Holyoak, 1980). For example, Einstein reportedly came to his key insight about relativity by imagining how the world would appear to someone traveling along a beam of light (Ghiselin, 1952). In counseling, people are often encouraged to examine their problems in terms of metaphors, as a way of reframing those problems and seeing them from entirely different perspectives (e.g., Ivey, Ivey, & Simek-Downing, 1987).

In ordered thinking, one often considers problems using specialized terminologies or statements. The metaphorical qualties of chaotic thinking can provide a broader and more coherent conception of many types of problems. Metaphors also create a more personal involvement with a problem, which makes it easier to work on, as compared with responding to it in a purely technical way.

Compare, for example, the rigid, methodical approach of the laboratory researcher, trying to find a cure for a disease, with that of the field biologist who searches for meaningful insights in nature (Smith, 1980). The key to curing the disease might be found in something as unusual as what a witch doctor does, which the laboratory researcher would merely scoff at. The field biologist, however, might be more likely to consider such remote possibilities and thus uncover whatever insights they might provide.

Chaotic thinking often leads to incongruities and apparent contradictions. From the standpoint of ordered thinking, this would normally be considered a drawback, but it can often stimulate creative exploration and discovery. This is because apparent contradictions can result in an eventual synthesis, yielding sudden, emergent insights (e.g., Koestler, 1964). In fact, chaotic thinking frequently exhibits this quality of *thesis, antithesis,* and *synthesis.* A chaotic thinker might begin with some basic premise that is valid in the moment. Every new idea that follows is then in conflict with this premise, because the moment has changed. In order to assimilate the new ideas, the existing premise must adapt, resulting in an eventual synthesis and the emergence of new and deeper insights.

Sometimes chaotic thinkers purposely consider contrasting, alternative realities in order to look at a situation in a more complete and realistic way. For example, they might generate arguments in support of directly opposite points of view, and then attempt to synthesize those arguments into a more balanced perspective. This tendency to draw extreme contrasts intensifies and clarifies key issues, and helps to reveal the underlying principles behind them.

Ordered thinkers can have a difficult time with this notion, if they fail to see the need to accommodate their thinking to changing situations. They might take new ideas and either reject them or try to force them into their current under-standings. Considering other perspectives and possibilities, or trying to resolve the apparent contradictions, might simply detract from the momentum of their plans. This would inhibit their creativity, because any thoughts that did not immediately fit into the existing plans might be excluded forever.

Another way that chaotic thinking enhances creativity is through its playful-ness. In ordered thinking, ideas and plans are generally taken too seriously. This is rarely a problem in chaotic thinking, which allows considerable freedom to play-fully explore many avenues. Chaotic thinkers tend not to worry about taking risks or being wrong, and they often engage in the playful combination of thoughts and ideas (e.g., Shepard, 1978). Many of the techniques of surrealism, for example, emphasized the combinational play of words and concepts as a way of encouraging the emergence of new insights (e.g., Gooding, 1993).

This play ethic helps to promote creative thinking and discovery. Ordered thinkers often measure their days in terms of how much they have worked, what they have achieved, and whether they have taken the right steps. Because of their work ethic, they tend to avoid playing around with anything new, which they would normally consider a waste of time. Unless the work is serious, it is not really work. In chaotic thinking, one often tries to turn work into play.

Most chaotic thinkers like to follow interesting diversions. They are usually less concerned about making mistakes or pursuing false leads. In fact, it is because they are willing to make mistakes that chaotic thinkers are generally more likely to take risks, accept new challenges, explore new areas, and discover new answers. Ordered thinkers generally regard mistakes as indications that they are failing and not achieving, and thus are less willing to take those risks.

The relative lack of pride among most chaotic thinkers, which was also discussed in the last chapter, further contributes to their ability to enhance creativity. Pride often vents creative energy; it encourages rigid thinking, by enshrining past accomplishments. For example, after achieving a major success, one might be hesitant to try again, for fear that the next attempt will not be as successful.

In addition, pride encourages one to protect a new idea, which often prevents it from expanding and growing. Chaotic thinkers are usually more interested in sharing ideas, and less concerned about receiving proper credit for them. They would probably not even care if their ideas were stolen, as long as the ideas were put to good use. To most chaotic thinkers, it would not matter who planted the seeds, as long as they could grow.

Modern theories of creativity have begun to incorporate many of the characteristics of chaotic thinking, such as considering multiple realities, exploring playful combinations, seeking out interesting contrasts and contradictions, developing useful metaphors, and discovering emergent properties (Finke, Ward, and Smith, 1992). They also have called attention to many of the limitations of taking a strictly ordered approach when trying to generate new ideas. For example, studies on creative imagination have found that it is often better to generate an image of a form before deciding exactly what function the form will serve (Finke, 1990). This promotes the discovery of emergent properties in the image, and often leads to more creative interpretations of it.

Ordered thinking can certainly be creative, but its creativity tends to be more structured and deliberate, and usually develops more slowly over time. Ordered thinkers tend to be more concerned with building something new and making it last. When they have creative insights, those insights usually come after considerable reflection. In general, they need more time to understand and integrate things, and their insights come mostly as afterthoughts. The creativity of chaotic thinking is usually much more intense and spontaneous.

As a rule, ordered thinking tends to be more creative when a person knows in advance what he or she wants to create, whereas chaotic thinking tends to be more creative when a person wishes to open up new possibilities and achieve new insights. Ordered thinking generally adopts a "form follows function" approach to creative invention, whereas chaotic thinking usually adopts a "function follows form" approach (e.g., Finke, 1990). In addition, creative achievements in ordered thinking can often be described as *clever*, whereas the creative insights in chaotic thinking are often described as *moving*. There is often an intense, emotional quality to the spontaneous insights of chaotic thinkers.

Chaotic thinkers can help ordered thinkers to achieve more spontaneity in their creativity by providing them with novel associations, suggesting new ways of seeing things, opening up interesting avenues of thought, and encouraging them to take tasks less seriously. They can also help by pushing ordered thinkers into the moment, getting them away from their previous plans, and opening them up to new, imaginative possibilities. Ordered thinkers, in turn, could help to edify the creative ideas of chaotic thinkers, which are often loosely connected and continually changing.

## ENCOURAGING CHANGE

Chaotic thinking often helps to bring about change, not by trying to force it but by encouraging it through creative and nonconfrontational means. This is especially useful in situations in which change is badly needed, but where direct approaches are likely to fail. For instance, suppose one were involved in a romance that seemed to be going nowhere, and wanted to do something about it. With ordered thinking, the usual procedure would be to sit down with the person and discuss the problem, perhaps pointing out how important changes needed to be made in order to make the relationship work, or explaining how the lack of progress in the relationship seems unfair.

Chaotic thinkers would rarely use such a direct, head-on approach. Instead, they might respond by doing simple, unexpected things, like suddenly cutting their hair, wearing funny clothes, or playfully rearranging the furniture. These actions could help to stimulate change in the relationship by loosening up the other person, but without having to raise and confront the person's inadequacies.

Chaotic thinking can encourage change in many static situations by helping to break up rigid patterns and routines. To most chaotic thinkers, the world is in a state of constant change, and the stability that many ordered thinkers strive for is mainly an illusion. Introducing playful, chaotic behavior is a natural way to avoid becoming stagnated. The opportunities for change and new insight that chaotic reactions often create can be particularly helpful when a person feels stuck and there are no simple or obvious solutions.

Suppose you found out that one of your supervisors had been lying to you. A typical ordered reaction might be to accuse the person of lying, and confront him or her with the evidence. However, this would usually result in denial, anger, threats, and counteraccusations. Instead, a chaotic response might be to compliment the supervisor's honesty and integrity, but then express concern that there are others in the company who lie and cheat to gain advantage. You might suggest that the two of you join forces to initiate a formal investigation of these individuals, to save the company from moral degeneration. You could even suggest giving lie detector tests to all workers, including the highest executives. The company could then set the standards for personal integrity for the entire industry. Your supervisor would thus be forced to confront the hypocrisy between promoting honesty but not practicing it, and you would avoid having to make any direct accusations.

Calling attention to multiple points of view is often useful in bringing about constructive changes, for it allows a person to experience new perspectives on a situation. Consider again the example of someone who is locked into a static relationship. A chaotic thinker might try to explore multiple ways in which the relationship is stuck, as a way of introducing possible changes. For instance, it might be sexually static, requiring creative efforts in that regard; it might be financially static, with both partners feeling that they are at career standstills; or it might be emotionally static, containing dull schedules and routines.

In pointing out these multiple perspectives, chaotic thinkers can often provide others with concrete options for initiating change. At first, they may have no clarity about the situation; they may not even know what the trouble really is. By providing them with multiple choices, chaotic thinkers can help people to narrow down and define precisely what it is that is causing the problems, which often leads to more precise and appropriate solutions. It is usually more effective than the scatter-gun approach often taken in ordered thinking, in which a person might simply declare that because they are having these problems the entire relationship is ruined.

The effectiveness of chaotic thinking in affecting change results in part from a heightened awareness of changing trends. For instance, chaotic thinkers who work in the automotive industry could probably tell you what consumers really want, what new technologies are generating interest, or what safety devices are likely to be important. They are likely to be more acutely aware of new developments that are needed in the industry, because they are usually able to feel change almost as it is happening. In contrast, ordered-thinking workers might be less aware of these changing trends, especially if their attention was focused on ensuring that everything was running efficiently.

Another way in which chaotic thinking can stimulate change is by helping to unstructure events that are overly planned. Consider, for example, the different ways in which ordered and chaotic thinkers might take vacations. Ordered thinkers often want the freedom of a vacation, but they usually end up overstructuring it. They might make plans to travel along certain routes and see particular sights, all according to specific timetables. Chaotic thinkers usually take vacations impulsively and without particular agendas, treating them more like adventures. The spontaneous, impulsive quality of chaotic thinking can often encourage people to become curious about having new experiences and to consider departing from their original plans.

As a rule, chaotic thinking promotes change by taking a person into the moment, away from their singular perspective on the past or the future, and then helping the person to focus on what they want presently. The person is then forced to begin to think about what they can do at that moment to bring about those changes (e.g., Fagan, 1970). As we explain in chapter 6, this can have many advantages in therapy and counseling.

## REFINING INTUITIONS

Most chaotic thinkers rely heavily on intuition, which allows them to respond rapidly to sudden and unexpected events. They feel comfortable knowing what to do in a situation without necessarily knowing why, or being able to explain their actions to others (Schooler & Melcher, 1995). Most ordered thinkers, in contrast, want to know exactly why a method works or why an action is appropriate.

Chaotic thinking thus encourages the development and refinement of intuitive judgment (Bowers, Regehr, Balthazard, & Parker, 1990; S. M. Smith, 1995). Chaotic thinkers are constantly refining their intuitions, by testing them out and allowing them to fail. In effect, they prefer to learn the rules as they go, so that their intuitions can develop naturally. Most ordered thinkers are less willing to put their intuitions on the line, and as a result, they often have a less developed intuitive sense for things. They thus tend to rely more on careful planning.

The refinement of intuitions in chaotic thinking illustrates again the principle of letting the structure emerge. As a rule, most chaotic thinkers avoid prejudging people and situations, and allow their insights to emerge naturally as a result of their ongoing interactions and experiences. The tendency in ordered thinking is to want to enter into situations with advanced knowledge, careful preparations, and clear expectations, so that unexpected developments or sudden surprises are minimized. However, by making the situations more closed and predictable, one also reduces the opportunity to learn from the experiences and to sharpen one's intuitions.

Sometimes chaotic thinkers purposely avoid reading criticisms of books, movies, or works of art until after they have experienced them for themselves. They would prefer to form an uncontaminated impression. Ordered thinkers are more likely to want to read a criticism in advance, so that they will know what is supposed to be good or bad about the work. From a chaotic perspective, this inhibits one's ability to experience and appreciate the work in a natural and genuine way.

Because they are more open to refining their intuitions, chaotic thinkers are often more willing to accept a novel idea, especially if it gives them new insights and understandings. Ordered thinkers, however, often want external proof before accepting an idea. They tend to be more skeptical and resistant, in part because accepting a new idea would usually require modifying their original principles or changing their previous plans. In chaotic thinking, new ideas are often accommodated more easily, because there is seldom the need for massive restructuring of prior concepts and beliefs.


## ENCOURAGING RATIONALITY

Another benefit of chaotic thinking is that it can encourage irrational people to behave more rationally. By intensifying the moment and calling attention to its complexity or absurdity, chaotic thinkers can often get a person to begin to deal with the reality of a situation. Ordered thinkers, by contrast, are often frustrated by irrational people. They normally try to confront the irrationality, and this seldom works.

To illustrate, suppose a friend of yours had an irrational fear about going to the dentist, even though you tried to explain that regular dental care helps to prevent cavities and tooth loss. A chaotic strategy would be to accept the person's irrationality and then do playful things that encouraged a more rational response. For instance, you might bring the person an oversized toothbrush from a joke shop or a year's supply of dental floss. You might offer to buy the person a lollipop for going to the dentist, or mention that most people only like kissing people with white teeth.

Instead of confronting irrationality, chaotic thinkers often try to immerse it within a playful atmosphere. The irrational person can then feel less pressured, and can begin experimenting with the idea that they really could do those things they have been avoiding, such as going to the dentist. Once they let into their minds the possibility that they *could* go, they can then work toward actually going. This is a general principle that many chaotic thinkers employ. They first accept an irrational response and then introduce unexpected complications into the situation, which eventually lead the person to have more rational insights on their own.

Suppose your husband or wife had a drinking problem. When you tried to discuss it, he or she refused to admit the problem and responded by getting angry and making unflattering allegations. Whenever you tried to be rational, your spouse insisted on being irrational. A chaotic thinker might respond to this situation by videotaping the spouse while he or she was drunk and then threatening to play the tape to others, explaining that they simply wanted to show all of their friends what having fun is really all about. This response accepts the drinking problem but utilizes it in unacceptable ways.

In such cases, ordered, judgmental tactics normally fail. By telling people that they are ruining their careers, their health, or their marriages, they will usually feel threatened and will be pushed further into denial. Chaotic thinking is generally more effective in bringing about rational behavior because it removes personal threats from the situation while forcing the person to confront reality. You are saying, in effect, "I'm going to give you a picture of reality which will be shared by others. This is not to say that you are a bad person, or a drunk. Nevertheless, your denials are going to fail, because you will actually see the consequences of your drinking, and witness firsthand how others feel about it. You are going to be brought inescapably into the here and now, where you can no longer deny reality."

In these types of situations, chaotic reactions make the person confront what they have been avoiding, without directly challenging them. Instead of arguing with the person over the issue, most chaotic thinkers would try to create circumstances and complications that allowed the person to come to his or her own rational decisions. Instead of being judgmental or vindictive, they would try to create a playful and positive effect.

Another way that chaotic thinking encourages rationality is by expressing extreme points of view. This often intensifies the moment and brings about a more rational compromise. If one starts out by expressing a moderate point of view, people often respond by being unreasonable, as a way of challenging for position or control. Suppose, for example, that you ran a business and could no longer afford to pay the entire medical insurance costs for your employees, and felt that under the circumstances it was only fair for them to share at least some of these costs. If you were to propose this to them directly, they would almost certainly reject the idea, inasmuch as you have been paying for these costs all along. Instead, you could propose that your employees should now pay the entire cost of the insurance, pointing out that they can always obtain bank loans in order to do so. After rejecting this outrageous proposal, they would then be more willing to pay for a part of the costs, which is the reasonable compromise you desired.

By providing multiple choices, some of which are sensible, and some outrageous, chaotic thinking allows for a more flexible and realistic acceptance of things. People might start out with certain irrational beliefs and expectations, but by having them consider multiple choices, they are often encouraged to adopt a more realistic perspective and select the more rational alternatives. People tend to be less rational around ordered thinkers, because they usually offer them only yes-or-no choices. One action is right; the other is wrong. One decision is correct; the other is stupid. These choices are often so absolute that a person has no middle ground. Such inflexible, black-and-white standards eventually lead to problems and conflicts, and usually prevent others from responding in honest and realistic ways.

Chaotic thinking expresses an openness that invites honest responding and rational behavior. By being open and flexible, chaotic thinkers can often get people to appraise a situation in more than one way, which allows them to make realistic choices. People who rely on ordered thinking often have trouble eliciting rationality, because they tend to take one point of view and then exclude any thoughts or ideas that do not fit in with that particular point of view.

## REVEALING SECRETS AND INTENTIONS

Chaotic thinking can often be used to gain insights about a person's true intentions or secret desires, by placing the person in a chaotic situation and observing how he or she responds. This can help to expose the thoughts behind a person's plans, without having to ask point-blank questions. Instead, chaotic thinkers often try to obtain this information indirectly, by encouraging chaos, complexity, and uncertainty.

For example, suppose you suspected your husband or wife of cheating on you. An ordered approach might be to make direct accusations or devise specific strategies for catching the person in the act. A chaotic approach, however, would usually avoid such confrontational methods. Instead, you might alternate between showing lots of affection and then not showing any affection. At a party, you might talk about a famous movie star who was cheating on his or her spouse. You might take your spouse to a movie in which cheating was the prominent theme. The way he or she responded to these situations would then begin to reveal how they were actually feeling.

When chaotic situations arise, the stress of the moment usually weakens a person's defenses, especially those of highly ordered thinkers. Having suddenly been cast into a crisis, they might become so distracted by the crisis that they momentarily forget about the consequences of exposing their plans. They are then more likely to reveal things that they ordinarily would not reveal if they had had more time to think.

If a crisis does not occur naturally, chaotic thinkers often manufacture one. For instance, they might take a person out to dinner at a fine restaurant but then pretend to have left their wallet at home so that the person will have to pay for the meal. Or they might disconnect a spark plug, to create the impression that their car has broken down. If their companions become sufficiently frustrated over these incidents, they will probably reveal their true feelings and intentions. They may say, for example, "I only went out with you tonight because I expected you to pay for dinner," or "I thought you could afford to keep your car in better condition."

By creating an artificial crisis, chaotic thinkers encourage people to relate to them at a more personal level. Ordered thinkers often prefer dealing with an "abstract" person, someone whom they feel they can easily fit into their plans. They therefore tend to avoid becoming personally involved with others when putting their plans into effect. Most crises, however, encourage these involvements, and thus help to bring one's plans to the surface.

Sometimes chaotic thinkers can get people to reveal their true intentions by getting them to react to a *potential* crisis. To illustrate, suppose you suspected that your boss was thinking of firing you, but had not yet said anything to you about it. You might mention that you were considering changing careers or moving to another city. You could bring up a news article about a major firing at some other plant, and comment on the coldness and cruelty of it. You could say something like, "They must have been very nasty to have fired all those people without any warning or notification." The way your boss responds to this can provide insights into what his or her true intentions are.

In this same situation, you could also mention that your cousin had just been laid off from his job, and that he was very angry at first, but eventually realized that his boss did what he had to do, and ended up respecting him for it. Your boss might then say something like, "You know, I'm having to make some hard decisions like that myself. I hope my own employees will be that understanding." This gets your boss personally involved with the issue, and thus more likely to reveal what he or she is really planning to do. Most people find it harder to conceal their intentions when forced to deal with potential problems on a personal level.

These chaotic methods are often effective because people who have secret agendas are normally split between what they want to tell others and what they want to hide from them. By providing what appear to be harmless outlets, chaotic thinkers give them opportunities to open up these hidden parts of their personality, and to reveal their hidden truths.

As mentioned previously, direct confrontation is generally avoided in chaotic thinking. Sometimes, however, directly confronting a person is the best way to find out what they really know or feel, especially if this is unexpected. Consider, for example, the way a clever detective might confront a suspect with a crime, after talking about irrelevant issues, by suddenly asking, "By the way, how did you come up with such an ingenious idea for robbing that bank?" Or, as another example, if concerned about the status of a romance, a person might suddenly ask his or her partner, "By the way, do you really love me?" This forces the issue into the present, rather than allowing it to remain at a distance and dwell within an ambiguous and uncertain future.

When ordered thinkers confront someone, there is often a righteous or judgmental quality to the confrontation. On those rare occasions when chaotic thinkers confront somebody, there is usually a distinct lack of judgmental tendencies. It is more an expression of intense interest than a need to impose criticism. A chaotic thinker would almost say to the person, "I don't care that you did something wrong; I would just be interested in knowing about it." This lack of value judgment makes it easier for people to reveal their secrets.

Sometimes chaotic thinkers try to increase complexity as a way of revealing a person's intentions. For instance, if they were called into somebody's office, and sensed that the person was not being entirely honest with them, they might begin to play off certain aspects of the conversation in order to complicate the situation. When the person tried to speak, they might suddenly shift their position or adjust their seat. When the person mentioned irrelevant things, they might raise their own irrelevancies. If the person was skirting the issue, they might skirt in return. The person might then begin to feel that they were never going to arrive at what they had planned to say, which would encourage them get to the real point sooner.

By increasing complexity, chaotic thinking often encourages people to fight against their own irrelevancies. To take another example, if your boss or supervisor asked you an irrelevant question like "How is your family?" in order to avoid telling you what was really on his or her mind, a chaotic reaction would be to respond with questions like "How is *your* family? How is your dog? How is your house? How is your lawn?" until finally your boss is ready to scream out what it is he or she is really thinking. By not forcing the issue directly, you allow it to build up pressure, which gives others little choice but to be completely honest with you.

Chaotic thinkers sometimes ask people for their advice, especially if they suspect duplicity. In fact, they even do this with their competitors or enemies. They might flatter them, ask them what they think, and then try to assess their true emotions or expectations. For instance, if competing with someone else for a key position, a chaotic thinker might go to the person and say, "You know, I really value your judgment. You are probably one of the better people in this department. I know the boss is considering both of us for the position, but I would really like your opinion on how I could improve my presentation."

This allows one to assess a number of things. If the other person was very eager to suggest a certain strategy, one could probably assume that it was unlikely to be successful. If the other person was critical of certain strategies, one could explore why the person thinks that those strategies would not work. The person might then reveal positive or negative attitudes towards the company, which could be useful in increasing one's chances for obtaining the position. Chaotic thinking can often uncover a large amount of information in this manner, and lead to insights into what the better choices and alternatives might be.

Sometimes ordered thinkers have an overwhelming desire to announce the cleverness of their plans, even against their better judgment. Although ordinarily they might be able to restrain themselves, when they get around chaotic thinkers, who seem totally playful, open, and nondevious, they usually have a harder time holding onto these restraints. Especially if their pride is challenged, these restraints can become severely weakened, and they will often begin to unmask their plans and aspirations.

## CREATING FAVORABLE ILLUSIONS

The relative freedom to explore alternative realities in chaotic thinking and to make them seem entirely believable can often be used to create effective illusions. This can help one to generate favorable impressions, avoid confrontations, and discover other dimensions of one's personality.

One way chaotic thinking can be used to create favorable illusions is by identifying with some truthful aspect of another person's point of view. As an example, suppose you had a jingoistic neighbor who wanted to run all of those godless non-Americans out of the country. To avoid having confrontations with this person, you might tell him how much you loved your country, how much you valued the land, and how much you respected the brave men and women fighting for it. Instead of mentioning that you find many flaws with the country, you could celebrate with him the joys of being an American. The person will then likely regard this single incident as overwhelming evidence that you are totally in agreement with him, and that you are a fine, outstanding person. Although this is an illusion, in that you really do not share his extreme views, you have not actually lied, for everything you have said was true.

When chaotic thinkers meet an interesting person whom they would like to get to know better, they often try to focus on some small part of the person's perspective and then elaborate on it. Suppose a person commented, "I really like the color green." Instead of simply agreeing or disagreeing with the person, one might describe the shades of the leaves outside, or the beautiful sheen of the ocean. This then allows one to have a meaningful conversation with the person about something he or she has shown an interest in. The impression is created that one is sensitive and understanding.

Sometimes chaotic thinkers create favorable illusions by doing something nice for an adversary. For example, they might suddenly give the person an unexpected and unwarranted present, like a cake or a pie, in a manner that seems totally harmless and without ulterior motives. This may not convince the person to like them, but other people will likely remember the gift, and will think of it as a gracious gesture.

When confronted with dogmatic or presumptuous people, chaotic thinkers might begin describing unusual experiences. For example, they might describe how they went to an energy zone in the desert and sat on a magical rock for days, or followed a drop of water for hours, until it reached the river. These seemingly pointless acts can often keep such people off balance, particularly when they have become convinced that they already know everything about a person.

On ocassion, chaotic thinkers also try to create the opposite impression, that they fit perfectly into someone else's plans and expectations. For example, if a man announced that he wanted to date a woman who had certain very specific qualifications, a chaotic thinker might try to convince him that she was the perfect match, by creating and elaborating on alternative realities that fit those expectations. This would normally be done not simply to fool the person but to create an interesting fantasy that could be mutually shared and explored.

To intensify the moment and encourage creative exploration, chaotic thinkers sometimes invent imaginary facts and create counterfeit realities. They might then invite people to consider these facts and try to explain them, especially if they seemed plausible. For example, they might mention that they had just read in the newspaper that scientists have succeeded in breeding a new type of elephant that has two trunks, but they cannot understand why. A person might then try to explain that this actually makes good sense, because having a second trunk would enable the elephant to hold onto a tree while it drank from a river, or to sound warning cries while it was eating. Again, this would usually not be done to fool or make fun of the person, but to create opportunities for considering and exploring interesting possibilities.

Similarly, chaotic thinkers sometimes create imaginary strengths and talents when describing a person to others. For instance, they might mention that the person is a champion body builder or has a wonderful singing voice, especially if these qualities contrast with the person's true characteristics. They might describe an overweight person as a world-class rock climber, for example. These illusions often create interesting effects when others try to reconcile the person's actual features with what they have come to believe.

It should again be emphasized that most chaotic thinkers would not create these counterfeit realities solely for the purpose of ridiculing or exploiting others. Rather, they would see them as opportunities for sharing and exploring alternative possibilities, often from novel or unusual perspectives. Moreover, these counterfeit realities can often begin to seem just as real to chaotic thinkers as to those for whom they were created.

Historically, chaotic thinkers have often been the creators of myths that others repeat and preserve. For instance, many of the great myths in our society, such as believing in the existence of magical or supernatural powers, were probably started by chaotic thinkers, who created alternative realities and made them irresistably appealing. Ordered thinkers were often the ones who then solidified these myths, by building entire belief systems upon them.

## FRUSTRATING THE NARROW MIND

Chaotic thinking has the further benefit of helping people to deal effectively with narrow-minded individuals who try to impose their principles or expectations on others. Chaotic thinkers often respond to these pressures by allowing the principles or expectations to be imposed, and then gradually introducing complications that divert them from their original paths. From a chaotic thinker's perspective, this is usually more effective than directly confronting the person, because it draws upon and utilizes the natural momentum of their plans.

Suppose, for example, that you were eating in a restaurant, and some self-righteous person came over and started complaining about your clothes or your eating habits. An ordered response might be to respond indignantly, making statements such as "Why don't you mind your own business!" or "You have no right to tell me that!" Usually, this would result in further arguments and an escalation of the problem.

Most chaotic thinkers would take a less direct approach, by intensifying the moment. For instance, they might agree wholeheartedly with the person, and then insist on seeing the manager to have bums like themselves thrown out. Or they might simply thank the person for their helpful comments, and then pretend to pick up some food off the floor and eat it. If dining alone, they might pretend that they were deaf, and make random hand gestures, or give the person a pen and some paper to write on. Instead of confronting such people, they would let them become increasingly embarrassed or frustrated in their efforts to further impose their principles or criticisms.

Introducing unexpected complications can often be highly effective in these types of situations. To take another example, suppose you had a petty, dictatorial boss whose rigid policies and endless, irritating memos were making life miserable for all employees. A chaotic response might be to distribute counterfeit memos, at first welcoming new employees or thanking everyone for the fine job they have been doing. Later, the memos might schedule meetings between supervisors and employees at odd hours, or even complain about the recent problem of false memos, perhaps telling employees to ignore all future memos that did not contain a special seal.

These chaotic reactions have several benefits. First, they keep one's spirits up and restore a sense of fun and hope. Second, they encourage creative expression in others. Third, they help to force things to a crisis point, where rational choices must be made and effective changes can then occur, so that an intolerable situation does not drag on for years and years.

Some people might react to ideas like distributing false memos with protest, regarding them as too undermining or damaging to the organization. But from the standpoint of chaotic thinking, one can simply ask, "Which is the better organization? One in which the workers joke, laugh, and work in harmony, or one in which the workers are angry, sullen, and paranoid?" Although seemingly silly and sometimes outrageous, these chaotic reactions often encourage the beneficial, playful qualities that many organizations desperately need.

Another way in which chaotic thinking can often deal with narrow-minded tendencies is by providing seemingly helpful but mostly unwanted information. For instance, if someone started questioning them about something they did not want to reveal, chaotic thinkers might give the person more information than they wanted, but not the information they needed. This would effectively complicate matters, for the person would then have to sort out the relevant information from the irrelevant information. For example, if you were being probed by hostile relatives about your latest personal relationship, a chaotic response would be to give them some relevant details, such as how long you had known the person, but lots of irrelevant details, such as the color of the person's car, where the person likes to eat, or whether the person knows how to use a computer. This would make it appear as if you were trying to be as honest as possible, but without having to reveal too much.

A common problem in our society is that people often presume that that they have an inherent right to change others, regulate their lives, or solve all of their problems. Most chaotic thinkers hold to the view that nobody has a right to tell others what they should or should not do. When they intervene in a person's life, it is usually to provide an alternative perspective, but this is normally done without making value judgments on the person's behavior.

In attempting to appear objective and flexible, people sometimes ask very open-ended questions, but without really wanting an honest response. Instead, these questions are merely the first step in imposing their expectations. By raising new and unexpected possibilities, chaotic thinking can often help to stifle these attempts and encourage people to be more receptive to other, more realistic alternatives.

For example, suppose a person asked you, "What do you feel like eating for dinner?" as the first step in trying to manipulate you into going to a particular restaurant. You could frustrate this plan by making a request such as: "I'd like a hamburger with peanut butter and sliced carrots," which you could repeat and insist on. You could then introduce alternative choices that reflected your true preferences, which the person would be more likely to accept. Even the most narrow-minded person will usually become more open and reasonable, and less interested in imposing his or her expectations, when faced with the prospect of having to deal with chaotic complications.

## REVERSING PRECONCEIVED NOTIONS

A related benefit of chaotic thinking is that it can reverse preconceived notions that often prevent people from relating to others as unique and genuine individuals. For instance, if they felt they were being stereotyped, chaotic thinkers might begin mentioning various episodes in their lives that revealed new and unexpected aspects of their character. They might describe, for example, how one night they decided to take their clothes off and swim out to the middle of the bay, because it seemed like an interesting thing to do. They might mention that they went downtown and played their guitar on a street corner for several hours. Or they might describe how they once spent all summer traveling around the country on a bus, without any specific destination. Such stories make it difficult for others to categorize them in any simple way.

When telling these stories, chaotic thinkers usually try to connect them in such as way as to promote a particular image of themselves. Random stories, no matter how interesting, tend to be dismissed. But when each story adds a new layer to that image and helps to create an alternative reality, it builds up in one's mind until one begins to see the other person in a totally different manner. This is often effective in destroying the original stereotype.

A common problem that chaotic thinking can often deal with is when people make decisions about a person's future that denies that person the right of individual choice. Suppose, for example, that your father was intent on having you enter a particular profession, and he refused to discuss the matter. You might respond by making bizarre choices that made your actual intentions more attractive. If you wanted to become an artist, for instance, and your father insisted on your going to medical school, you might pretend that you have just joined a cult, and begin wearing strange clothes and reciting chants. After a while, if you then hinted that you were rethinking your involvement in the cult, and were contemplating becoming a serious, professional artist instead, your father would probably breathe a sigh of relief and welcome this decision.

Chaotic thinking can also help to discourage people from making assumptions that are unrealistic or unwarranted. This is illustrated by the following anecdote. Two students who were doing very well in a chemistry class decided to drive to another university to party the weekend before their final exam. By the end of the weekend, it was clear that they were in no condition to return, and they decided to simply tell the professor that they had gotten a flat tire and were stranded. Upon arriving late the next day, they explained the situation to the professor, who was apparently satisfied and agreed to let them take the exam on the following day. The next morning, he gave each student a copy of the exam and placed them in separate rooms. The first question, worth 5 points, was very easy, much to their delight. The students, however, were unprepared for the second question: "95 Points: Which tire?"

Another way in which chaotic thinking can be used to reverse preconceived notions is by introducing multiple perspectives on a situation or problem. For instance, suppose a husband complained that his marriage was over because he had just discovered that his wife had been cheating on him. A chaotic thinker might suggest that there are actually a number of alternative possibilities. There could simply be a problem in communication. The husband's job could be interfering with their relationship. The wife could be worried that she is no longer attractive.

Or, she could simply be angry with him and be having an affair to get even. These other perspectives could help the husband to realize that the marriage may not actually be over, and even if it is, that there are other issues that need to be examined. This can leave the person with a more realistic grasp on the situation, as compared to simply concluding that the marriage is over and that is that. Getting people to set aside preconceived notions is often a prelude to exploring alternative, creative solutions to persistent problems.

## HELPING TO UNRAVEL MYSTERIES

Chaotic thinking can also help one to gain insights into how to solve mysteries. With a chaotic approach, one collects all the facts, considers a range of alternative possibilities, and then allows the solution to emerge. In so doing, one avoids making unwarranted assumptions, limiting oneself to a single possibility, or coming to conclusions prematurely, which are often drawbacks of an ordered approach.

When suddenly confronted with a mystery, chaotic thinkers often try to increase its complexity by collecting as much information as possible, talking at length with any witnesses, and exploring a wide variety of scenarios and interpretations. In ordered thinking, one usually tries to reduce the complexity of a mystery in order to simplify matters, but this often prevents one from seeing it in a broader, more complete, and more realistic context. There is also a tendency in ordered thinking to try to force solutions, whereas with a mystery it is usually better to let the solutions emerge as more becomes known. This is encouraged in chaotic thinking, and helps to keep a person from becoming overwhelmed by the complexity of a mystery.

In a sense, chaotic thinkers often allow themselves to become part of the mystery, to become players in it rather than observers. This intensifies the moment and increases their personal involvement in the mystery. Whereas ordered thinkers typically remove themselves from situations in order to study them, chaotic thinkers tend to thrust themselves into those situations, particularly when they generate considerable excitement or intrigue.

Consider, for example, the methods of Sherlock Holmes, who apparently exhibited many of the qualities of chaotic thinkers. Holmes was often bored until a complex and intriguing problem came along, whereupon he became intensively and personally involved. He loved crises, which helped to focus his energies into the moment, and would sometimes purposely create a crisis purely for dramatic effect. He had a remarkable ability to observe meaningful details, and delighted in exploring alternative realities. Yet he took very little credit for any of his accomplishments, and usually left it to Watson to record his cases (Doyle, 1930).

Modern methods for solving mysteries and crimes also employ many of the principles of chaotic thinking. Detectives, for example, are now taught various techniques for noticing minor clues and incidental details, entertaining multiple hypotheses, avoiding premature inferences, relying on their intuitions when the evidence is inconclusive, and getting suspects to reveal what they really know. Ordered approaches to solving crime often work best when the evidence clearly points towards a single hypothesis, when formal methods of analysis are available, or when there is a master plan at work. Chaotic approaches are usually more effective when the crime is relatively unstructured and the evidence points in many different directions.

Chaotic methods can also be useful when trying to diagnose a mysterious illness. With an ordered approach, a physician might listen briefly to the patient's complaints, run some tests, and then make a diagnosis. But the physician would usually remain detached from the patient, and might even become defensive if the symptoms persisted. With a chaotic approach, the physician would become more personally involved, consider multiple possibilities, and try to explore other things that were going on in the person's life that could be relevant. By accepting the complexity of the illness, the physician would stand to gain a deeper understanding of it.

Even when trying to solve everyday puzzles, most chaotic thinkers show a preference for personal involvement and increasing complexity (e.g., Levine, 1987). They often respond to puzzles playfully, and try out various novel or unconventional approaches for solving them. For example, they might try to solve an anagram by sounding out the syllables, and then rearranging the sounds to form words, instead of simply trying to rearrange the letters. In chapter 5, we consider other examples of problem-solving strategies that are based on the principles of chaotic thinking.

## INCREASING ATTENTION TO MEANINGFUL DETAILS

Because chaotic thinkers are usually more in touch with what is going on all around them, they are often the first to notice and recognize the significance of subtle details, hints, and cues. For instance, they can often recall various details about a person, such as whether the person was wearing a certain type of ring, how tightly their shoes were tied, whether they had minor scars or other markings, or whether one of their eyes was a slightly different color than the other. These incidental but potentially meaningful details are often overlooked by those who rely on ordered thinking, and who only focus on things that are directly relevant to their plans.

Chaotic thinkers also tend to be the first to notice early warning signs, such as the subtle noises a car makes when it is about to break down. Ordered thinkers are often less aware of these warning signs, especially if they have convinced themselves that they have already taken care of any such problems in advance. A common habit in ordered thinking is to carry out periodic inspections, and then to turn one's attention away from potential problems if no flaws are found. Chaotic thinkers tend to notice the tiny cracks and odd sounds right away, and to immediately recognize their implications.

Many chaotic thinkers are able to recall extensive details from books they have read or movies they have seen, such as the names of minor characters or minor incidents connected with the plot, even long afterward. This is not to imply that they have "photographic" memories in any literal sense (e.g., Loftus, 1979), but rather that they are more likely to attend to these details and consider their possible significance, and are thus more likely to remember them (e.g., Craik & Lockhart, 1972; Craik & Tulving, 1975).

Chaotic thinkers also tend to be more sensitive to the nuances of conversations and their ramifications. They are often acutely aware of the meanings behind a person's words, as well as the body language the person is using. Body language often counts for more than the words themselves (Ekman, 1982; Mehrabian, 1972), and many chaotic thinkers take full advantage of this. For instance, a woman might suddenly ask her spouse a direct question like, "Do you really love me?" and then notice his reactions, such as how he moved his hands or feet, whether he blushed, or even whether his pulse rate increased.

This attention to personal details can often be put to good use. For instance, it enables one to form better intuitions about what people are really like and how they are likely to respond. It also helps one to become more aware of the needs and feelings of others. This is both a strength and a weakness, however, for chaotic thinkers are sometimes willing to help people even before they ask, having already picked up on their needs. Those whom they are trying to help might then come to believe that the chaotic thinkers can see right through them, and are sensing things that they might not want to reveal (e.g., Haley, 1973).

The various details that chaotic thinkers tend to notice and absorb are probably less extensively organized than the facts collected by most ordered thinkers (e.g., Bower, 1970; E. E. Smith & Medin, 1981). In chaotic thinking, there seems to be an almost "random access" quality to the way memories are stored and retrieved. Chaotic thinkers are often able to recall various details with surprising speed and accuracy, seemingly without having to conduct lengthy memory searches or follow traditional retrieval pathways. But although they tend to notice and remember many subtle details, they usually avoid cluttering their minds with exact numbers or figures, which is one reason why there are so few chaotic accountants.

Because ordered thinkers are generally less sensitive to subtle details, there is probably a greater tendency in ordered thinking to fill in those details in memory. This would typically be done in using memory schemas, scripts, and other organizing structures (Barlett, 1932; Neisser, 1967; Schank & Abelson, 1977). As a general rule, the more organized a person's memory becomes, the less likely it is that incidental details will be remembered accurately, particularly those that do not fit in with existing principles, categories, or plans. In chaotic thinking, memories for details would therefore be less affected by the conventional organizing tendencies of the human mind.

# 4

## Basic Techniques of Chaotic Cognition

We next consider some of the basic techniques of chaotic thinking and provide examples of how they might be applied in general types of chaotic situations. Although these techniques represent only a small part of the total, integrated nature of chaotic thinking, they provide some insight into the kinds of methods that chaotic thinkers often employ. We emphasize, however, that only by studying chaotic thinking in its entirety can one begin to understand how and why these various techniques work. In any situation, the most appropriate response depends on the total context of what is happening, as well as on the abilities and talents of the individual.

For this reason, chaotic techniques should never be applied as part of a preconceived plan. Rather, it is important that they remain open-ended. When these techniques are used for specific purposes or to support a specific plan, they often give people something to focus on, anticipate, and counteract. This is when they are most likely to fail. Similarly, when chaos is employed destructively, as when a person sets out to ruin someone else's plans or to get even with them, it often backfires. When chaotic thinkers react to something someone has done, it is usually to demonstrate the futility of trying to impose plans that are blatantly unrealistic, inappropriate, or quixotic, and to encourage the person to acquire a more realistic perspective.

When properly used, chaotic techniques allow one to intensify the moment and create new opportunities for insight, rather than to achieve specific goals. In retrospect, they might seem brilliantly planned, but this is usually an illusion, for chaotic situations can unfold along many paths. These techniques might be employed for general purposes, such as to restore harmony to a situation that has become unbearably structured, but most chaotic thinkers would avoid using them to achieve a particular end. In fact, chaotic techniques are often used merely to gauge how someone might respond to an unexpected event.

We have already touched upon some of these techniques in previous chapters. The present chapter expands upon them in greater detail, and describes particular ways in which they are often used. Again, however, these techniques should be considered merely as illustrations of chaotic behavior, and as general guidelines or principles for what chaotic thinkers typically do. In fact, most chaotic thinkers would seldom actually follow any of these principles as rules per se. When dealing with specific situations, they usually just respond according to their instincts for what should be done in that moment. For this reason, most chaotic thinkers would benefit by learning about these techniques only insofar as they make explicit certain aspects of chaotic thinking that they might not have previously recognized.

In ordered thinking, one often needs to pause and ask, "What principles or rules are appropriate here?" Ordered thinkers are thus usually better at following principles and applying specific techniques, but they often apply them blindly, especially if they do not have sufficient understanding of them. It is therefore important to consider the entire spectrum of chaotic thinking when employing these methods.


## BECOMING UNFOCUSED


The first technique, that of becoming unfocused, is often one of the hardest things for people to learn, especially those who have become accustomed to thinking only in ordered ways. Most ordered thinkers want to keep their minds focused on some pressing issue or problem, as this is normally what drives them to achieve their goals. Most chaotic thinkers, however, usually strive to become unfocused and to experience the richness and complexity of the moment. They generally avoid thinking about the future and its consequences; in fact, they often think about nothing in particular. They might go walking for hours and just observe and absorb this or that without dwelling on any issues or problems. They might simply notice their bodily motions, such as the way their arms move back and forth as they walk. They might become engaged in swinging a key chain, bouncing a ball, or counting the cracks on the sidewalk. They might simply stare at cars or tree limbs. These simple activities help them to attend to what is happening in the moment and allow their minds to wander freely.

The old analogy of seeing the whole forest and not just one particular tree applies to much of chaotic thinking. As one looks at the forest, one gets a better sense of what a tree actually is, because one then sees a variety of trees. If one focuses on only a single tree, then one tends to assume that every other tree is identical to it. By becoming unfocused, chaotic thinkers are thus able to acquire a broader, more realistic perspective on things.

Ordered thinkers sometimes recognize this need to be unfocused and to escape temporarily from the stress of planning and structuring their lives, but they usually look for a system to help them do so. They often want a precise recipe, like meditation or self-hypnosis, that they can follow in an ordered, step-by-step manner. Most chaotic thinkers seek natural ways of becoming unfocused and would tend to regard such methods as overly structured or ritualized.

When ordered thinkers walk into a situation, they tend to focus on certain things right away. For example, they might focus on how they want the conversation to go, or how they want a relationship to develop. From the very outset, they often have specific expectations for exactly what should happen. In many of these situations, however, it is often better to try to expand one's awareness and avoid trying to isolate, regulate, or define what is happening.

In learning to become unfocused, it helps to ask oneself, "How many things do I see right now, and what is the relationship among these things?" It also helps to engage in activities without having a specific goal or purpose. For instance, one might go to an art exhibit or a museum and simply wander around. Or, one might go to see a movie that one never intended to see, merely for the experience of being in a situation that is unplanned.

The unfocused qualities of chaotic thinking promote an increased openness to new experiences. By and large, chaotic thinkers are more open to experiencing new things and seeing situations from new perspectives. Their ability to consider multiple realities and interpretations stems from their tendency to broaden their focus and explore many possibilities.

Incubation, which was discussed in chapter 2, is also encouraged by the unfocused qualities of chaotic thinking. By defocusing one's attention away from a problem, one is often in a better position to see the inherent, underlying structure behind it. In ordered thinking, one often wants to force a solution and to be in control of the problem at every phase, but this can prevent the emergence of new insights. To use an analogy, once ordered thinkers plant a seed, they often want to push the roots down and pull the plant up, instead of letting it grow naturally. Similarly, most ordered thinkers want to be in control of their ideas at every point, making sure they turn out in just the right way instead of letting them develop naturally. In general, they often have trouble letting go of the reins and just allowing things to happen.

Once one has all the information that bears on a problem, instead of sitting down and saying that one is now going to solve it, it might be better to try to become unfocused and refuse to think of anything that might be directly related to it. For example, one might simply take an undirected walk and, if necessary, count street lights or people to occupy one's mind in other ways. This would help to shift one's focus away from initial biases and expectations and to achieve a broader perspective on the problem.

Another way to encourage unfocusing is to practice unstructured daydreaming. For instance, if one were worried about losing one's job, one might daydream about going on a vacation, discovering a hidden treasure, or meeting an interesting person. By fantasizing about many different and seemingly unrelated things, it is often possible to gain new and unexpected insights into current problems.

There is already an enormous literature on the benefits of nondirected thinking of this sort (e.g., Adams, 1974; de Bono, 1975; Edwards, 1986; Hilgard, 1977). We stress, however, that becoming unfocused represents only one technique that chaotic thinkers employ, and it would not necessarily be used in all situations. In particular, chaotic thinkers tend to become highly focused in crisis situations, where it is usually important not to become distracted or allow one's attention to wander.

## SEEING MEANING IN THE MEANINGLESS

Chaotic thinkers often try to see beauty and significance in ordinary things. For instance, they might look at a neon light and make it seem special and meaningful. They may be fascinated by the swirling patterns on the surface of a lake or swimming pool. They see meaningful shapes in clouds. Their metaphors invite creative explorations and provide meaning to things that might otherwise be overlooked or regarded as meaningless.

As discussed previously, there is often a rich and unstructured interconnectedness among ideas and symbols in chaotic thinking. Everything is connected to everything else, which helps to make each event seem meaningful. For example, chaotic thinkers might notice that a particular melody reminds them of how trees sway in the wind or how certain people walk. They might notice that there are certain things all of their friends have in common. By exploring these multiple connections and their implications, chaotic thinkers often promote the emergence of new insights and discoveries.

Seeing meaning in the meaningless is a multiple reality exploration. Chaotic thinkers usually try to discover a variety of different ways in which something that is ordinary might become meaningful. When somebody does something that seems irrelevant, instead of simply dismissing or criticizing it, they often consider ways in which it might be significant. Instead of judging things as facts, they tend to explore alternative possibilities and interpretations. Whenever new events occur, they often speculate on their multiple implications.

For example, suppose a minor earthquake struck somewhere in California, and computer stocks fell on the very same day. Chaotic thinkers might ask if it were possible that investors were worried about Silicon Valley being damaged by the quake. They would not consider this as a necessary or likely connection, but merely as an alternative reality that might be worth exploring.

Ordered thinking often excludes such remote connections and possibilities. Many ordered thinkers, for instance, limit their world to things that have direct, causal connections and are thus very predictable. But this predictability begins to block out all other possibilities. In one sense ordered thinkers often prefer this, because it simplifies things, but over a lifetime it can empty their lives of all of its meaning. The structuring tendencies of ordered thinking frequently serve as a substitute for that meaning, but it is usually a poor substitute.

## CREATING APPARENT STUPIDITY

Chaotic thinking is inherently playful, and most chaotic thinkers are not overly concerned about making minor errors or embarrassing mistakes. As a result, they often engage in apparently stupid behavior on purpose, especially if it helps loosen up rigid patterns or routines. For example, when walking with friends, they might suddenly jump into a puddle and claim to be a tidal wave, or pick up a stick and begin twirling it like a baton. Besides encouraging openness and levity, these apparently stupid acts keep others from responding to them in habitual ways or placing them into pigeonholes.

As an example of how this technique might be used, suppose you were involved in a relationship that had become stagnant, and you wanted to encourage more honesty and flexibility. You might begin wearing a pair of extremely dark sunglasses that made you look silly, but which you claimed made you more attractive. You might then pretend to accidentally bump into people or trip over furniture.

By doing these apparently stupid things, one can often return the novelty to situations that have become rigid and devoid of meaning. It makes one more interesting and less predictable, and it opens up new possibilities. By doing things that appear stupid and pointless, one also begins to take chances and to experience a greater sense of freedom.

An ordered response to problems in relationships is often to complain to the person or to try to make him or her jealous. But this generally results in unnecessary confrontations and further misunderstandings. By making the situation less serious, these problems can be avoided, and one can usually increase the chances of bringing about constructive changes.

Chaotic thinkers sometimes purposely misunderstand people in order to create apparent stupidity. For instance, if repeatedly told by a supervisor that they needed to be more concerned about improving their attitude towards work, they might begin wearing a shirt with an enormous smiling face on it, saying "I'm a happy worker." These chaotic misunderstandings often discourage people from making further, arbitrary demands on them.

Another form of apparent stupidity is to pretend that someone else has convinced one to do something stupid. For example, suppose that your spouse did not approve of your present job, which you really liked and did not want to give up. You might mention that a friend of yours has just talked you into giving up your steady job and becoming a traveling salesman for a company that makes vacuum cleaners. This would require that you spend a lot of time away from home, but your friend has made it sound really exciting. Your spouse would probably get angry at the other person for trying to corrupt you and would then be more willing to accept your present job.

Creating apparent stupidity is an excellent way of dealing with those who believe that they can manipulate others with impunity. For example, if two people had jointly purchased a car, and one of them suddenly refused to share it, a chaotic response might be to paint the car a bizarre color, claiming that this would now make it look brand new. Or suppose someone insisted on teaching you how to play golf, even though you tried to explain that you really were not interested. You might let go of the club each time you swung. Instead of openly confronting these attempts at manipulation, the chaotic response leads them down strange and unexpected paths.

Doing apparently stupid things often causes people to underestimate one, and thus allows one to disguise one's true strengths. If people think you are incompetent, that you pose no real threat, they usually lower their guard. A good example is the detective who comes up with a stupid solution to a crime, and proposes it in earnest to the suspect who, in ridiculing it, reveals that he or she is guilty. Consider, also, the classic ploy in which a spy deliberately lets himself get caught, which then provides him with an opportunity to acquire the important information he needs. For instance, the spy might intentionally allow the other person to easily take his gun, in what appears to be a stupid blunder, but then the person discovers that the gun has no bullets.

Allowing oneself to appear foolish at times also helps keep one's pride in check, which is especially important for many ordered thinkers. By deliberately doing something that is apparently stupid, one no longer has to worry about always being right. One can thus cast off the hobgoblin of never making a blunder; having already been stupid, one can now risk being insightful and innovative.

## DOING THE NEXT BEST THING

One of the principles of ordered thinking is to try to do the very best thing in every situation. Accordingly, an ordered thinker's plans are usually designed to produce the optimal result or effect. In chaotic thinking, one often does the next best thing and avoids making the obvious choice.

There are three rationales for this. First, it makes one less transparent and predictable. Second, it enables one to step outside any unreasonable plans or structures that are being imposed onto the situation. Third, it helps one to consider a wider variety of options without necessarily ruining one's chances for survival or success.

As an example, suppose your boss had just decided to have you do something that you considered unethical. The next best thing might be to call in sick that day and obtain a medical excuse from your doctor. This would buy you time and allow your boss to reconsider matters. It would also allow you to survive the situation without seriously endangering your job or career.

Doing the next best thing can often help to forestall unpleasant confrontations. Suppose someone wanted you to marry him or her and expected you to make a firm decision one way or the other, which you were not yet ready to do. You might do the next best thing by going off on a vacation by yourself. The person might be angry with you for taking the vacation, and perhaps accuse you of being selfish, but this would allow you to explore other dimensions of the relationship and would give you new things to talk about when you returned.

In general, doing the next best thing is often effective when people are trying to provoke you into doing something you do not want to do. For example, a group of bikers approached a truck driver who was eating lunch at a restaurant. They first took a jar of sugar and poured it into his soup, asking him, "What are you going to do about it?" "Nothing," he replied. They then unscrewed a salt shaker and poured salt into his drink. "What are you going to do about it?" "Nothing," he replied. Then they poured pepper into his lap. "What are you going to do about it?" "Nothing," he again replied. Finally he got up, paid his bill, and walked out. One of the bikers turned to the waitress and said, "He wasn't much of a man, was he?" "He's not much of a driver, either," she replied. "He just ran over all your bikes."

Sometimes doing the next best thing can create surprisingly favorable impressions. Suppose your son broke something and expected you to punish him for it. Instead of following through with the punishment, you might come in and say, "Well, people have accidents and bad days. I know you've been feeling really bad about this, and I think this time we'll just let it ride." Having spent the day anticipating that you would do something bad to him, your child is likely to be fascinated by your unexpected understanding and insight. He might end up having much greater respect for you than if you had merely punished him, which would have been the most obvious response.

Thinking that something always has to be done in a certain way can limit a person's ability to develop and express new ideas. For example, if you were trying to write a story, instead of thinking about the very best way to write it, you might think about other ways which, although not so ideal, would still be acceptable. This often helps reduce writer's block and allows one to find alternative methods of expression (Elbow, 1981; Leader, 1991).

Always doing the most obvious thing can keep one from exploring creative possibilities, whereas doing the nonobvious thing can often lead to unexpected discoveries. When stuck on a problem, for example, it often helps to take an approach that is less than ideal and that others might not approve of, but that might conceivably lead to the missing insight (e.g., Levine, 1987; Wickelgren, 1974).

This is why novices sometimes make discoveries that experts overlook, being less aware of the best approaches.

Suppose you and your fellow employees had not had a decent raise in many years, and the obvious response of complaining to management had no effect. You might do the next best thing, such as taking an embarrassing, part-time job at a fast-food restaurant and ocassionally wearing your uniform to work. If management objected to this, which they almost certainly would, you could simply explain that you had no choice; the cost of living had increased, and you had bills to pay. This method is often more effective than simply trying to give logical arguments for why you deserve the raise, which the management is usually prepared to counter.

This technique can sometimes allow one to create interesting situations and opportunities in relationships. For instance, suppose that while on a date, it became clear that a woman was not really interested in seeing you again, although you still wanted to see her. The obvious strategy of trying to convince her to go out with you again would probably fail. In such cases, a chaotic thinker might do the next best thing by creating an alternative reality that opened up new possibilties. For instance, he might casually mention, in the course of the date, that he had a twin brother. He might then call the woman several days later and claim to be this twin, explaining, "My brother has told me all about you, and you sound very interesting. I would really like to meet you, especially since my brother thought that we would have much more in common." The woman might then go out with him merely out of curiosity, which would allow them to explore entirely different aspects of the relationship.

Consider the case where a teacher might be trying to give an exam, and several students insist on talking outside the classroom. The teacher might deal with this situation by doing the next best thing and creating an alternative reality, instead of simply telling them to stop. For instance, the teacher might tell the disruptive students, "I'm trying to give an exam on ESP, and although I don't mind if you talk, several of my students have complained that your thoughts are disturbing them."

As a further example that illustrates this technique, suppose one of your neighbors at an apartment complex had been harassing you. You might consider confronting the neighbor directly or complaining to the management, which would be the most obvious response, but this could lead to retaliation or revenge. Instead, you might do the next best thing, such as screaming at imaginary people late at night. This would intensify the moment, raise new uncertainties about you, and increase the complexity of the situation. You could then leave a large note on your own door several days later, supposedly from the managers, stating that they heard that you have been making violent threats against other tenants and were recently involved in several fights, and that they are planning to evict you if there is any further repetition of this violent behavior.

At the very least, doing the nonobvious thing allows one to escape the stagnation and stigma of always being predictable. The directness and predictability of ordered thinking usually enables one to take the initiative, but it often lets others jump ahead and gain the advantage later on. By doing things that are not so predictable, one's actions are less likely to be anticipated or exploited.

## DOING THE OUTRAGEOUS

Occasionally, chaotic thinkers are tempted to do something truly outrageous. Besides the obvious effect of generating large amounts of chaos, doing outrageous things can provide opportunities for exploring novel situations and discovering creative solutions to problems. It can also encourage rational behavior in others. It is important, however, that people know, at least implicitly, that one is doing these things in a playful and understanding way and not merely to harass or make fun of them.

Most chaotic thinkers would normally do outrageous things to intensify the moment, to call attention to important needs, or to try to restore lost harmony to a situation. For instance, one might begin wearing a large bandage wrapped around one's head for several days, as a way of making life more interesting, exploring people's reactions, or perhaps to symbolize that his or her current job situation is causing him or her headaches.

Doing outrageous things can have many practical uses in everyday situations. Suppose you were called into someone's office to be reprimanded for something that was not really your fault. As the person began to lecture you, you might suddenly pretend to have a cramp, which became so severe that you had to take off your shoe and begin rubbing your foot. Or you might begin scratching uncontrollably and then mention that you have been having a problem with one of your neighbor's pets. At this point the person will likely forget about wanting to criticize you, and instead will be thinking of some excuse for getting you out of the office.

Suppose the situation were more serious, and your boss or supervisor wanted you to do something illegal, and you were made to feel that you could not refuse. You might schedule an appointment at your local hospital to explore the possibility of minor surgery, or set a court date to appeal a recent parking ticket. This would provide you with a perfectly legitimate excuse for not having to commit the illegal act. You could then explain, "I really wanted to help you out with this, but I simply couldn't get away." Besides protecting your position, this allows the other person to reconsider the consequences of his or her plans.

Although often effective in disrupting another person's plans and keeping the person from manipulating others, doing outrageous things also has a more general, beneficial purpose. It encourages people to reassess whether those plans are really appropriate, given the bizarre and unexpected complications that have suddenly occurred. This often causes them to pause and think about the situation in a more reasonable and rational manner.

An example of this is when chaotic thinkers pretend to espouse extreme positions in defense of policies they are actually opposed to. For instance, if someone were defending capital punishment, they might argue that all criminals should be electrocuted, even for a first offense. They might suggest that the criminals be made to hold the wires in their teeth, so that the electricity will reach their brains more quickly. They might even suggest that the circuit should be connected to a fireworks display, so that the moment of death will be celebrated. Such outrageous proposals can often cause people to reconsider the wisdom of their original views.

As mentioned previously, ordered thinking tends to promote highly polarized, "yes/no" choices and perspectives, which often leave one with less and less freedom. In considering outrageous possibilities, chaotic thinking can open up other options, alternatives, and points of view, which can restore choice and freedom to a situation that has lost them.

Even minor forms of outrageous behavior can sometimes be very effective. For instance, suppose you were receiving annoying phone calls that could not be traced. You might put a message on your answering machine for a week, in the voice of an operator, saying that your phone has been disconnected and is no longer in service. Besides frustrating those who have been making the annoying calls, leaving such a message creates an interesting effect with other callers. For example, you might gain new insights into whether certain people really cared about you by seeing whether or not they made an effort to contact you in some other way.

Ken Kesey, the well-known novelist, once said that if you paint it bright enough, most people will not see it. This is generally true of the seemingly bizarre things that many chaotic thinkers do. When chaotic thinkers intensify the moment and create bizarre effects, the bizarreness often fades once the moment has passed. In contrast, using a more moderate or direct approach, as in ordered thinking, tends to result in greater visibility over time.

Bizarreness is usually easier to accept when it occurs honestly and up front, rather than insidiously. Compare, for example, the person who immediately tells you that they do psychic readings based on the shape of a person's nose, which they might even be able to laugh about, versus the person who slowly reveals their irrational beliefs over time, and dares you to criticize them. The latter tends to occur more often in ordered thinking, whereas most chaotic thinkers are less concerned about having their fanciful ideas exposed and evaluated.

We should emphasize that most chaotic thinkers do not go around doing outrageous things merely to disrupt the lives of others or as a matter of habit. Much of the time they are relatively passive and would generally engage in such actions only in response to an unstimulating or irrational situation. As a rule, they usually start out by trying to deal with a person simply and rationally, without engaging in bizarre behavior. If this fails, they might then resort to doing outrageous things as a way of intensifying the moment and creating alternative realities. And even when they do employ bizarre methods, they usually try to leave people with a good feeling about them. Even though they might be outrageous, they can be funny, lovable, and nonthreatening at the same time.

## AVOIDING REPETITION

Ordinarily, chaotic thinkers try to avoid repeating the very same behaviors or patterns of thought. Like an artist who explores different styles of expression from one painting to the next, chaotic thinkers usually prefer to vary their methods. By avoiding repetition, they intensify the moment, increase complexity, promote creativity, and keep others from predicting what they are likely to do next.

By frequently varying one's responses, one can cause people to wonder about one's true interests or intentions. This can make it difficult for others to manipulate or take advantage of one. For example, if a fellow employee had been planning on taking over your job, and began doing various things to annoy you, you might respond by creating unpredictable surprises for the person—some good, like a nice gift; some bad, like a stupid joke; but never the same. The person would then be caught off balance and would always be guessing what the next surprise would be. And even when the surprise was good it would arouse suspicion. By varying the nature of the surprises, one encourages chaos rather than vengeance and increases the chances of ultimately restoring harmony to the situation.

As a rule, chaotic thinkers tend to do worse on repetitive tasks, whereas ordered thinkers tend to do better. Unlike chaotic thinkers, ordered thinkers usually do not get bored with the predictability of a repetitive task; in fact, they generally like doing things in the same way, and usually improve with practice. This contributes to their sense of accomplishment and pride. However, having discovered an effective way to do something, ordered thinkers might conclude that it is the only way to do it, which could rule out exploring other, possibly more efficient ways.

Most chaotic thinkers, given a task and told that it must be done in a certain way, quickly become bored. Having already performed the task a particular way, they are likely to ask, "What is the point of doing it the same way again?" This is why many chaotic thinkers try to discover novel ways of doing a task, even if it seems to be a waste of time.

From the perspective of chaotic thinking, every situation is unique, and thus repetition is seen as pointless. What worked in the past may not work in the present. One cannot step in a river in the same place twice, because the river is always changing. Although this tendency to avoid repetition may lead to inefficiency, it can also lead to the discovery of new and sometimes better ways of doing things. For this reason, chaotic thinkers usually try to vary the methods they had previously used in similar situations, even if those methods had been highly successful. Ordered thinkers tend to rely on the same, proven methods over time, and are usually reluctant to change things that seem to be working. They are thus usually more consistent and reliable, but they tend to be less innovative.

There is also a greater tendency in ordered thinking to repeat past experiences. Ordered thinkers might see the same movie or read the same book over and over, to savor its ideas and replay its structure. When chaotic thinkers see a movie or read a book, it usually becomes a part of them, and they rarely feel the need to repeat the experience.

In learning to avoid repetition, it often helps to practice doing even simple, routine tasks in original ways. For example, one might begin to vary how one ties one's shoes, what one eats for breakfast each morning, or the particular route one takes while driving to work. These simple departures from routine habits can help one to move away from thinking about every situation as a narrow, predictable, and often meaningless event.

## INCREASING PURPOSEFUL CLUTTER

In the previous two chapters, we described how chaotic thinkers often try to increase complexity in a situation as a way of intensifying the moment and keeping their options open. One of the most effective ways of doing this is to increase purposeful clutter, adding little complications here and there in response to someone's efforts to impose excessive amounts of structure. The clutter is "purposeful" in that it is tailored to these structuring tendencies.

This technique can often help dissipate the momentum that an ordered plan has acquired. One would initially accept the plan, introduce purposeful clutter, and eventually try to slow it down. Because many ordered thinkers prefer to lead uncluttered lives, they normally want to simplify situations, which helps them to conrol things. Chaotic thinkers often respond to this by adding unexpected complications and thickening the plot.

Suppose your supervisor was reluctant to give you a raise and was prepared to counter your rational arguments by keeping the discussion simple and under his or her control. To increase purposeful clutter, you might comment on how interesting you found the various items on the person's desk, or ask where some of the items were bought. You could also ask for advice on various problems that you were having at home. These digressions would gradually complicate his or her strategies for how to respond to you, and he or she might then welcome an opportunity to resolve the issue of the raise instead of debating you over it.

Another way that chaotic thinkers often slow down rigidly structured plans is by giving inaccurate compliments, which a person will then feel compelled to stop and correct. For instance, you might say to someone who is trying to pressure you into doing something, "I really like the way you are handling this situation. It is the same method George Washington used to deal with his troops at Valley Forge." They would first have to stop and figure out what you meant, and then explain that they were really using a different method. This would increase the complexity of the situation, not only by cluttering and interrupting the flow of the plan, but also by forcing them to reexamine their own behavior.

A related method for increasing purposeful clutter is to suddenly ask people simple, casual questions that disrupt the flow of conversation and make them stop and think. For example, you might suddenly ask someone whether today is Thursday when it is actually Friday, or how to spell an unusual word, like "hiccough." These innocent questions often provide sufficient clutter to keep the person from effectively controlling the conversation.

Creating purposeful clutter is also helpful when one wishes to avoid answering direct, probing questions. For example, if someone insisted on knowing what you really thought about a certain political candidate, you could say that one of the things the candidate said about eliminating leaks in government reminds you of a time when you were 7 years old, when your older brother told you that the milk carton was leaking and you tried to repair the leak but could not find any tape, so you had to use chewing gum. In using this method, you would try to create the impression that you wanted to give as complete an answer as possible and were not merely trying to avoid the question. You could then continue to bring in multiple associations and digressions, until the person finally gave up. As with most chaotic techniques, this method has the advantage that it is nonconfrontational.

Chaotic thinking often makes use of multiple realities in creating purposeful clutter. Suppose you were upset by the way you had been treated at work, for instance. You might respond by telling different people different complaints so that your supervisors kept hearing new, conflicting things every time they spoke with someone. You could tell one person that you were angry about not getting a raise, another that you were thinking of complaining to the union, a third that you wanted better benefits, and so on. This would make it difficult for your supervisors to plan specific rebuttals to your concerns.

This last method usually works best when the complaints are tailored to the biases of those to whom you are complaining. For example, you might complain about your salary to someone who had not had a recent raise. If someone had a personality conflict with your supervisor, you might mention that you had just had an argument with this supervisor and could not understand why he or she reacted that way. Not only would the listener tend to remember your complaints more accurately, he or she would also tend to become a passionate sympathizer. You might also go to some people who like your supervisor, and describe him or her as wonderful and caring. Your supervisor would then hear that even though you have some complaints, you also think highly of him or her.

As with most chaotic techniques, the purpose of increasing clutter is to encourage rational thinking and beneficial change. Chaotic thinkers almost never introduce clutter merely for the sake of causing problems. Rather, their intention is usually to stimulate reasonable insights in those situations that have become structured to an unrealistic degree, and to restore the harmony that those structures have removed.

As a further illustration, consider how chaotic thinking might be used in the following situation: Suppose that a sandwich shop began to tow away anyone who parked in their parking lot for longer than 10 minutes, because they had a contract with a local towing company and were making a large profit. If one's car were towed away unfairly, an ordered response might be to confront the owner of the sandwich shop or make a formal complaint. A chaotic response to this unreasonable policy would be to create purposeful clutter. Chaotic thinkers might take down the license plates of some of the cars parked in the lot and then call the towing company, identifying themselves as an employee at the sandwich shop, and insist that those cars be towed away. They might continue to make such calls for several days, sometimes giving fictitious descriptions of cars so that the towing company would not be able to find them. The people whose cars were towed would become angry, the towing company would become frustrated, and the owners of the sandwich shop would become perplexed.

If this did not bring about a change in the towing policy, chaotic thinkers might then call the towing company and report that someone has been playing a phone prank and has been making phony towing requests. They might claim to be the assistant manager, and request that from that point on, the towing company was to ignore all towing requests that were not made by him or her personally. The employees at the sandwich shop would then begin to wonder why the tow trucks stopped coming. Finally, chaotic thinkers might distribute hundreds of apologetic flyers on the windshields of cars parked in the surrounding area, supposedly from the sandwich shop, saying how sorry they were for all the inconvenience their recent towing policy had caused and offering to give a free sandwich to anyone who brought in the attached coupon.

In using this technique, it is usually better to introduce clutter gradually, so that the complications seem natural and do not immediately overwhelm people. This allows them to react to one complication at a time and slowly draws their energy away from their original plans. They are then more likely to have realistic insights into the consequences of their actions and policies.

There are many variations on the general technique of increasing purposeful clutter. Consider, for instance, how it might be used when driving in heavy traffic. People who have made plans to arrive somewhere at a certain time often become intolerant of any unexpected delays and may begin to drive impatiently and tailgate. If this happens, instead of simply hitting the brake and possibly creating a dangerous situation, one might respond by weaving back and forth, under the pretense of trying to make it easier for the person to pass, but which increases the complexity of the situation and makes it harder to pass. This should be done in such a way that it appears that one is actually trying to help the person, so that the person does not retaliate. The technique is often effective with those who believe that they have an inherent right to drive fast, especially after having been delayed, and are entitled to make up for the lost time by disobeying traffic laws or intimidating other drivers.

Practicing chaotic techniques can help one to become more comfortable with complexity and to get out of the habit of always trying to reduce it, which is a common tendency in ordered thinking. Encouraging purposeful clutter also gives one access to a variety of different options at any given moment, which increases one's flexibility. This can be especially useful if it appears that a chaotic technique has backfired.

For instance, suppose it became clear that you were the one who had circulated humorous, playful memos at work, and your supervisor came to you and said, "I know you did this. Don't try to deny it." You might respond by saying, "You know, a lot of people have been telling me that you don't have a good sense of humor. I thought that if I put out these memos, people would start laughing and realize that you really were a pretty funny person. I did it because I really care about you." By responding in this candid, chaotic fashion, instead of simply pretending that you knew nothing about the memos, you could create a whole new level of complexity. Whereas before you might have been perceived as an enemy, you could now be perceived as a possible ally. Whatever started the problems to begin with would likely be forgotten as the person tries to figure out this alternative reality that you have suddenly created.

One of the reasons why chaotic thinkers are often so difficult to manipulate is that they can quickly put people into situations that they no longer understand and in which there are no obvious rules. This often causes them to put their original plans on hold and attend to these new and sudden complications. Eventually, this can lead them to explore alternative perspectives and possibilities that they might never have considered otherwise.

## UTILIZING NATURAL EVENTS (GOING WITH THE FLOW)

As we have mentioned, a central principle in chaotic thinking is to try to utilize whatever is happening in the moment and to avoid direct confrontation or active resistance. Chaotic thinkers rarely try to run uphill, swim against the current, or fight city hall. Instead, they usually accept and work with the existing forces in a situation, and try to go with the natural flow.

Excessive reliance on ordered thinking often causes one to resist the natural flow. Once ordered thinkers have a plan in mind, they might stick to that plan no matter what. For instance, they might sit indefinitely waiting to make a left turn against heavy traffic, having already made the plan to turn there. After deciding that they want something, they might go straight for their object, and devise specific plans for how to get it and how to meet any resistance they might encounter. When chaotic thinkers want something, they often do not go directly for it. Instead, they often "dance" around it, advancing and retreating, until whatever is defending it gets exhausted. They would first try to dissipate whatever was blocking their way, without confronting or attacking the resistance.

As an analogy, ordered thinking is like a fish that goes directly for the bait—and often gets caught. Chaotic thinking is like a crab that sidles up to the bait, nibbles at it, lets the fisherman jerk the line, then nibbles some more, until at last the crab has taken all of the bait off the hook without getting caught. In trying to snatch the whole bait all at once, those employing an ordered approach often become trapped.

Consider again the contrast between ordered and chaotic driving styles. When rushing home on a crowded freeway, ordered thinkers often drive straight ahead and press on until they encounter a traffic jam and become stuck. Chaotic thinkers usually look for small openings and work themselves slowly through the traffic by picking their spots, seeing opportunities, and staying in the moment. This allows them to avoid becoming stuck. Drivers employing a highly ordered approach often succumb to traffic jams because their whole strategy is usually to drive as fast as they can and to challenge any cars that get in their way.

The chaotic technique of utilizing natural events can help one to accept and deal with many everyday problems. Consider, for instance, how you might deal with manipulative in-laws who have decided that they know how to raise your children better than you do. An ordered reaction might be to confront them, arguing that they have no right to meddle in family affairs, or claiming that they do not know enough about the children to be giving any advice. This is fighting against the flow, because the in-laws are unlikely to change their habits. Instead, you could take the easier route of simply asking for their advice. You could mention, for example, that you will try to raise your children in a way that shares their fundamental values. You could tell them that you appreciate their wisdom and that you will try to incorporate it into your style. Instead of challenging and confronting them, you would now have them on your side.

Chaotic thinkers often try to blend in with those around them, so they will not be regarded as a threat. They usually prefer to remain invisible, as discussed in chapter 2. Ordered thinkers often resist blending in, believing that it would compromise their principles or values. In many situations, however, taking a hard-lined attitude does not work, at least in proportion to what one stands to gain.

For instance, suppose your clothes or hairstyle offended potential employers. An ordered reaction might be to stand by the principle that people have the right to dress any way they want. One might be tempted to say, "I will not cut my hair in order to get this position. If they won't hire me on the basis of my actual qualifications, then I'm not interested." With a chaotic approach, however, changing your clothes or cutting your hair really does not change who you are. Most chaotic thinkers would simply dress for the job and blend in, if that is what is required, knowing that they would not be abandoning their individuality by doing so.

This technique of accepting a situation and utilizing it might seem to contradict that of doing outrageous things to disrupt rigid policies and affect change, which was described earlier in the chapter. However, both techniques serve the same general purpose. When chaotic thinkers do something outrageous, their intention is usually to create freedom in a situation where all freedom is drained away, and where they have few other choices. They are not really confronting people, but are simply trying to open up the situation so that they can survive in it. In trying to utilize natural events, they likewise avoid confronting people, and are responding in such a way as to survive within that situation.

There are many cases where refusing to go with the flow has led to disastrous results. Consider the farmer who decides to plant a big-money crop in a climate where it will not grow, or the entrepeneur who establishes a business in a location where no customers are likely to come. These endeavors might fulfill a person's lifelong dreams and ambitions, but they usually end up failing.

Going with the flow also means not arbitrarily changing something that is currently working. If one finds a winning strategy against an opponent, it is often a mistake to purposely change that strategy just for the sake of changing it. In ordered thinking, one is often tempted to stop doing what has been successful up to that point in order to confuse an opponent, but this usually backfires. When chaotic thinkers change their strategies or routines, it is usually done impulsively and to intensify the moment, rather than as part of a deliberate plan.

We mentioned that most chaotic thinkers avoid trying to "fight city hall." But even when they go along with city hall, and thus go with the flow, they try to use that flow to their advantage. Ordered thinkers tend to fight city hall, and gain a certain amount of satisfaction in doing so. Yet this often results in eventual frustration, fights to the death, and the collapse of long-range plans. Compromise can often get one where one wants to go, as long as one is willing to make small adjustments. This does not necessarily mean defeat, just that some of the plans may need to be modified.

Because chaotic thinkers generally believe in multiple realities, they seldom worry over the issue of compromise. One method of achieving something can be just as good as another. They thus tend not to limit themselves to certain preconceived notions about what is right and proper, which can sometimes create problems in ordered thinking. By going with the flow, one implicitly accepts many alternatives and possibilities that extend beyond the boundaries of personal pride.

Chaotic thinkers often combine the techniques of utilizing natural events and increasing purposeful clutter, which was described in the previous section. For example, suppose you were a teacher, and one of your students complained that he needed to get at least a "C" in your class in order for his parents to buy him a new car. Although you tried to explain that this did not seem like a good enough reason to warrant special consideration, he was relentless, and continued to beg and argue. Instead of fighting with him, you could go with the flow and accept his arguments, and then complicate the situation in unexpected ways.

For instance, you might offer to let him take three additional exams over the summer, and if he passed the exams, you would give him a "C" in the course. You could say that you have never made an exception like this before, but because he was so obviously concerned about it, you were willing to give him this special opportunity. You could also point out that you were allowing him to do this without having to pay any summer tuition. In fact, you would be sacrificing your own free time this summer, just for his benefit. This would make it appear that you were being extremely fair and reasonable, while having complicated matters considerably. Like most chaotic techniques, this should have an overall positive effect, and the student should emerge from the experience having learned some important lessons about requesting special privileges.

As a further example, suppose a heartless city official had decided to cut funding for animal shelters, a move that you strongly opposed. Instead of simply writing a nasty letter, you could utilize the fact that there are a lot of stray cats in your neighborhood that needed love and care. You might put collars on the stray cats, with tags that said, "My name is Fluffy. If you find me, please call _____" and then give the name and number of the city official. The official would then get dozens of calls from different people, each claiming to have found his cat. This would make your point more effectively than direct confrontation and protest. It utilizes the situation in a chaotic manner and creates purposeful clutter that exacerbates an unfair policy.

The chaotic complications that often arise in everyday situations are neither inherently good nor inherently bad. Ordered thinkers, however, tend to see the worst in them, and thus overlook opportunities to utilize the complications in flexible and creative ways. By going with the flow, one can often see unexpected changes in a positive light and turn apparent failure into fortuitous success.

## INTENSIFYING A PROBLEM

Related to the technique of utilizing natural events is that of intensifying a problem in order to draw attention to it. This is sometimes the best way to encourage effective reactions to problems without becoming directly involved in their solution. In such cases, one not only goes with the flow, one turns up the rate of flow.

Many common annoyances can be dealt with in this manner by allowing them to become magnified into larger issues. For example, if the barking of your neighbor's dogs was disturbing you, you might record the barks and then play them back at high volume late at night. This would cause others in the neighborhood to become more aware of the problem, and it would eventually get resolved without your having to resort to direct confrontation.

As another example of intensifying a problem, suppose certain people were always criticizing you. Instead of fighting the criticisms, and trying to show how they have misjudged you, you might make up your own criticisms about yourself and distribute or display them. You could even invent criticisms that were more outrageous than the ones your critics had made. This would help to make you immune to any further criticism and might even generate sympathy and support.

For instance, suppose your supervisors came to you and complained that your paperwork was ocassionally late, that you did not always come to work on time, and that you sometimes took too long at lunch. You might simply accept these criticisms and then intensify them. You could begin spreading exaggerated rumors that your paperwork was the shoddiest paperwork that anyone on this planet had ever seen, that you were always late for everything, even to pick up your paycheck, and that you spent at least 3 hours a day in the cafeteria. When these rumors got around, your supervisors would almost come to your defense, wanting to present a more realistic picture. You have painted the picture totally black, and they are forced to shift and try to paint it white.

A common problem in the modern workplace is when those in charge try to micromanage every aspect of a worker's performance. A chaotic approach to this problem would be to encourage these tendencies to an absurd degree. For instance, one might suggest that all employees be required to record the number of sheets of paper they had used each day, indicate the type of food they had for lunch, or log in the number of water breaks they took. This would intensify the problem of trying to impose excessive control over how the workers performed their jobs, and would encourage more flexible and reasonable policies.

This technique can also be used to publicize secret plans and agendas, especially those of deceptive or overly ambitious people. For example, if someone were subtly trying to acquire power within an organization, one might create and distribute campaign buttons or bumper stickers with the person's name on them. The person would then be put in the position of having to publically deny wanting power while secretly desiring it.

Intensifying a problem can also help when you suspect that one is about to push for an undesirable policy change. For instance, if someone at work was about to argue strongly in favor of the rights of smokers, and propose that smoking be allowed in the workplace, instead of trying to counter those arguments directly, you could distribute flyers giving the standard, specious arguments from the tobacco industry, so that people would then say, "Yes, we've heard all that before."

## MAKING RAPID DECISIONS (GOING NOWHERE FAST)

In chaotic thinking, to use a common expression, it is usually better to go nowhere fast than nowhere slow. Why take more time to get to a place, if that is where you seem to be headed anyway? Making rapid decisions reflects the impulsive quality of chaotic thinking. Chaotic thinkers seldom waste time contemplating various choices or their hypothetical outcomes. They usually act on their impulses and discover the consequences of those actions right away.

Going nowhere fast helps one to quickly see which paths are unlikely to be rewarding. For instance, if you were out on a date and felt a sudden impulse to kiss the person, and if the moment seemed right, you might simply act on your impulse. At least, if you were rejected, you would know how things stood with that person right away. If you thought that your boss might want to fire you, you might suddenly demand a large raise, to see how he or she reacts. By responding rapidly and impulsively, one pushes an uncertain situation to a crisis point, where unspoken plans and feelings are often then revealed.

Going nowhere fast also helps one to avoid debating the wisdom of decisions that have already been made. Instead of hesitating, or dwelling on what might have been, one simply keeps on moving. Reflecting on the past is a common habit in ordered thinking, but for most chaotic thinkers it serves little purpose and merely prevents them from experiencing the total complexity and intensity of the moment.

Most ordered thinkers instinctively avoid making rapid decisions. They like their plans to unfold at a rate they are comfortable with, and hate to be rushed. As a result, the rhythm of their plans can often be disrupted if they are forced to respond quickly to sudden, unexpected complications. Because they seldom anticipate these complications, they will usually be caught off guard and may not have enough time to respond to them.

Suppose someone had proposed a new plan for reorganizing your department, which they thought would save alot of money, but which would actually disrupt the department and cause serious problems. If you were to carefully point out the obvious flaws in the plan, the person would probably have time to think of ways to respond to your concerns. Instead, you might start out by praising the plan, then rapidly raise a series of questions about it. You might mention, "I think it's an intersting plan, but what will we do about retirement payouts? What will we do about part-time workers? How will we handle labor union objections?" These sudden, unexpected concerns will usually cause the person to pause, ponder, and perhaps reconsider the entire plan.

As this example illustrates, chaotic thinkers can often exploit the initial enthusiasm that ordered thinkers might have for their plans. They might start out by seeming to approve of the plans, then quickly introduce alternative realities and concerns that can cause ordered thinkers to realize that their plans are less than ideal. Because the plans seem flawed, they might then decide to abandon them.

Making rapid decisions can also help one to see relations among things as they exist in the moment, and to keep from falling back on old, inappropriate plans. Whenever old plans start to fail, it helps to begin making rapid, intuitive decisions, playing off hunches, and responding impulsively to whatever happens, so that one does not end up dwelling on the fact that the old strategies no longer work or that one is falling behind. Making rapid decisions often pulls people forward into the immediate present. This keeps them from blaming themselves for past mistakes or worrying about how things will eventually turn out.

Many chaotic thinkers are highly skilled at making quick assessments of people, and can often judge their inner qualites and potentials shortly after encountering them. Ordered thinkers sometimes make rapid judgments about people, but these tend to be based on rather superficial criteria and can result in classifying people in relatively simple ways. For example, an ordered supervisor might classify all employees as either good workers or bad workers. The rapid decisions and assessments in chaotic thinking are more likely to be based on the essential characteristics of a person.

When given lots of time, chaotic thinkers usually take more risks and explore less promising options. When they must respond quickly, however, as in a crisis, they tend to do the most sensible or essential things. Ordered thinkers tend to be more sensible when given lots of time to think things out, but in a crisis they often do things that are risky or inappropriate. As a general principle, chaotic thinking is less effective when one is forced to slow down, whereas ordered thinking is less effective when one is forced to speed up.

## CREATING USEFUL SYMBOLISM

Because most chaotic thinkers tend to see the symbolic meaning in things, they are usually looking for new and better metaphors to express their ideas and experiences, and to explore how seemingly unrelated things might be related. They might notice, for example, that a palm tree is like a basket, because its leaves can be woven together. These metaphorical explorations often provide starting points for achieving new insights and discoveries, as was discussed in chapter 2.

Generating symbolic expressions can provide a powerful technique for dealing with excessive literal-mindedness or subtle attempts at manipulation. Particularly in conversation, metaphors buy one time, as the listener has to figure them out and sort through all of their possible meanings. For example, if you were engaged in an argument with someone, you might suddenly refer to a familiar fable or quote some obscure expression, such as John Wilkes Booth's "Sic semper tyrannis!" Most listeners would then have to stop and sort through the unexpected symbolism and its implications.

In this regard, metaphors are often more effective than direct statements or complaints. To suggest to someone that your relationship is "like an octopus" is usually more effective than simply stating that it is tying you down or clouding your future. To describe your job as a "utopia for gremlins" can worry your boss or supervisor far more than any direct complaint about the many things that have been going wrong.

Oftentimes metaphors function like looking glasses, in that people tend to project their fears and hopes into them. To tell someone a metaphor that bears indirectly on an important problem in his or her life often enables the person to examine the problem through the metaphor and to explore creative solutions. For example, if you knew that a person was afraid of getting out of a bad relationship, you might talk about what it must be like for the animals at the local zoo to be caged up all the time and what someone could do to set them free.

Chaotic thinkers sometimes send people abstract symbols, which, like ambiguous figures in visual illusions, allow for multiple explorations and speculations. For example, they might send someone an unusual rock, a strange vegetable, or a black rose, so that the person will try to uncover its underlying meaning. They might place chess pieces in the mailboxes of their friends or fellow workers, to give them an opportunity to explore their symbolic implications. They sometimes write poems for people, even total strangers, expressing some important insights about the person through the metaphors. These poetic metaphors then allow the person to project their wishes and desires into them.

We should again point out that chaotic thinkers would generally use these various techniques to intensify the moment, invite creative exploration, or restore lost harmony, and not merely to disrupt the lives of others. When they complicate a person's plans or intrigue them with metaphors, they are usually reacting to excessive or unnatural rigidity in a situation. The irony in this is that ordered thinkers often convince themselves that they are the ones creating the harmony, by imposing order and structure onto a chaotic world. But their plans can often have the opposite effect. From a chaotic perspective, those plans are never sufficiently flexible or complete.

We also should reemphasize a point made at the beginning of the chapter, that these techniques represent only some of the methods that chaotic thinkers might actually use. Most chaotic thinkers would constantly improvise new techniques in response to the total, changing context of a situation or problem. Hence, the particular methods we have described in this chapter should be considered only as general illustrations of how chaotic thinking might be applied.

# 5

## Strategic Applications

The next three chapters concentrate on specific applications of the techniques of chaotic thinking in practical, real-life situations. In this chapter, we focus on chaotic strategies that are often effective in games and sports, solving everyday problems, responding to acts of aggression, engaging in corporate competition, marketing new products, winning debates and negotiations, developing effective legal strategies and political campaigns, and finally, dealing with pranks and other forms of petty harassment.

These strategies are based on many of the chaotic techniques described in the previous chapter. They have also been touched upon in various books that have explored winning strategies in sports (e.g., Fuoss & Troppmann, 1981; Holtzman & Levin, 1973), general methods for solving problems (e.g., Hayes, 1981; Levine, 1987; Wickelgren, 1974), and practical techniques for dealing with crises in business and management (e.g., Fink, 1986; Peters, 1992).

### CHAOTIC STRATEGIES IN GAMES

In many types of competitive situations, the direct, confrontational approach commonly taken in ordered thinking often fails, because it plays into the hands of an opponent's strengths. A chaotic approach, with its emphasis on playful, nonconfrontational tactics, often provides better chances of winning, especially when faced with an obviously superior opponent. Besides helping to break up the concentration and confidence of an opponent, a chaotic approach minimizes the frustration of making mistakes or falling behind.

Instead of focusing on winning the game, chaotic thinkers often explore ways of increasing the game's complexity. For example, if you were playing against a superior opponent in tennis, instead of trying to win every single point, you might complicate the game in unexpected or unusual ways. You might take frequent time outs because a bug keeps getting into your ear, pretend that your racket keeps slipping out of your hands, pause to constantly test the wind, grunt at inappropriate times during the volley, or kiss the ball whenever you made a good shot. If the game were hopelessly lost, you might begin to attack anyway, pretending you were close behind and then celebrating every point. This may not give you a victory, but it would help to maintain your interest and energy level and keep you from becoming demoralized.

In highly competitive situations, instead of always trying to make the best possible play at all times, you might sometimes make the next best play instead. This can help to make you less predictable without sacrificing the game. The other players would then begin to wonder about your true strengths and intentions, and they might even employ an inappropriate game plan or counter strategy.

Sometimes it helps to do something that is apparently stupid or even outrageous. In a game of basketball, for example, you might suddenly take a desperation shot from midcourt when there is no obvious reason to do so. You might argue with the referee when he calls a foul on the opposing team. You might stage a mock fight between two of your own players. Such tactics tend to disrupt your opponents, not only because they seem bizarre and pointless, but also because they cause your opponents to wonder what you are really up to. They also help to shake up your team, especially if they have been playing poorly.

If your opponents had particular strengths, you might constantly challenge those strengths, so that they would have to prove them to you. This might result in a quicker defeat, but if your opponents suddenly had trouble demonstrating those strengths, they might begin to doubt themselves. For the same reason, you might continue to fight even in lost causes. At the very least, this would make you or your team feel better and would encourage further doubts among your opponents.

These tactics are usually more effective against ordered opponents, who tend to take games too seriously. For many ordered thinkers, every game can be a life or death, win or lose struggle. By doing unexpected or playful things, one can often frustrate their plans and strategies and cause them to question or reconsider them. By responding chaotically, one becomes unpredictable and harder to intimidate.

Another chaotic strategy is to play off excessive pride, by creating exaggerated expectations in the minds of one's opponents. For instance, you might praise your opponents excessively, pointing out how they never seem to make any mistakes. Your opponents will likely absorb the praise, reflect on how good they are, and come to have unrealistic expectations for how they should perform. They might then get angry or frustrated at the slightest mistake or blunder.

One could also employ multiple realities, by redefining an opponent's strengths as weaknesses and one's own weaknesses as strengths. For instance, if the opposing basketball team had a strong fast break, you could point out ahead of time how this is actually a tremendous vulnerability, how anyone who wants to can simply neutralize it by slowing the game down, using a full court press, and fouling at every opportunity. Your opponents may then respond by adopting a split strategy, having assumed that you are going to try to counter their strength. This begins to complicate the game plan, and your opponents can be caught, in effect, between two horses. Should they rely on their usual strength or go with a different strategy?

You might also suggest that their fast break is actually taking away from their shooting game, which is causing their basic shooting skills to deteriorate. You could point out that by doing so much running, their guards are too tired to play a strong defense. You could say that their players are becoming lax and undisciplined because of the haphazard, unstructured way in which a fast break unfolds. And you might conclude by suggesting that you therefore do not consider this a real strength, but rather a liability that has not yet been properly tested.

If there were a single outstanding player on the other team, one whom the opposing coaches always worried about stopping, a chaotic coach might respond by not even trying to stop him. Instead, the coach might simply go with the flow and try to shut down the other players on the team. In fact, the weakest player might be used to defend this person, a player whose sole responsibility would be to show him no respect, no matter how many points he scored. This would place an entirely different perspective on the situation. Eventually, the coach could point to the fact that even though the star player has been scoring lots of points, it does not seem to have done much good, because the other players are doing so poorly.

Most professional teams and athletes may be reluctant to adopt these chaotic tactics because they seem to violate the accepted "rules" of the game. There are standards of fair play and dignity that all players are supposed to observe, and these techniques may be seen as unfair or unethical. But this comes from viewing the game from only a single perspective. By considering multiple perspectives, one realizes that there are many other things going on in addition to the game itself. In disrupting the normal, structured flow of the game, these alternative realities can then emerge and can begin to redefine the situation.

A similar variety of chaotic strategies can be employed when playing board or card games. For example, in bridge or poker, you might begin by complimenting your opponents on their playing, and then follow this up by making a series of distracting statements or comments such as "You won't believe this, but my nose has been itching all day." You might take out a Walkman and put on the headphones, explaining that this helps you to concentrate, or wear a pair of dark glasses, explaining that you have an eye infection. Again, these chaotic tactics would complicate the game in unexpected ways and would likely disrupt your opponent's strategies.

As a general rule, it is usually better to hold off at first and avoid revealing your strengths early in the game. Instead, you might begin by playing inconsistently, which would allow you to learn about your opponents' strengths. If you made a good move, you could follow it up with a stupid one, to see how your opponents respond. This also encourages your opponents to overestimate their own strengths and to acquire unwarranted confidence in the effectiveness of their plans.

If you were playing against highly ordered opponents, you might try moving the game along at a fast pace, keeping as many options open as possible. This tends to disrupt the opponents' game plans, and encourages them to hesitate or make mistakes. The situation would be reversed if you were an ordered thinker playing against chaotic opponents, in which case you would want to keep the game moving at a slow. deliberate pace, simplify things wherever possible, and narrow down the options.

In board games such as chess, ordered thinkers are normally at a disadvantage whenever the positions are complicated and there are still many pieces left on the board. or whenever there is little time left to think. Chaotic thinkers, in contrast, are normally at a disadvantage whenever the positions are relatively simple and there are few pieces left in play, or whenever there is lots of time to think. For this reason, chaotic thinkers might want to insist on shorter time limits, make moves that invited complicated positions, and avoid the end game.

Most ordered thinkers prefer to see games as discrete events, separated from all other events. Chaotic thinkers tend to see games as complex events with multiple realities. They often notice, for example, how the other players are feeling, or what else is going on in the room. At any point in the game, a variety of unexpected circumstances might arise, and most chaotic thinkers would try to utilize these to affect the outcome of the game. Ordered thinkers usually think that the game is just about the game, instead of realizing that there are all kinds of psychological battles that are also being fought.

In any type of game, luck usually favors chaotic thinkers. This is because luck is unpredictable and spontaneous, and resonates naturally to the chaotic thinker's style. Because most ordered thinkers depend on predictability for success, they usually want to eliminate the element of luck altogether and thus often fall prey to it. Chaotic thinkers, with their heightened sensitivity to how things are changing in the moment, can usually adapt or escape if luck goes bad, or utilize the opportunity if luck suddenly improves.

Ordered thinkers might convince themselves that their actions completely determine the outcome of the game, even if their success is due entirely to luck. They thus tend to overestimate the amount of control they actually have. Chaotic thinkers are usually more willing to attribute their success to luck; however, they may not realize that they can sometimes gain control of the situation.

Because ordered thinkers tend to play the entire game using one particular method or strategy, they often fail to take advantage of those moments when they happen to be playing at peak level. Instead, they might continue to play conservatively. Chaotic thinkers are usually more attuned to these moments and often do riskier things in order to take full advantage of them.

As a rule, ordered thinkers are at a disadvantage if the game is close at the end, where luck and unexpected events can have a greater impact. At such times, they often make the mistake of trying to sit on their lead, which takes away from their momentum, normally one of the strengths of ordered thinking. In such cases, most ordered thinkers would probably be better off trying to maintain control and actively dictate the course of the game.

With a chaotic approach, one usually learns to play games without studying their formal principles or strategies. This often causes chaotic thinkers to start out poorly, but it also allows them to quickly adapt to the other player's style. As a result, the strategies they employ are usually not the familiar, expected strategies, and this adds to the game's complexity. They also tend to be better at reading the other players and using this information to improvise novel strategies.

In general, chaotic thinkers tend to do better when they are underdogs or are expected to lose, whereas ordered thinkers tend to do better when they are expected to win or have established a winning tradition. Because most chaotic thinkers like to intensify the moment, they often prefer having to catch up. In comebacks, all of the emotional factors begin to favor them. The game is suddenly forced into the present, where most chaotic thinkers are at their best and can perform at peak level. They can then "rise to the occasion." Ordered thinkers generally prefer to play a more consistent game and to be ahead from the very start.

The intensity of chaotic thinking often feeds upon itself, especially in the excitement of competitive situations. When chaotic thinkers get rolling, it is usually a mistake to try to confront or directly challenge them, as many ordered thinkers are inclined to do. This would only serve to increase their intensity and encourage them to rapidly utilize the confrontation to their advantage. In such cases, it is usually better to simply back off and allow the intensity to burn itself out.

In terms of overall strategy, it is usually important, when playing against ordered opponents, to break their will and confidence. If one can make them hesitate, doubt themselves, or suspect that their plans have failed, one will at that moment have a distinct advantage. This can often be achieved merely by staying with the opponent and keeping the score uncomfortably close.

There are also several things that ordered thinkers could do to improve their chances of winning against chaotic opponents. First, they might try to loosen up their plans, especially if a chaotic opponent has begun to frustrate them. Second, they might try to structure the game in such a way that it reduces the number of options. Chaotic thinkers usually prefer to have multiple choices at every opportunity. Third, they might try to exploit a chaotic thinker's natural tendency to try new ways of doing things, which can sometimes happen at the wrong moments. Finally, they might try to get them to pause and reflect upon what they are doing. Most chaotic thinkers are at their best when they react spontaneously and often get into trouble when they start to analyze their choices.

## PERCEPTUAL TRAPS

Chaotic thinkers sometimes make apparent blunders that call attention to promising but misleading features of a situation, which then convince a person to make certain choices that ultimately backfire. These apparent blunders often exploit the tendency in ordered thinking to focus on specific, salient details related to a plan, as discussed in chapter 2. Hence, we refer to them as *perceptual traps.*

Perceptual traps are especially effective against ordered opponents who are determined to carry through a particular plan at all costs. In a game of chess, for example. if an opponent has initiated an attack and begins to anticipate victory, a chaotic thinker might set a perceptual trap by making an apparently foolish move that allows the opponent to quickly snatch up a piece, where the price for doing so is to be checkmated.

These traps can be employed in a variety of competitive situations. If you were about to play in a tennis tournament, you might let it leak out that you have been attending a special clinic to develop a powerful backhand. You could then pretend to be angry over the leak because you were hoping to unveil this new "weapon" at the tournament. When you first arrived, you could warm up by hitting nothing but backhands, pretending to be enormously pleased. Then, once the tournament began, you could rely on your forehand, your true strength.

People are more likely to fall into perceptual traps when they believe that an opponent is using a specific plan or strategy against them. This usually makes the trap more effective, because they begin to focus on irrelevant features of the situation in order to counter the supposed plans of the opponent. Chaotic thinkers can often use this almost as a pivot point to increase a person's faith in his or her own plans, and to lead him or her down the wrong path.

Perceptual traps frequently have a strong disorienting quality. Once the trap is sprung, a person is often unsure about what has actually happened. Because ordered thinkers tend to reason in a logical, step by step fashion, they often have trouble reconstructing the situation and understanding what went wrong. The plan should have worked, but it did not. They often cannot see why the plan failed, because every step seemed correct. They might then continue to replay the event over and over in their minds, becoming even more confused.

One way to enhance a perceptual trap is to increase the level of excitement and anticipation, which intensifies the moment. For instance, you might begin to praise and flatter your opponents as they approached the trap. You could then begin to act indecisive and confused, pretending that you were worried about your opponent's next move. You might even pretend to get upset with yourself for having been so stupid.

The more things you can do to intensify the moment and create the illusion of imminent victory, the more likely your opponents will raise their expectations. For example, a common tactic in boxing is for a boxer to suddenly act tired and dazed, and stagger backwards, to get his opponent excited about the prospect of a quick victory. The opponent might then lower his defenses and move in for what seems to be an easy "kill." That is when the trap is sprung, and the knockout punch is delivered.

Normally, it is better to make perceptual traps as subtle as possible, so their purpose is well disguised. Sometimes, however, the best way to create a perceptual trap is to set it up well in advance and to make it so obvious that your opponents can clearly see it, and then to distract them with some other tactic. They will then forget about the trap as the situation becomes more complex and will blunder into it at some later point.

The basic principle behind all perceptual traps is that you encourage people to see what they want to see, and not to see what you do not want them to see. Once you determine what the person is planning, you allow those plans to unfold, creating the illusion of certain success, and then set the trap. This strategy illustrates the chaotic techniques of going with the flow, creating favorable illusions, and doing the next best thing.

Chaotic thinkers are usually less susceptible to perceptual traps because they consider multiple realities. Instead of focusing on one particular plan or point of view, they usually try to see a situation from many sides. The apparent gain may be true, or it may not be true. For most ordered thinkers, the illusions created by perceptual traps become their only reality, and they are thus more likely to fall prey to them.

As one might expect, perceptual traps form the heart of many types of confidence games (e.g., Maurer, 1974). A good con artist is a master at making the fantastic seem attainable, at creating the illusion that you can get something for nothing. A good example of this is the "pyramid" scam, in which people are convinced that their investments will guarantee a high yield. The con artist then pays the interest out of their investments, and keeps the rest of the money, until the pyramid collapses.

Ordered thinkers often make the mistake of assuming that because something is attractive or predictable, it must therefore be real. In setting perceptual traps, a chaotic thinker might encourage this by allowing them to make several correct predictions at the very start. They are then likely to conclude that because their previous predictions were correct, things will continue to proceed as planned. This is the essential fallacy that eventually traps them. For instance, in the notorious "pea and shell" game, victims are led to believe that they have discovered a method for how they can beat the game, having been successful the previous times. When they then lose, they are likely to blame themselves for the error, thinking that they must have overlooked something, and will usually want to play again.

These traps often achieve their effects by presenting partial truths in logical progression, which the person is led to believe are whole truths. For instance, a perceptual trap might be structured to imply that if A is true, then B, C, and D are also true, thereby blinding the person from considering alternative possibilities. For example, if someone happened to miss an important shot in a basketball game, a chaotic thinker might point out that (a) the shot clearly missed the basket, (b) missed shots are usually a sign of fatigue, (c) a fatigued person should slow down and try to conserve energy, and (d) a good way to conserve energy is to relax on defense. Thus the player might become trapped into concluding that his shooting will improve if he relaxes on defense. Of course, each of these steps represents only a partial truth, but one can be taken in by the apparent, logical progression of the entire sequence.

In addition to relying too heavily on predictability and logical progression, ordered thinkers are often overly concerned with wanting to see their plans carried out to the very end. They usually want the satisfaction of the grand finish and might therefore decide to stick with a plan in spite of obvious risks. For many ordered thinkers, it is therefore important to know when to take the small profit of the moment and leave. In particular, they should probably be wary if they are seeing only good things in a situation. If the game seems too good to be true, if they begin to feel that their pride is being flattered, it is probably time to quit.

Good poker players are very much aware of the workings of perceptual traps (e.g., Hayano, 1982). They usually let the other players win a little at first to make them think they can win a lot later on. They encourage them to imagine large profits and to think they are better players than they actually are. Then, after winning their money, they will try to make it seem as if it was simply due to luck, and to leave the other players with the impression that they are still the better players.

As mentioned, chaotic thinkers are generally less susceptible to these traps. Most of them prefer to think in terms of short term rewards, rather than long term advantages; they prefer to take the small profit today rather than the big payoff tomorrow. They will usually defeat a con game by not believing in it or by seeing it as only one of many possible realities.

Not all perceptual traps, however, necessarily work to a person's detriment or defeat. In chapter 6, we discuss examples of how these same types of traps can often be used to help people acknowledge important things about themselves that they are not yet seeing. In effect, people can often be trapped into having valuable insights by using similar kinds of chaotic methods.

## PROBLEM SOLVING STRATEGIES

As discussed in chapter 3, one of the benefits of chaotic thinking is that it often helps a person discover creative solutions to perplexing problems and puzzles. For instance, instead of always taking a direct or logical approach to a problem, one might apply the chaotic principle of increasing the problem's complexity. This often works better than trying to simplify the problem, which can sometimes make it harder to solve.

An everyday example of this is trying to untie a knot. By loosening various parts of the knot and thereby making it more complex, one can often find a way to untie it, whereas by pulling on the knot in an effort to simplify it, one often tightens it and makes it harder to untie. This concept can be extended to many types of problems, including those in science, management, and human relations. By keeping problems open and loose, one can often begin to explore their intricacies and discover new ways to solve them.

As mentioned previously, this same strategy is also helpful when trying to solve mysteries. Valuable insights into mysteries can often be gained by increasing their complexity, such as by examining every clue, suspecting anyone who might have been involved, and looking down all the paths. By trying to simplify the mystery prematurely, one risks going down the wrong path. This usually forces the evidence to fit the theory, instead of allowing the theory to emerge once all the evidence is in.

Many studies have shown that there is a tendency to confirm one's initial biases by attending to only part of the evidence (e.g., Wason & Johnson-Laird, 1972). This tendency, known as *confirmation bias,* would be lessened with a chaotic approach. By letting structures emerge naturally, one would minimize the risk of committing oneself prematurely to a particular theory on the basis of only a few suggestive clues. For this reason, chaotic thinkers are probably less likely to form misguided impressions based on incomplete information.

With an ordered approach, one usually tries to simplify problems in advance to make them more manageable. As a result, one might overlook important hints or clues that would have emerged from the complexity of the problem and that could have provided valuable insights into how to solve it. This tendency to oversimplify a problem often renders it insoluble, as there may be many subtle factors affecting it that must also be taken into account.

Meteorology is a good example. Early attempts at weather forecasting often failed because the forecasting techniques were oversimplified. It is now well known that even very small effects and disturbances can merge together to have enormous consequences on weather patterns (e.g., Gleick, 1987). For instance, slight changes in humidity or the amount of sunshine can have dramatic effects on the weather, especially over the long term. Many early forecasters mistakenly assumed that large changes in the weather must necessarily result from large causes.

To return to the example of untying a knot, if you take the knot and forcefully pull on both ends of it, you often end up making it so tight that it becomes almost impossible to untie. The same thing often occurs when trying to solve mysteries or other types of problems. If you try to force the solution, you tend to make the situation so rigid that the solution is delayed or prevented. If you were questioning suspects in a murder case, for instance, and directly accused them of lying, they would tend to cling more tightly to their alibis. However, if you pretended to accept their alibis and encouraged them to provide you with additional details, you might be more likely to establish their innocence or guilt (e.g., Royal & Schutt, 1976).

By accepting and reinterpreting certain annoying features of a problem, one can often discover the key to its solution (Levine, 1987). When encountering a minor difficulty that seems to stand in the way of solving a problem, people tend to put the difficulty aside, assuming that it does not really count in the overall scheme of things. Yet many important breakthroughs have come from studying these little difficulties, looking at them in a different light, and asking what they might mean. For example, the discovery of relativity resulted in part from Einstein's having recognized the significance of certain inconsistencies in the laws of nature (e.g., French, 1979). Avoiding or dismissing the disturbing features of a problem can inhibit the discovery of creative solutions. It is usually better to take those features into account and to postpone arriving at a solution than to try to force a solution prematurely.

When one focuses only on one aspect of a problem, one often misses the fact that it is really part of a much larger problem. Consider, for example, what often happens when one tries to put a brand new part into an old car. Many of the other parts then begin to break down because the new part works so well that it increases the stress on the old parts. In ordered thinking, there is a tendency to want to replace every part with the newest, best part available. Yet sometimes an old car needs old parts.

Chaotic thinking can also be helpful when having to answer questions or solve problems on exams. When taking tests, people often assume that every question, in principle, can be answered correctly. The drawback of this is that if one happens to get stuck on one small question, one risks sacrificing the whole test. By accepting the notion that every question has multiple, possible answers, one can avoid falling into this trap and worrying about having to get a perfect score.

*Brainstorming* is another problem solving strategy that is based on many of the principles of chaotic thinking. It emphasizes looking at problems from many different perspectives, generating multiple ideas in an unstructured manner, and allowing possible solutions to emerge in a natural and uncritical way (Osborne, 1953). However, as it is typically used, it tends to focus on solving particular problems, rather than as a means to explore new possibilities. It also tends to result in *groupthink,* which can cause people to adopt impractical or unrealistic solutions (Janis, 1972).

## WARFARE STRATEGIES

Perhaps not surprisingly, strategies based on chaotic thinking also have many uses when one is forced to respond to the aggressive actions of others. Chaotic techniques, in fact, form the basis of most modern guerrilla tactics. In using these tactics, one pretends to confront the enemy but actually goes around, thereby avoiding direct confrontation. One counterattacks in places where the enemy least suspects. One fights not to win but to complicate and prolong the war (e.g., Chaliand, 1982; Laqueur, 1976).

We mention several applications of chaotic techniques in warfare to emphasize that they are not necessarily frivolous or harmless. Some of the previous applications of these techniques, such as using them to frustrate opponents in games, might create the impression that they are fatuous, impish, or fun loving. But sometimes they can have deadly serious consequences.

A basic chaotic strategy in warfare is to complicate the battle in any way possible. A chaotic army might strike at random and never repeat a maneuver, unless the enemy expected them to. They might disrupt the enemy's supplies so that they arrived at irregular, unpredictable times. If necessary, they would violate every rule of war and fair play that the enemy believed in, as Hannibal did when he used charging elephants to terrorize the Romans.

Pride encourages most ordered thinkers to play by the rules, even in times of war. But these rules seldom apply to chaotic thinkers, who usually respond according to the situation, without regard for established principles. For instance, in the Revolutionary War, the ethics for fighting at that time were that you marched into battle, forming neat and orderly formations. The patriots, however, simply picked off the proud British soldiers, who eventually became demoralized by these chaotic tactics.

When chaotic thinkers engage in warfare, they generally do not set limits on how long the war will last or on what tactics they might use. The war becomes like a poker game with unlimited stakes and uncertainties. This can often be unsettling to an ordered aggressor, who would probably plan on the war lasting only a certain amount of time. Yet wars are chaotic by nature and rarely unfold according to schedule.

Ordered thinkers often fail to realize that their actions could set into motion chaotic events that might continue indefinitely, without rules, limits, or schedules. This can often happen, for example, when one starts a war simply to gain some small advantage, and the war becomes chaotic, in spite of the many careful plans, and drags on and on. The resulting cost of the war can then far exceed whatever the aggressor had hoped to gain from it.

There are two other chaotic strategies that are often effective against a superior military force. One is to demonstrate to the enemy that they are not invincible, that they have weaknesses and foibles like everyone else. Consider, for example, Doolittle's raid on Tokyo. The raid did little actual damage, but it was effective in demoralizing the Japanese. Such tactics often cause an enemy to question the basis for their confidence and pride.

The second strategy is to employ passive resistance, allowing invaders to take over a country, but then making things as difficult for them as possible. The classic example is the "scorched earth" policy that Russia used in response to Napoleon's invading armies. This strategy is based on the combined techniques of utilizing natural events and increasing purposeful clutter. Eventually, the invaders either give up, realizing that it is not worth the effort, or they become assimilated into the culture of the country they have invaded.

In most repressed societies, chaotic thinkers would tend to employ the latter strategy. Ordinarily, they would prefer to take a passive approach and avoid actual conflict by simply adapting. But at some point, if a critical mass were reached and the situation became sufficiently oppressive, chaotic thinkers could be driven to rebel. They would then likely engage in unlimited guerrilla tactics.

## CORPORATE AND MARKETING STRATEGIES

The modern business world is inherently chaotic, and as in warfare, it is often risky to think of it as ordered and rule governed. Chaotic thinking can help one survive in many types of competitive markets by intensifying the moment, raising unexpected complexities, exploring multiple realities, and stimulating favorable changes.

Suppose that you ran a company that was engaged in a major battle with another company for control of a valuable market. Instead of directly competing against their strengths, you might try to increase purposeful clutter, perhaps by supporting their labor unions, encouraging local environmental groups to oppose their waste management policies, or spreading rumors that they might be going bankrupt. Although this would ignore the normal rules and principles that usually define fair business practices, it might enable your company to survive, especially if the competing company was intent on taking over your business.

Perceptual traps, considered earlier in this chapter, can also be useful in many types of business situations. As the president of a large corporation, you might send your top sales people to one location, to make it look as if an important deal were taking place there, and then send your real negotiators someplace else. You could tie up the competition by making them think about one deal while arranging another. If you were negotiating for the purchase of a particular company, you might suddenly break off negotiations and pretend to be interested in a different company, in order to shift the competition in that direction.

The techniques of chaotic thinking can also be used to market new and unusual products, especially products that might be considered controversial. Chaotic advertising strategies can often create a sense of freedom associated with a product, that many people find irresistable (Mandell, 1984; Sandage, Fryburger, & Rotzoll, 1983). This is especially true if the product allows one to "break the rules," in effect, by engaging in chaotic behavior.

For example, imagine a product called "Death Cookies," which contained beef fat, refined sugar, and lots of salt. One might claim that although they tasted good, they were deadly. The box could have a skull and crossbones above a label that said, "Eat one and die." Commercials could show kids eating death cookies when their parents were not looking, cheating death once again. Naturally, parents and nutritionists would howl in protest and might try to boycott the product, but one would benefit from any negative publicity.

You could also take the weaknesses of your product and transform them into strengths, by creating multiple realities. For example, suppose your company made an inferior light bulb that was not very bright. You could advertise it as creating a romantic atmosphere or an early American look. You could also produce television ads that showed normal light bulbs exploding in their sockets because they were too powerful.

Advertising and marketing specialists are, of course, already familiar with many of these strategies (e.g., Cooper, 1986; Urban & Hauser, 1993; West, 1992). Even so, the desirability of a product could be enhanced considerably by bringing the full methods of chaotic thinking to bear on a marketing campaign.

## DEBATING STRATEGIES

There are a variety of chaotic strategies that can be employed when debating someone (e.g., Keefe, Harte, & Norton, 1982; Lee & Lee, 1989). Although ordered thinking usually gives one an advantage in the preparation phase of a debate, where one can organize arguments and anticipate responses, chaotic thinking usually gives one the advantage during the debate itself, where one can suddenly turn the arguments in unexpected directions.

Chaotic thinkers often try to make the points in a debate more complex than their opponents expected. They muddy the water, bringing in things that seem relevant but actually are not. For instance, if an opponent argued that we needed to conserve water, chaotic thinkers might point out that conservation itself is a rather complicated process, with many steps and procedures, and then talk about what each of these procedures might actually involve. This can make irrelevant points in the debate seem important and important points seem irrelevant.

Another version of this strategy is to disrupt the logical flow of an opponent's arguments. Suppose someone wanted to argue that we ought to be sending food to a starving, third world country. The logical flow of their argument might run like this: (a) People in that country are starving; (b) we have lots of food; (c) we should therefore help by feeding them. A chaotic response might be to interrupt this logical flow by asking questions like, "But should we feed them for all time? Should we send them our very best food? If we feed them, won't that prevent them from growing their own food? Won't they then have more children, creating additional problems?"

Your opponents may then be stuck, not only by having to respond to these little attacks you have made, but also by having to address the bigger issue of whether or not their whole argument is essentially flawed. You have trapped them, in effect, by getting them to defend against flaws that do not really exist. They might then waste time responding to these bogus arguments.

By forcing your opponents to argue in the abstract, the debate may end up far from where it began. You might then conclude by saying, "I see that my opponents are confounded by this, which must be due to the unsoundness of their basic premise. Because there are so many flaws in their arguments, there must be an inherent underlying weakness at the heart of their ideas. An unflawed thesis would never have as many weaknesses as my opponents'."

For many ordered thinkers, these unexpected developments could be devastating. Their whole argument may fall apart as they then try to explain themselves out of this corner. They will likely feel that they must now demonstrate that their argument really is coherent in order to restore their pride. They might therefore spend the rest of the debate trying to prove the rightness of their position. But the more they try to do so, the more they prove your point, for you would only need to remind them that if their argument really was sound, it would stand without need of constant defense.

Essentially, you have moved this from a reasoned debate, which ordered thinkers tend to win, into a transactional, unpredictable situation. Instead of laying out an orderly framework, you are now debating moment to moment. You are raising unexpected issues and your opponents must respond to them. They are no longer building their logical edifice, for you have intensified the moment and have sped things up. Instead of calmly debating the issue, you have turned the debate into an immediate, rapid interplay of statements and rebuttals, which goes against their strengths and can leave them floundering in a sea of complexities and irrelevancies.

If there are weaknesses in your own arguments, you could try to argue them as virtues by considering multiple realities. For instance, if your plan for industrial development would clearly result in polluting the local waters, you could acknowledge this, but then give reasons for why pollution is not always such a bad thing. You might say, for example, "If we pollute our waterways now, nature will adapt. But if we try to keep the pollutants out, then nature won't be able to adapt later on, when even more serious forms of pollution could occur." Such arguments often trap your opponents into debating issues that are pointless.

Instead of trying to confront your opponents' arguments, it is usually better to accept their arguments initially, but then lead them down unexpected paths. For example, if you felt that the pollution controls proposed by your opponents would cost too much money, you might begin by praising these controls, then subtly raise questions about who will end up paying for them, how long they will last, or exactly how they will be implemented, which utilizes their arguments to your advantage.

Another debating strategy that uses chaotic thinking is to express ideas in terms of metaphors. Against highly ordered thinkers, this almost always grinds the debate to a halt. It forces them to stop and work through the various possible meanings and interpretations of the metaphor, which then allows one to redirect the debate in any number of alternative directions. For example, a metaphorical statement such as "Pollution controls are like thought police for the environment" might be made in response to a carefully reasoned and logical argument.

Although most ordered thinkers prefer direct statements and literal interpretations, they often avoid being pinned down about exactly what they believe or what they intended to say. They usually fear being trapped by vagueness or inconsistency, which they tend to regard as having made a mistake. This can sometimes be exploited in debates. For instance, you might suddenly interrupt the debate and ask your opponents whether they were using the word "valuable" in the sense of "having monetary value" or "having desirable characteristics," and then press them for additional clarification.

Yet another strategy would be to take what your opponents say and exaggerate it, using the technique of intensifying a problem. For instance, if your opponents argued that we all had a moral obligation to feed hungry people, you could ask, "Do we also have the same obligation to ensure that other people are happy? Are we required to see that every dog is fed? Are we required to see that every crop receives adequate fertilization?" Although this argument is totally ridiculous, you have gone from the immediate point, which might have had some validity, to an abstract image of having to go out into a field and spread manure. At this point, the best thing an opponent could do would be to simply declare that this is a specious argument and to not respond to it. By responding, they risk becoming trapped in the logical flow of the argument and being led further astray.

In applying chaotic strategies in debates, the main objective is to react to and utilize an opponent's plans or goals, and to regard the debate as a kind of game in which many alternative realities can unfold. In debating against chaotic thinkers, ordered thinkers might therefore try to disguise their plans for as long as possible and to resist the temptation to take pride in them, which often results in their plans being easily exposed and exploited.

## LEGAL STRATEGIES

Lawyers have often made use of many of these chaotic strategies, especially in the courtroom (e.g., Bailey, 1971, 1982). Unlike corporate lawyers, who tend to focus mainly on the formal principles of law, courtroom lawyers tend to focus more on the sentiments of the judge or jury. They try to get jurors personally involved with the issues and concerns facing the defendant. Chaotic strategies are very useful in such situations, where purely logical arguments often fail.

For instance, if a client were accused of assaulting someone, a lawyer might try to make the jurors reflect upon how they, too, have had misunderstandings with people from time to time and how easily this can occur. The lawyer might constantly remind them what it is like to be goaded and teased by others. This invites them to consider multiple realities and alternative perspectives.

As a defense attorney employing chaotic methods, you would stay away from true logic as much as possible. Instead, you would try to make your arguments *seem* logical, while actually appealing to the jurors' emotions. For instance, if your client were arrested for drunk driving, you might make the following argument: "Yes, my client was arrested, but how many of us have never been in a bar and had a beer, or have never been driving home when a policeman pulled us over? Any of us could have been in this situation, and it is just a random occurrence that my client is here today. How would you feel if you were sitting here in this docket because some police officer had pulled you over just for having a beer after work? How would you like this to threaten your career, your honor, and your future?" Such arguments might sound brilliantly logical, yet their true purpose would be to appeal to one's deepest emotional sympathies.

As another example, consider a case in which parents were being accused of neglecting their children and were about to lose custody. One of the worst things the parents could do would be to appear defiant and try to give rational arguments for why they still deserved custody. In these types of situations, ordered thinkers are often tempted to make such arguments, and these almost always backfire or fall short.

Instead, a chaotic strategy might be to advise the parents to appear emotionally distraught, in order to generate as much sympathy as possible. For example, you might tell the parents to stay up all night prior to the hearing so that they would look tired and pitiful. You might tell them to cry whenever a sensitive question is asked. You might have them say things like, "We love our children. We know we did wrong. We want to get counseling. Our own parents neglected us." These types of responses are contrite, nonconfrontational, and encourage compassion and understanding.

When questioning a witness, chaotic lawyers often raise doubts and uncertainties by creating favorable illusions. A classic technique is to suddenly point to someone in the courtroom who is dressed to look like the defendant and ask, "Could it have been *this* person?" whereupon the witness might respond, "Well, I suppose it might have been." The lawyer can then argue that if there is one person whom the witness confuses with the defendant, there are likely to be many others.

A standard courtroom strategy for defense attorneys is to try to establish that there are other possible interpretaions of the evidence. A chaotic lawyer can often do this effectively by creating alternative realities and making them seem convincing. They can often get witnesses to admit that these other scenarios are in fact plausible, thereby raising doubt about the guilt of their clients.

Prosecutions are almost invariably ordered operations, where the primary goal is conviction. Defenses, in contrast, are almost always chaotic operations. This is why most defense attorneys should try to encourage novel and unexpected developments wherever possible. The prosecution is intent on establishing one reality: This is the guilty person; he or she did it and deserves punishment. The defense must consider alternative realities: It might or might not have been my client, he or she could have had other reasons for doing it, or there may have been extenuating circumstances.

A legal office could benefit by having a combination of ordered and chaotic lawyers. Ordered lawyers would normally be better at structured activities such as doing legal research or filing motions. However, with an intense case that was being fought in a courtroom, where the outcome would depend on the sentiments of a jury, a chaotic lawyer would probably be the best choice. Ordered lawyers might not want chaotic lawyers on their staff because they are usually not very good at doing paperwork and are sometimes not reliable. But once they get into a courtroom, where they can intensify the moment and explore alternative realities, chaotic lawyers often achieve brilliant effects.

## POLITICAL STRATEGIES

As with debates and legal cases, chaotic strategies can often assist political campaigns. If you were running against an incumbent, for instance, you might try to raise various issues that would get the person to respond to you. Because your opponent will naturally be reluctant to do so, you could try to make this unavoidable by using various chaotic techniques.

For example, you might publically criticize his or her actions, presenting them in the most outrageous terms. You could use bizarre symbolism, such as saying, "My opponent's views are like sewer water, which you are being forced to drink." When your opponent finally does respond to you, you could then point out that there must be something to your criticisms, since he or she seems so disturbed by them.

You could also try to raise doubts about your opponent by creating favorable illusions. For instance, you could say something like, "My opponent's brother in law is a slumlord" if the person happened to own some apartments on the bad side of town. You could raise questions about whether or not the candidate was a good father, pointing out that he never went to his son's Little League games or that he had not attended his daughter's graduation. You could claim that he hated animals, because he once spanked his dog with a newspaper.

Your hope is that your opponent would respond to at least some of these allegations, whereupon they would become an issue. If this happens, you can then ride the issue until it becomes a dead horse and your opponent's name becomes synonymous with it. This gives you the press coverage you need, which is essential if you are an underdog with little campaign money.

On the other hand, if you were the incumbent, you might try to ignore your opponent for as long as you could and then try to make that person the issue. You might argue that the person was unfit for office because he or she had no experience, was of questionable character, or was acting in a rude manner. As the incumbent, you do not need a real issue, you only need to remind voters how wonderful you are.

If your opponent began attacking you for something you once did, you could use the chaotic strategy of intensifying a problem by spreading exaggerated rumors about yourself. You could then offer to clarify which ones were probably true and which ones were not. This would create purposeful clutter and make you immune to further allegations and innuendos.

For example, suppose your opponent learned that you had once cheated on your spouse. You might let other stories leak out about how you have cheated but have airtight rebuttals for them. You could then announce, "I'm doing the best I can to disprove all of these stupid allegations. I can't possibly do so, but most of them are pure baloney." You could then say, "I don't know where all these attacks are coming from. I'm deeply sorry for the one time it happened, but the rest of this scurrilous garbage is just invented by my opponents." The impression is created that, here is a person who did it once, who is sincerely sorry, and now people are simply jumping on him or her with these hundreds of phony stories. The effect of the first charge would be tempered by the irrelevance of all the others.

As a related example, suppose you were caught cheating on your taxes, which threatened to ruin your campaign. You might respond by creating as many other allegations as possible and then denying each of them, pointing out that they were scandalous and without substance. People would tend to forget the central issue of the first story and concentrate on the later ones. You would thus have diluted the original issue.

In previous chapters, we discussed how chaotic thinkers can often avoid unnecessary arguments, confrontations, or revelations by going with the flow, creating favorable illusions, and responding to questions without really answering them. This is what successful politicians are often so good at. They generally know how to sidestep a difficult issue without actually lying, how to appear insightful without getting specific, and how to appear forceful without getting upset (e.g., Grey, 1994; Melder, 1992; Simpson, 1981).

Although it may help to win political campaigns, chaotic thinking may not be the best way to create or operate a government, at least one that is likely to endure. Politicians who are skilled at using chaotic techniques often turn out to have poor planning and organizing skills, which are the usual strengths of ordered thinkers. In the final chapter, we consider further the contrasting roles that these two styles of thinking might play in various forms of government.

## STRATEGIES FOR NEGOTIATION

Many of the tactics that facilitate successful negotiation are also based on general chaotic principles (e.g., Nierenberg, 1973; Raiffa, 1982; Rubin & Brown, 1975). For instance, when negotiating with someone, it often helps to begin adding little demands as the negotiations continue. If you were negotiating to buy a house, for example, you might point out how nicely the house has been kept up and that you really liked the kitchen and the bedrooms, but mention that you would want just a few things repaired. You might comment on the beautiful lawn, but mention that you would have preferred an additional tree or bush. You might observe that the house was just the right color, but add that the doorbell needed to be replaced. This tends to complicate matters and encourages the other person to close the deal.

Doing the next best thing is also useful when negotiating for something. For instance, if you were interested in buying a car, you might start out by negotiating for a car you did not want. After haggling over the price, you could then switch your interest to the car you did want, saying something like "Well, how much for that junker over there?" This helps to derail the plans of salespeople by forcing them to use their tactics on an illusory goal. It also encourages them to become more reasonable when your true preference is then revealed.

In most negotiations, ordered thinkers usually begin by trying to impose their proposals on others and challenging anything others propose. Chaotic thinkers often anticipate this by making outrageous proposals they do not want, while subtly alluding to the sensible ones they do want. After the outrageous proposals are rejected, they would then suggest that the sensible proposals might be acceptable, even though these were really not what they had in mind. They thus let the other party have their victory, while getting the outcomes they wanted all along.

Another negotiation strategy is to try to get a person caught up in having to defend his or her pride. For example, recall the story of the genie who threatened to destroy the hero after he had just been released from the bottle. The hero responded by issuing a series of challenges: "I bet you can't create a golden horse, I bet you can't make yourself ten feet tall," and so on. After the genie had met all of these challenges, the hero issued the final challenge: "I bet you can't get back into that tiny bottle."

Whenever chaotic thinkers are pressured or pinned down in negotiations, they usually respond divergently. They might then decide to intensify the moment and raise a whole spectrum of alternative issues or possibilities that could complicate the negotiations considerably. When ordered thinkers are pressured, they tend to strive for simple convergence in their negotiations.

In formal negotiations, chaotic thinkers are often good mediators for others, but they may not be particularly good at negotiating on their own behalf. In such cases, they are sometimes too willing to go with the flow and give away things they do not really want. In contrast, the proposals that ordered thinkers make are often more calculated and tactical: For instance, they might deliberately hold on to something just because the other person wants it, and use this as a bargaining point. When chaotic thinkers are negotiating on behalf of others, however, the situation is more like a game, and they can then be much more effective.

## DEALING WITH PRANKS

Although a seemingly frivolous topic, pranks and related forms of petty harassment can be very destructive to an individual. Many types of pranks can be dealt with effectively, however, by using chaotic countermeasures. Oftentimes the best overall strategy is simply to elaborate on the prank in order to take the fun out of it. For instance, if somebody kept writing silly messages on your car, you might cross out the messages and write better ones over them. This would prevent the prank from having its intended effect.

The point of responding chaotically to a prank is to frustrate those who are intent on hurting or upsetting you or making you the butt of a joke. Instead of being bothered by this, you could take the prank and twist it in such a way that it is no longer recognizable as a prank. This often allows you to have more fun with the prank than its perpetrators.

If you were a frequent victim of phone pranks, for example, you might set up the following message on your answering machine: "Due to recent obscene phone calls, all conversations are being recorded and traced. If you have a legitimate reason to contact me, please stay on the line." Another strategy would be to keep a tape recorder near the phone that contained a recording of static noise. The next time the person called, you could turn on the recorder and play the static into the receiver, explaining that you must be having a bad connection. Instead of becoming annoyed by such pranks, you can often turn them around.

These chaotic strategies can also be effective in dealing with various forms of juvenile behavior in school or at work. Suppose you were a teacher, and one of your students was always cutting up in class. Every time you asked this student to behave, he promised to do so but then resumed his irritating mannerisms, knowing that you could not actually fail him merely for misbehaving. You could, however, do the next best thing. One morning, you might put a small patch of glue or some chewing gum on the student's seat. When he got stuck and complained to you, you could express outrage at this shameless act, telling the class, "I'm tired of these childish pranks, and I'm going to find out who's responsible for them." You could then apologize to the student and promise to conduct an investigation. Of course, the student would know you really did it, but you would seem to be on his side, sharing his anger. You would have created a counter prank while appearing completely sympathetic.

Most chaotic thinkers would do such things not to seek revenge, but to make the person deal sensibly and realistically with a naturally chaotic world. Their real intention would be to disengage the person's plans, preventing them from exerting any more control over their lives. In the case of the disruptive student, you would demonstrate that his actual control over what happens in your class is in fact quite limited, and that there are always unexpected, chaotic developments that await him should he begin to feel invincible.

Even if they do not completely solve the problem, these chaotic methods often allow you to equalize your own aggravation with that of your tormenters. At the very least, you can take satisfaction in knowing that you have not merely put up with the many vagaries that are thrust upon you by insensitive people, but have done something to make yourself feel better.

By and large, ordered thinkers are usually more likely to pull pranks than chaotic thinkers. They often enjoy planning the prank, anticipating its effects, and seeing it unfold. When it succeeds, they take pride in its success. At the same time, however, they also are more likely to be victims of pranks and to become upset by them.

When chaotic thinkers respond to pranks and disruptive events in general, they usually do so without specific goals or schedules. They might continue to create alternative realities or purposeful clutter indefinitely, involving the person more and more deeply, until he or she is forced to withdraw from the situation.

When employing these strategies, it is more effective to become involved as a player than as a director or controller. Ordered thinkers usually want to remain in control of a situation so that they can continue to cause things to happen and anticipate the results. Once chaotic events are set into motion, however, it is usually better to relinquish that control, so that events can unfold in a natural and unstructured way.

## ETHICAL ISSUES

Many of these chaotic strategies might seem unethical and even a bit cruel. As we have stated previously, however, most chaotic thinkers do not simply go around disrupting things or retaliating against people. On the contrary, their primary interest is in restoring the harmony to a situation, which ordered thinkers often disrupt through their structuring tendencies. By doing chaotic things, chaotic thinkers often contribute to the ultimate failure of what they perceive to be irrational plans and principles.

Chaotic techniques are neither inherently good nor inherently evil. Most of them simply create interesting and dynamic situations that promote insight and change. When chaotic thinkers do playful or bizarre things, it is usually to create alternative realities, which can often result in a deeper awareness of what is happening at the moment.

In fact, there is a strong Machiavellian quality to many chaotic techniques. Most chaotic thinkers are unconcerned with the moral question of whether a particular method should or should not be used, as long as it seemed practical and expedient at the time. Ordered thinkers often feel that methods must be justified according to rules or principles. They are therefore inclined to think that chaotic reactions consist of little more than dirty tricks and thus might consider them to be unethical. Yet most chaotic thinkers would place human needs and harmony above society's rules and prescriptions.

Chaotic techniques can certainly seem ill spirited when taken out of context or when described in insufficient detail. When properly used, however, they take into account the total context of the moment, and have a playful rather than malicious quality. A technique that seems mean or spiteful in a narrow context can become reasonable and enlightening in a broader context, especially if it is used compassionately rather than for individual gain.

Instead of using chaotic techniques to achieve specific goals, most chaotic thinkers would use them to create new opportunities, promote a sense of playfulness, and keep their options open. When one applies these methods too narrowly, it takes away the creativity and freedom that they normally encourage. The person then becomes just as predictable as before. This also allows others to focus on the techniques and retaliate against them, instead of having the desired effect of increasing chaos and stimulating new insights.

Ordered thinkers could reduce the temptation to use chaotic methods improperly by trying to become less focused in these situations. Instead of taking the actions of others personally, and possibly plotting revenge against them, they might think of ways in which they could make the situation more interesting or playful. Among other things, this encourages the creative exploration of alternative realities.

Finally, we should consider the further objection that chaotic methods might be unfair to those who have put their trust in someone to perform a job or task in a certain way. However, if that trust is based on selfish motives, unrealistic expectations, or manipulative intentions, it should no longer hold. In general, in cases where a person has become obstreperous and unyielding, where polite requests and importunate gestures have failed, and where one has few other options, then chaotic methods are usually called for.

# 6

## Interpersonal Applications

Some of the most important applications of chaotic thinking come into play when dealing with interpersonal problems and situations. These include times in which one wishes to form or improve personal relationships, wants to encourage personal growth, has to deal with irrational or irresponsible people, or is engaged in a therapeutic setting. The chaotic methods described in this chapter are therefore of general interest to most people, and of particular interest to counselors and therapists.

There has been an increasing tendency in modern society to try to structure human interactions. Personal relationships, for example, are often placed on an agenda and are regarded in much the same manner as any other structured activity. This is due in part to the need to coordinate work schedules, but it also derives from the idealism of ordered thinking. We have come to expect that relationships should develop in predictable, ideal ways and should fit into one's long-term plans. However, when this denies the inherent, chaotic qualities of relationships and prevents them from changing or growing, it usually causes problems.

When these problems arise, the typical manner in which most ordered thinkers try to deal with them is to impose even more structure. Instead of making their relationships more flexible, they tend to regulate them more tightly. This is encouraged, to some extent, by the many popular self-help programs that employ structured plans for developing interpersonal skills and achieving new insights (e.g., Gartner & Riessman, 1984). But for those who already rely too heavily on ordered thinking, imposing additional structures only contributes to the problem. As this chapter shows, chaotic thinking can often help to unstructure ordered relationships and encourage more effective ways of interacting.

## ORDERED AND CHAOTIC RELATIONSHIPS

Special problems often arise when ordered and chaotic thinkers are involved in the same relationship. Ordered thinkers usually want to make extensive plans for the relationship. They expect others to share in those plans, whereas chaotic thinkers usually desire freedom and spontaneity. This often results in frustration and misunderstandings when the two styles of thinking begin to clash.

Typically, ordered thinkers are the first to become frustrated. Consider the following situation, in which a man who is a highly ordered thinker is about to go on a date with a woman who is a highly chaotic thinker. Like most ordered thinkers, he has a specific agenda for the evening. He will pick her up at 6:00, they will eat dinner at 7:00, they will go to see a particular movie at 8:00, they will return at 10:00, and he will give her a goodnight kiss.

When he arrives to pick her up, however, she is not ready. This causes them to miss their dinner appointment, and he starts to fume. She suggests that they simply go somewhere else for a quick meal. Over dinner, he is thinking that the date may now be ruined. She says they can still go to the movies, but when they get to the theater, she wants to see a different movie from the one he had planned on. He is now in a virtual rage, and she has no idea why he is so angry. At this point he has all but given up on the goodnight kiss, which he probably would not get in any event.

Similarly, many chaotic thinkers become frustrated in their relationships with ordered thinkers. Even when they appear to go along with the plans that ordered thinkers have made for the relationship, they may secretly find them unbearably restrictive and may regard their future-oriented idealism as cold and impersonal. This often leads to sudden, impulsive rebellion, which ordered thinkers usually regard as a sign of instability, or even betrayal. The relationship suddenly ends, and they cannot figure out what went wrong, since they stuck to the plan exactly as intended, and everything seemed to be working just fine.

One reason ordered thinkers are often drawn to chaotic thinkers initially is that they see them as being easier to fit into their plans as compared with other ordered thinkers, who would normally have competing plans of their own. They also tend to see chaotic thinkers as being rather childlike and in need of supervision and guidance. Chaotic thinkers often try to tell them to slow down, to let them have their freedom, but this is usually very difficult for ordered thinkers to accept. And even when they agree to allow them this freedom, most ordered thinkers eventually come back to their original plans.

For instance, chaotic thinkers might try to explain that they need to have more space and some time to themselves, but then an ordered thinker might call them up the next day and ask if they would like to go out. When they try to explain, again, that they need their freedom, perhaps by saying, "Didn't we agree that I needed some space?", the person might then reply, "But we didn't do anything yesterday."

This illustrates a curious aspect of the interpersonal style of many ordered thinkers. They often pretend to be willing to listen to and negotiate with you, but they then keep returning to their plans and continue trying to impose them. Chaotic thinkers are often then forced to resort to the kinds of techniques we have been describing in an effort to keep themselves from being swallowed up by those plans.

Those who rely too heavily on making plans for a relationship can display dramatic mood swings when those plans are frustrated. For instance, they might alternate between expressing outrage at the person and expressing guilt over their anger (Shapiro, 1981). In such cases, the guilt may function as a vehicle for trying to salvage the plans that the anger has endangered.

When people become overly attached to their plans, they might relentlessly press the other person for a committed relationship. If this happens, chaotic thinkers might try to stretch the situation out as far as possible. From their point of view, the longer one waits, the more likely it is that unexpected events will intervene, which will complicate the person's plans. Conditions will inevitably change, new perspectives will likely emerge, and the plans will ultimately slow down and lose their obsessive qualities.

There are several things that ordered thinkers might do to begin to unstructure their relationships and avoid many of these problems. One is to build more flexibility into their plans, so that they are not so easily frustrated when those plans do not unfold as expected. Another is to let the other person know in advance exactly what their expectations are. A third is to become more aware of the other person's mood at any given moment.

For instance, in the date example, the man could mention ahead of time that he has a dinner arrangement at a particular time, then ask the woman what time he should pick her up. He could then consider more than one choice to fall back on. In case they could not have dinner at the restaurant he had planned on, he might think about what other restaurants would be good alternatives. He might avoid assuming that she will want to see the same movie he wants to see. Also, he could try to be more aware of her mood at the end of the date, when he wants his goodnight kiss. If he has been insulting or boring, he should not expect to get one.

The need, in ordered thinking, to add flexibility to one's plans is particularly important when trying to develop or maintain long-term relationships. For example, couples often place themselves on rigid schedules for sharing activities; this can make the relationships overly structured. Many times these activities have to be scheduled because of job constraints or the simple fact that there are many other things that have to be done. Even so, it helps to try to maintain some openness and adaptability.

In planning every aspect of a relationship for the rest of all time (as in "We will get married, we will have two children, I will go to school, you will raise the family, and then we will retire to Florida"), ordered thinkers may inadvertently offer chaotic thinkers the dullest life they could possibly envision. When this plan is rejected and regarded as unrealistic or even ridiculous, most ordered thinkers might take the rejection personally, because they have put so much time into thinking about it. But few relationships can ever be successfully micromanaged, especially over the course of many years.

It is usually a good idea to try to set some time aside just to have fun in a relationship, without spending that time in activities that necessarily involve winning and losing. Those couples who frequently play competitive golf or bridge, or who spend their spare time engaged in other forms of competition, are not really playing together. It is often better to take part in genuinely playful activities in which there is nothing to win or lose, especially when trying to unstructure a relationship that has become excessively rigid.

This can be a difficult concept to accept for those who take a highly ordered approach to relationships, because it involves having a sense of proportion. Consider, for example, the person who might begin screaming at his or her spouse simply because they had lost a game of bridge or charades. This can end up endangering the whole relationship, because a realistic perspective has been lost. At such moments, one might stop and ask oneself, "Is it really worth sacrificing my marriage over a game of bridge or charades?" Or, "Is it absolutely necessary for me to always be blatantly honest about exactly how I feel?"

In such cases, it might help to employ the technique of going with the flow. Ordered thinkers often feel that they are being less than honest in their relationships if they do not provide constant criticism where they feel it is needed. If a husband does not like the dress that his wife is wearing, for example, he might feel an uncontrollable urge to tell her so. It is usually better, however, to accept the situation as it is, imperfections and all, than to try to correct it.

Chaotic thinkers sometimes allow themselves to get trapped in relationships by acquiescing to the strength of an ordered thinker's plan. If they are then given any opportunity to escape the relationship, however, they are likely to do so. For example, if his or her partner suggested that they should take a short break from one another and do a few things on their own, a chaotic thinker might leave and never come back, especially if the other person's expectations had become too intense.

Most chaotic thinkers usually do not forgive affairs. Unlike many ordered thinkers, they tend not to put them into a long-term perspective. An ordered thinker might argue that the affair was insignificant or that it will make the relationship stronger in the future, but these arguments seldom work with chaotic thinkers. They would likely see the affair as changing the whole meaning of the relationship, and conclude that it can never be the same again.

When chaotic thinkers are wronged in a relationship, there is usually no going back, no "erasing" the deed. The other person may try to ask for forgiveness, or may want to know what they can do to make things right again, but most chaotic thinkers would simply tell them, "This has changed our relationship forever, and it can never be as it was." For most chaotic thinkers, a single cheating incident can be worse than a divorce, whereas the opposite is often true for most ordered thinkers.

When forming a new relationship, chaotic thinkers are relatively unconcerned about a person's past or why the person behaves the way he or she does. Instead, they usually make a rapid assessment as to whether or not they can live with the person's behavior, whatever might be causing it. They are more likely to consider the person's character as manifested in the moment, and to regard their past, even a sordid one, as largely irrelevant. Most ordered thinkers, in contrast, would want to know a person's history before committing themselves to a relationship.

In ordered thinking, there is a tendency to consider each new relationship in isolation and to try to formulate specific plans for it. But although they often regard new relationships as unique, ordered thinkers tend not to think of the other person as unique. Chaotic thinkers often view a new relationship as connected to all other relationships, but they tend to regard each person as a unique individual. They often discover those common things that seem to work across their relationships, such as going on trips, sharing poetry, or seeing romantic movies, and then apply these broad insights about relationships to each individual person.

## OVERCOMING PERFECTIONISM

The expectations for a successful relationship that typically arise in ordered thinking tend to be excessively idealistic. Ordered thinkers tend to have an ideal mate in mind and might expect to find those qualities in every person that comes along. They might might join a dating service and list dozens of highly specific requirements that the other person is expected to fulfill. Or they might constantly try to correct another's faults and weaknesses.

Many ordered thinkers strive for perfection in their relationships, as in other aspects of their lives, and often end up trying too hard to achieve that perfection. They would almost rather pursue a perfect relationship that did not really exist than have an actual relationship that was less than perfect. Chaotic thinkers tend to be more realistic about their relationships. If one relationship did not work out, they would usually do the next best thing and begin another. If a relationship seemed unsatisfying in some respects, they might explore novel ways of trying to make it more interesting.

When people commit themselves to finding an ideal person, they tend to get bored with those who do not measure up and quickly move on to someone else. As a result, they often find themselves on the "rebound." Chaotic thinkers are more likely to focus on one person and stay with that person, at least until they begin to feel that they are losing their freedom.

Once they have convinced themselves that they have found an ideal person, ordered thinkers often pursue the relationship blindly, believing that if they are simply persistent, the relationship will ultimately succeed. When these efforts reach a dead end, however, and they realize that their intuitions about the person were wrong, they might then try to provide a detailed analysis of why the relationship failed or recount all of the ways in which the person fell short of their expectations.

Sometimes ordered thinkers will give up on a relationship if some minor thing goes wrong. At other times they might press a relationship beyond reasonable limits. Which of these occurs usually depends on how they view their plans. As long as they can move smoothly from one step to another in the plan, and feel that they are still in control of things, they will usually press on. But if something suddenly happens that prevents them from moving on to the next step, they are likely to think that the plan is contaminated and will probably then abandon the relationship.

In a sense, many ordered thinkers are Promethean. They want to give people the "fire of the gods," but then suffer the pain of never reaching their ideals. They are thus seldom completely happy or satisfied with any situation. There is always something wrong with their job or relationship, and they usually end up being disappointed. Most chaotic thinkers, in contrast, are Dionysian, for they tend to pursue pleasure and stimulation and are usually satisfied to simply be a part of the natural flow of life.

In ordered thinking, there is often a tendency to fantasize about future possibilities after meeting a person. One might visualize exactly how the relationship will develop, imagine all the things they can do together, or mentally rehearse what they will talk about. However, this encourages one to idealize the person and to form unrealistic expectations about the relationship. For most ordered thinkers, it is probably better to try to suppress these fantasies and simply focus on how things are developing within the moment.

## IMPROVING INTERPERSONAL COMMUNICATION

Another reason why ordered thinkers frequently have problems in relationships, particularly with chaotic thinkers, is that they are often lacking in interpersonal communication skills. Unlike most chaotic thinkers, they often do not attend to what is actually being said at the moment or recognize the importance of body language and nonverbal cues.

Chaotic thinkers are often good conversationalists, not merely because they use words effectively or have interesting ideas, but because they are usually able to create a genuine transaction with people. They typically listen to what others say and expand upon their ideas. Ordered thinkers have a tendency to impose their own ideas or correct others' mistakes, which often disrupts conversations. By focusing more on declaring their opinions, they often become detached from the natural flow of sharing ideas and insights.

A related problem is that many ordered thinkers do not expect people to actually respond to what they are saying. Their words and ideas are sometimes expressed almost in the form of ultimatums to the listener, instead of inviting discussion. They often talk as if there were only one correct point of view, whereas chaotic thinkers often talk as if they had no particular point of view at all.

In their initial encounters with people, ordered thinkers often begin by using the "asking questions" approach. This typically consists of simple yes or no types of questions such as "Do you have a job?", "Do you like Chinese food?", or "Do you like classical music?" The reason for asking these questions is to reduce complexity and arrive at an instant summation of the person. This approach quickly turns off most chaotic thinkers, who would likely feel that they were being categorized.

Sometimes ordered thinkers try to rely on their reputations or past achievements as a basis for forming new relationships. For instance, they might think of themselves as being defined by what they have accomplished or by what they do well. Chaotic thinkers usually try to express who they are by the way they interact with people. Instead of talking about what they have achieved, they usually talk about interesting things that have happened to them or things that they notice about the person. Whereas most ordered thinkers want to be appreciated for what they have done, most chaotic thinkers want to be appreciate for who they are, and for their insights and ideas.

Most ordered thinkers believe that conversations should follow certain patterns or rules. Chaotic thinkers are generally less sensitive to these rules but are usually more in touch with the subtle, interactive qualities of conversations. For instance, they often notice when people sigh at certain questions, have tears in their eyes, or hesitate when they respond to certain questions. They might watch to see whether people are tapping their fingers, tightening their legs, or clenching their jaws, and they would quickly infer what these responses might mean. At times, they are almost like human polygraph machines because they are so sensitive to the underlying meanings behind a person's actions and words.

Ordered thinkers often miss these signs and their meanings because they are generally focused only on those things that relate specifically to the success of their plans. For example, an ordered father might decide that his son is going to medical school and might begin telling him what he needed to do in order to prepare for this. As the conversation progressed, however, the son might be looking away, tightening his knuckles, and starting to perspire, but the father might continue to impose the plan, missing all of these important cues that indicate that this is not really what his son wanted to do.

A related problem is when people start to regard others as objects, rather than as individuals. For example, a husband might refer to members of his family not as special, unique people, but as "my wife," or "my son." These are "things," with various functions. In saying something like, "My wife should have my dinner ready by such-and-such time," or My son should be honoring the family by getting good grades," one is not really talking about a person, one is talking about an object and what the object should be doing.

Another reason ordered and chaotic thinkers often find it difficult to communicate is that they often have different ways of expressing their dissatisfactions. When something bothers ordered thinkers, they are more likely to complain about it up front, even when it might be inappropriate to do so. Chaotic thinkers tend to keep their complaints locked up inside until they are ready to explode with a whole rash of criticisms. An ordered thinker might then say, "Why didn't you tell me all of these things before?", whereupon the chaotic thinker might reply, "They were so obvious that you should have noticed."

Ordered and chaotic thinkers also tend to respond very differently to threats or ultimatums in relationships. As a rule, such tactics are usually more effective with ordered thinkers. For example, if a man were told by his wife, "Either you do what I tell you or leave," he would likely become very distressed and agonize over having to make a decision. Chaotic thinkers, forced to choose at that moment between freedom and the lack of freedom, would likely tell the person "Good-bye." Whereas ordered thinkers might experience the whole spectrum of emotions in such situations, chaotic thinkers would tend to make the emotionally simple decision of choosing freedom.

Ordered thinkers often try to be excessively reasonable with regard to their feelings. For example, they might say that they did not care if someone left them, after having thought the matter over, when in fact they cared very much. Chaotic thinkers tend to be much more candid and less reasonable when expressing their feelings. When ordered thinkers have trouble communicating their feelings, it is often because they analyze and debate them, which interferes with discovering what they really feel.

Some specific things that ordered thinkers might do to improve their skills at interpersonal communication include the following: First, they could try to get around the concept that every conversation is a matter of having to convince somebody. One of the best ways to do this is to make a point of really listening to what the other person is really saying, not just responding to them in terms of one's own plans or ideas. Second, instead of always asking direct questions, they might try simply mentioning things that they found interesting. This allows others to respond openly and without artificial constraints. Third, they could try to regard each moment in the conversation as unique, without a past or future. Finally, they could try to become more aware of the subtle, meaningful cues that occur in conversations, such as body language, and to be less focused on always trying to convey a certain impression or point of view.

## ENCOURAGING PERSONAL GROWTH

Ordered thinking places emphasis on making long-range plans, accomplishing goals, and improving things in the external world. Chaotic thinking places emphasis on intensifying the moment, gaining new insights, and improving oneself. It thus tends to promote personal growth.

Ordered thinkers generally prefer new things because they are unspoiled. Chaotic thinkers generally prefer used things, because they have the potential for improvement. A brand new thing can only get worse, whereas something that is old and used can often get better. This is why most chaotic thinkers are willing to accept people as they are, and to look for creative ways of encouraging personal growth and insight.

For instance, chaotic thinkers often create and share meaningful fantasies as a way of helping people explore their talents and come to new insights about their hidden qualities and potentials. If they encountered someone who had extremely romantic ideals about love, for example, they might describe how a deep, spiritual love transcends all lust, how they have been searching all their lives for that one special person, or how they have suffered at the hands of those who exploited and betrayed their trust. They would then encourage the person to explore the fantasy with them and to grow within it.

On the face of it, this might seem exploitive, or even dishonest, because the fantasies are not real; however, from a chaotic perspective, these fantasies provide a mirror into which people can project their innermost qualities and desires, which enables them to see themselves more favorably. In effect, chaotic thinkers are giving them a reflected vision of their own wonderfulness, which shows that they have the capacity to love, to care, and to share ideas and feelings.

These personal insights are no less valid just because they arise within a fantasy. Consider, for example, the Wizard of Oz, who gives the lion a medal so he will feel the courage that he always possessed. This is essentially what chaotic thinkers do when they share fantasies with people. They help them discover who they really are, and encourage them to explore qualities within themselves that they may not have been aware of.

One should draw a distinction here between misrepresenting oneself in order to take advantage of someone, which is clearly unethical, and exploring alternative realities as a way of helping a person find happiness or insight, which would be the intention of most chaotic thinkers. Technically, this might be regarded as a form of misrepresention, in that chaotic thinkers may not be disclosing everything about themselves when they share these fantasies. But from their perspective they are not really lying, for in that moment they are experiencing an alternative reality that is just as valid as any other.

We should note that creating alternative realities works both ways in chaotic thinking. It can bring a person's fantasies down to earth, which chaotic thinkers often try to do when the plans that stem from those fantasies become unbearably disruptive or irrational. On the other hand, it can often enhance those fantasies, raising them to higher levels so that new insights can follow. In this sense, the "mirror" that chaotic thinkers often provide for people can reveal both unrecognized virtues and unrealistic aspirations.

The idealisms of ordered thinking are often so rigid that they can inhibit people from exploring new possibilities within themselves. In contrast, chaotic thinking tends to bring out a person's natural qualities and talents. One of the reasons chaotic thinkers can often create such effective fantasies for people is that they usually have no personal goals or ulterior motives behind what they do. Their actions are usually motivated by curiosity or empathy, and they are mostly interested in creating opportunities for mutual discovery and growth.

In developing these fantasies, chaotic thinkers often tell people what they want to hear, but that they do not yet know they want to hear. If one tries to tell people things they already know, they usually feel that one is trying to manipulate them. For instance, a chaotic thinker might tell people that they have a warm innocence or passionate enthusiasm, rather than simply telling them that they have nice hair or a pretty smile. In general, they try to touch people in areas where they secretly aspire to be free.

One of the drawbacks of creating these illusions for people is that eventually they may ask for something that one is unable to provide. For example, a chaotic thinker might show a person how to be happy, but then the person might want the chaotic thinker to give them that happiness. From a chaotic thinker's perspective, you cannot give a person something that they already have. They must discover it within themselves.

Personal growth can often be inhibited by dwelling on the mistakes of the past. Ordered thinkers have a tendency to look back on many of their past decisions with regret, wishing they had done things differently. In doing so, they often overlook the possibility that other types of decisions might have turned out even worse or provided them with fewer opportunities than they presently have.

A common belief in ordered thinking is that the best relationships start out as friendships and then develop into romances at some later time. On the contrary, most romances begin with an initial, chaotic intensity and may then develop into more stable friendships later on, once one is past beyond the romantic "bifurcation point."

Although ordered thinkers often want to create romance, sometimes desperately so, they usually do not know how. They tend to fumble the romance in the intensity of the moment, or they keep waiting for the right moment, which never actually comes. In trying to create romance, it often helps to simply talk about the kinds of things that one thinks are romantic. For instance, you might talk about how you enjoy looking at shooting stars with someone, and how each time you see one, you like to tell the person something new that is special about him or her. By simply talking about romantic things in an unstructured way, the romance itself often then emerges.

Most chaotic thinkers prefer emotional simplicity in their relationships, which allows them to concentrate on the person, intensify the moment, and create romantic fantasies. They usually do not like having to compete with many other people for someone's time and affection, nor do they need a lot of time to sort out their feelings. They might typically say to someone, "Let's become intensely involved and see where it goes; at least we will have given it our best shot."

These chaotic approaches carry more risk, because they might offend some people or seem too bold. However, they present one as a real person who is willing to be vulnerable. One is not simply sending out a copy of one's resume, but is creating an opportunity for genuine growth and romantic potential. The other person is then free to accept or reject this opportunity.

Most ordered thinkers live for security but dream about freedom and romance, which they often deny themselves. On the other hand, most chaotic thinkers live for freedom and romance, but dream about security. For this reason, one should probably use different strategies when trying to create intimacy with ordered and chaotic thinkers. With ordered thinkers, it might be better to try to fit initially into the expected roles, to mirror their idealizations, and to offer them an opportunity to be free, but without endangering their plans. With chaotic thinkers, it might be better to try to arrange activities to some degree (but without overplanning), to focus on having fun, and to offer them an opportunity to be secure, but without endangering their freedom.

## DEALING WITH IRRESPONSIBLE PEOPLE

In spite of the many rules and regulations in our society, many people continue to act irresponsibly. For instance, they might avoid paying back their debts if they suddenly decide that the person does not deserve to be repaid, even though they are legally or morally required to do so. They might decide to run pedestrians off the road, merely for being in the way, regardless of the traffic laws. They might convince themselves that they can exploit or cheat others whenever it suits them and will never be caught.

Chaotic methods can often be effective in helping one to deal with irresponsible people and to encourage them to behave more responsibly, especially after ordered approaches have failed. The following example illustrates, for instance, how the techniques of increasing purposeful clutter and doing outrageous things might encourage a person who owes you money to repay the debt. Assume, for instance, that a relative has borrowed money from you and has promised to pay you back, but now denies that he or she owes you anything at all. You have made several polite requests for the money, but these have all been ignored.

You might have some flyers made up from an imaginary company called "Financial Relief Services," which advertise help for people who have many debts. These flyers could start out with nonspecific messages, such as "We can help you relieve your financial burdens," which you could leave on the person's car or mail to his or her home. Subsequent flyers could then become more specifically directed at the person: "Would you like to have your good name back?", "Are relatives trying to collect money from you?", "Are you a deadbeat brother/sister?", and so on.

The point of sending these flyers is to give the person innocent reminders that you are not simply going to forget about the debt, and to emphasize that irresponsible behavior often has chaotic consequences. If these methods failed, you might then consider more extreme chaotic methods, such has having helium balloons made up with the message "You owe me" printed on them, and then putting them in unsuspecting places.

Such methods are usually more effective than engaging in direct confrontation or threatening to take legal action, which irresponsible people are often good at countering, and which tends to exacerbate the situation. The chaotic reactions complicate the person's life in relatively harmless ways, but create entanglements and uncertainties that can be far more aversive than direct threats or more forceful measures.

Another situation in which chaotic methods can often be of help is when one encounters irresponsible drivers. For example, suppose someone purposely sped up and tried to run you down as you were crossing the street. You suspect that the person has probably been drinking and is doing this simply to harass you. Taking the usual approach of reporting the incident to the police would probably do little good, especially if there were no witnesses. Instead, you might use the chaotic technique of intensifying a problem.

If you were able to get the license plate number, for example, you might create several dozen notes with the following message: "I'm sorry I made a small dent in your car. My friends and I must have had too much to drink. My license number is _____ and I drive a (give description of vehicle)." You could then leave this message on various cars that were parked along the street. At least some of the owners are likely to notice some small dents in their cars that they had not noticed before, and will assume that this person did it.

The ensuing complications would help to counter the assumption, often shared among irresponsible people, that they can do whatever they want and there is nothing anyone can really do about it. By responding chaotically, you allow the situation to unfold in many unexpected and potentially enlightening ways, without ever having to become personally involved. The chaotic approach thus utilizes the irresponsible behavior and enables it to have a myriad of unanticipated consequences.

## DEALING WITH IRRATIONAL PEOPLE

Chaotic techniques can also encourage irrational people to behave more rationally, by forcing them to deal with the reality of a situation. We saw examples in chapter 3 of how chaotic thinking can promote rationality; here we consider some additional techniques that are especially effective when encountering irrational people.

Suppose that your boss would not let you take a vacation this year, even though your request was perfectly reasonable. After listening to the various reasons your boss might give for turning you down, you could then say that you understood these concerns and that you actually agreed with them. Then you could simply restate your desire—"I want a vacation." Instead of engaging your boss in a logical argument, which would usually fail in such cases, you could make the point, again and again, that this is something that you really need to do, in a way that your boss could not dispute. Instead of confronting the irrationality, you could allow the irrational arguments to simply exhaust themselves.

Irrational people sometimes get angry when you do not agree with what they are saying. When this happens, you could become angry, too, but not at them. Instead, you could get angry at other things. For example, if your boss got angry because you wanted a vacation, you could say that you were angry with the way the system was so unfair. You worked hard, and you needed some time off, but the system did not care. This helps to displace their anger. In fact, you can often get the other person to share your anger. Your boss might end up saying, "Yes, I know exactly what you mean. I'm sick of the way the system has been treating me, too."

Ordered thinkers sometimes become irrational when they have their minds set on a particular plan of action. They resist any attempt to question the appropriateness of the plan. In such cases, chaotic methods can often restore rationality to the situation. For instance, suppose someone had made extensive plans to take you on a vacation when you really did not want to go. This person might say, "We'll leave in two weeks and drive straight through to Las Vegas and then stay for seven days." If you resisted, or tried to explain that the plan was unreasonable, the person might become angry and tell you, "Look, I've already spent a lot of time planning this for us, and I'm even willing to pay for it. So this is what we're going to do."

Instead of directly confronting the person, you could accept and then complicate the plan, using the techniques of utilizing natural tendencies and creating purposeful clutter. For instance, you might agree to go on the vacation, but when you started out, you could explain that you had just gotten back from a plane trip and could only drive for a few hours. You might start to drift off the road and apologize for your lack of sleep. You might then insist on stopping along the side of the road so you could take a nap. If there were a river nearby, you could suggest that the two of you ought to go fishing because the fish should be biting this time of the year.

By introducing these simple distractions whenever possible, you would eventually slow the plan down, without having to directly oppose it. This goes with the flow and works within the structure of the plan. It is like being caught in a riptide and being pulled out to sea. Usually, the worst thing one can do is to fight the current. Rather, it is better to go with the current until it begins to lose its strength and then swim away.

What if you did not have the time to go along with the plan? In such cases, you could mention that you had certain prior obligations, such as a work project or a job interview. This usually works better than trying to explain that you simply did not feel like going. By saying that you had work that you had to complete, or a schedule that you had to meet, most ordered thinkers would understand and respect that, because you are responding to an external structure or authority.

Suppose you had relatives who insisted on coming down for an extended stay and who were intent on helping you to restructure your life. You have tried to talk them out of coming, giving rational arguments why this would not be a good time for a visit, but their plans have already been made and you are given no choice. They have made it clear that they expected you to clean your house or apartment, to get up at a certain time early each morning, and to hold to the daily schedule they have arranged.

You could utilize these expectations, introduce chaotic complications, and encourage a rational compromise by doing some of the following things: First, you might deliberately oversleep, explaining that you had stayed up most of the previous night. Then, you could agree to clean the house or apartment, but mention that you first needed to go to the post office and the store, which would result in unexpected delays and prevent you from getting around to the cleaning. Next, you could pretend that you were trying to get dinner ready on time, but arrange for a friend to call you at that moment, so that the dinner would be late. Finally, when your relatives were ready to watch television, you could explain that the set was broken, having previously removed the fuse.

You would therefore always have some legitimate excuse that kept you from holding to their schedule. After a few days, they would likely start to go "native," so to speak. They would begin to find it easier to behave as you behave than to continue following their plan. You have not directly stopped the plan, but you have taken the wind out of its sails by employing passive resistance. One of the strengths of ordered thinking is in anticipating and overcoming obstacles to plans, but you have provided no obstacles whatsoever. By seeming to go along with the plan, you have avoided the very confrontations that the plan was designed to meet.

Consider, as an analogy, what often happened to imperial forces after they successfully invaded a more primitive civilization. After a few years, the conquerors were often assimilated into the existing culture. Their original impetus for becoming invaders and ruling a great empire became diluted by the fact that they had now become members of that society, with families and cultural responsibilities. They were forced to adapt to a host of new customs and new ways of doing things, and as a consequence, their original plans and impassioned idealisms eventually faded.

Ordered thinkers tend to drive harder when they believe their plans are being challenged. However, they also tend to become frustrated when having to deal with continual and unexpected complications. By encouraging natural entropy and passive resistance, one allows misguided plans to collapse under their own weight. One is going with the flow, and the flow is towards chaos.

These methods are often effective in responding to people who think they can easily manipulate you, either by making irrational demands or by invading your privacy. They drive home the point that one is never really in complete control of a situation, as it can become chaotic and unpredictable at any moment. They thus encourage people to become more reasonable and realistic about their actions and expectations.

As another example, consider how you might respond to a series of loud parties your neighbors have been having at your apartment complex. You might begin by making a polite request to keep the noise down. If this did no good, you might then leave a notice on your neighbors' door one afternoon, ostensibly from the management, saying, "The maintenance crew will be repairing loose paneling in some of the apartments during the next few days. We apologize for any inconvenience." You could then get up very early the next morning, take a hammer, and begin pounding on the walls. The next time you saw your neighbors, you could complain bitterly about how the maintenance people have been disrupting your life, by coming into your apartment when you least expected it and making all that racket. This may not get your neighbors to have fewer parties, but at least you have made them aware of the effects of increased noise, and perhaps they will be more reasonable and considerate in the future.

In a related situation, suppose your downstairs neighbors insisted on chain smoking in their apartment, even though you tried to explain to them that the smoke rises up into your apartment and causes you respiratory difficulties. But they do not take you seriously, and the problem continues. You might make a recording of yourself coughing, connect the recorder to a timer, and then set it to play at full volume for half an hour in the middle of the night, while you would stay at a motel for the next few days. If your neighbors complained to the manager, you could simply explain that all the smoke was making you cough, and you could not get any sleep.

This last example illustrates the principle of doing the next best thing. The "best" thing would have been to convince your neighbors to give up smoking or to have the manager move them to another apartment. But these are not enforceable. So the next best thing is to create chaotic complications, and to demonstrate that there can be unforeseen consequences of their actions which are really not your fault.

## DEALING WITH FANATICS

Perhaps the most irrational person of all is the fanatic, someone who is committed heart and soul to a crystallized idea or glorious cause. Fanatics are never as concerned with actually convincing you of the virtues of their positions as they are with merely imposing them upon you. It is therefore better to avoid engaging fanatics in conversation or debating their views, and simply walk away, whenever possible.

Sometimes, however, the fanatics may be people you care about, or the situation may prevent you from avoiding them. In such cases, you might acknowledge and accept their beliefs, and then try to incorporate those beliefs into your own. In a sense, you could try to build a house within their irrational world, until they began to trust you. This would allow them to visit your rational world without having to leave theirs.

Because you have built a house in their world, they can no longer regard you as a threat or a nonentity. By continuing to rebuild the house, and involving them in the interaction, you can often create an indissoluble link and get them to know you as a person. For example, suppose you encountered a religious fanatic who was intent on converting you, and whom you could not avoid. You might start out by embracing their beliefs in a sincere manner, then permit them to share some of your feelings. This would allow them to see you as someone who understood and appreciated what they believed in or stood for.

The irrational beliefs of most fanatics can be thought of as offshoots that depart from a normal growth process. A chaotic strategy would be to protect those offshoots until other branches, that is other alternative realities, could begin to grow. Most fanatics will resist this growth, but you can encourage it by creating opportunities for temporary explorations. This is often effective, for example, with suicidal people, where you get them to postpone their suicide for just a week, which then gives them an opportunity to see things from other perspectives (e.g., Freeman, 1993).

Ordered thinkers often run the risk of becoming fanatics whenever they begin to defend their principles to the extreme, untempered by compassion or perspective. Their sole concern might then be to manipulate others into accepting those principles and to join them in a crusade. When this happens, they are often successful at attracting followers who lack goals and principles of their own (e.g., Hofer, 1951). They are then increasingly likely to become dictators or cult leaders, an issue we explore further in chapter 9.

Chaotic thinkers can also become fanatics, but usually in a different sense than ordered thinkers. When they suddenly feel the need to express any impulse, regardless of rules or constraints, they risk becoming out of control. They can then become easily distracted and intensely involved in irrelevancies, which can lead them to become passionately irrational. We have more to say about this in chapter 8, where we discuss some of the limitations of chaotic thinking, and also in chapter 9.

## DEALING WITH CHILDREN

Children, and childish individuals in general, often assume that they can do whatever they want around you. The methods of chaotic thinking are ideally suited for dealing with the mind of the child, which often frustrates the structured thinking of ordered adults. This is because chaotic thinking itself is childlike in many respects—as indicated, for example, by its focus on the moment, its unstructured qualities, and its spontaneity.

When children misbehave, one might respond by creating small, realistic consequences for each of their actions, in order to intensify the moment. One might want to avoid abstract, future consequences, such as, "If you bounce that ball in here, you will go without dinner." Such consequences are often unrealistic; the child probably knows, for example, that few children are ever really denied dinner.

Instead, it is usually better to say, "If you bounce that ball in here, you can't watch your favorite cartoon show." This imposes immediate, realistic consequences that are entirely believable.

In dealing with children, it is important to accept the chaotic aspects of their way of thinking. Children are usually very involved in the moment, so one should not waste time talking about what happened in the past or is likely to happen in the future. Suppose a child began to open a bag of cookies. Instead of saying, "You can't have any cookies because they will ruin your dinner," one could make a deal in the present, perhaps by saying, "You can have one cookie now, so pick out the one you want."

It is best to always be genuine with a child. Most children can tell when one is playing phony roles, like "adult" or "teacher," or making idle threats. Also, it seldom pays to engage the child in a struggle of wills, for most children naturally resort to chaotic tactics. They tend to focus on the psychological weaknesses of their parent's behavior and will usually use these weaknesses to their advantage.

As a rule, children are more likely to exhibit chaotic thinking than adults. Compared to most adults, they are in a relatively powerless position and have internalized fewer rules, which encourages chaotic responding. They are also less likely to draw upon their past or project their plans far into the future.

Ordered thinking adults should not expect children to understand their principles, at least not right away. For example, if you told a child not to play in the street, explaining that it was dangerous, the child might think that you meant right now. You might therefore have to repeat the warning as new situations arose and not assume that the child would automatically obey your rule. A common tendency in ordered thinking is to assume that children should do things correctly once a rule is explained to them, but this violates their chaotic impulses.

Creating alternative realities can also be very helpful in dealing with children, especially with the arrogant child who is constantly making small demands. For example, if you were at a restaurant, and a child suddenly came up to you and demanded that you get out of his or her seat, you could agree to do so but then sit down on the floor next to them. This would present an alternative reality that the child had not anticipated. The silliness of your behavior would draw attention to the child's immaturity, which most children cannot stand.

Another chaotic technique for dealing with children is to utilize their inherent distractibility. For instance, if a child wanted a candy bar and began screaming in the store, you might ask them if they would like to help you carry one of the bags out to the car. This would make them think that they suddenly had an important task to do, and their focus within the moment would then shift.

It also helps to look for emergent patterns in the child, such as their changing likes and dislikes, to show an awareness of these new patterns, and to become more flexible in responding to them. For example, you might notice the types of clothes that your child wanted to wear, the television programs that your child often watched, or the games that your child enjoyed. It is important to keep track of all these things because it shows the child that you are aware of them as a unique individual, instead of simply as a generic "son" or "daughter."

Modern society seems overly concerned with accelerating children into adulthood (Elkind, 1988). We now want our children to mature quickly and efficiently. The problem is that most children need time to grow up, to play, and to experience things in unstructured ways. By trying to turn them into adults sooner, in order to "improve" them, one often risks ruining the child.

## CHAOTIC APPROACHES TO PSYCHOTHERAPY

Chaotic approaches to psychotherapy are becoming increasingly popular (e.g., Butz, 1993; McCown et al., in press). They focus on the total context of a person's emotions and feelings, the gradual emergence of new insights, and the utilization of natural reactions. This is in sharp contrast to the more common behavioral or cognitive approaches, which tend to be highly structured. In these approaches, which are discussed in more detail at the end of the chapter, one tries to structure the therapeutic situation in advance and to direct it towards future change. With chaotic approaches, one focuses on the immediate present and allows the structure to emerge.

Most chaotic therapists try to play a passive role in the therapeutic situation and accept uncritically whatever their client says and feels. This is characteristic of all humanist or client-centered approaches (e.g., Rogers, 1951). Instead of imposing a specific plan or system, chaotic therapists would try to react to what is happening with the client at the moment and avoid challenging or confronting them.

For example, a chaotic therapist might start out by asking the person about a recent sporting event or the current political situation. By getting the client to focus on things that are likely to be meaningful or interesting, the therapist can help them acquire a sense of perspective. This draws them away from their problems, so they can begin to look at them in a new light. The therapist might then try to encourage a mutual, transactional pattern of responding, by involving the client in immediate, back-and-forth conversation, and look for emergent patterns in what the client tells them, which would help them link things together for the person.

For instance, suppose a client said, "I really don't have any problems. Although my father sometimes beat me up when I was little, I don't have problems now; although I got into an argument with my parole officer, it wasn't a big deal; although I got drunk last night, I really don't have a drinking problem." The therapist might call these various incidents to the attention of the client, pointing out how they seem to contradict the claim that he or she does not have any problems, and suggest that there seems to be something more going on. The person may have never put these things together before, but could now begin to see the connections and their implications.

Chaotic therapists might also encourage their clients to explore multiple realities. The clients may see themselves as mean, evil, or worthless, and the therapist would try to get them to see themselves in other ways and to interpret their problems from a variety of different perspectives. In doing so, they would try to keep the conversation focused on the present, which is the only time when you can ever really change somebody.

In addition, chaotic therapists might try to create a "metalanguage" when talking with people, in order to bring out those things that they want them to think about (e.g., Haley, 1973). For example, they might explore how other people are currently affecting the person, and what the larger picture looks like. After talking with the client, they begin to get a sense for the person's mannerisms, attitudes, and things the person considers important. They might then use this knowledge to interpret what the person is actually saying at a much deeper level. It has then become a metalanguage, because it is much richer and more meaningful than just an ordinary conversation.

There is an inherent, interactive quality to the metalanguage of most chaotic therapists. Instead of the therapist telling the client what to do, both the therapist and client react to one another and work towards emergent patterns. It is playful and exploratory, rather than directive. Most chaotic therapists therefore try to avoid getting caught in arguments with their clients. Their conversations are more like dances, rather than tennis matches.

Although therapy can have many serious consequences, chaotic therapists often try to approach it with a playful attitude. This allows the client to keep a sense of proportion, even though many tragic things might be discussed. It also keeps the deadly seriousness of the problem light enough so that therapeutic work can go on.

There are other chaotic techniques that therapists might employ. They might gradually increase the complexity of the conversation, introducing new and unexpected ideas and possibilities. This serves to keep the client off balance and less able to control the situation. Or they might express their ideas indirectly, using stories or metaphors, and purposely violate the normal rules of conversation. For example, suppose a client came in and said, "I'm feeling fine today. In fact, I was just out walking in the sun." A chaotic therapist might respond by saying, "You know, your face is as white as I've ever seen a face. And I notice that your hands are trembling, and that you're holding one hand in front of your mouth." This ignores the rules of conversation, which say that one should always respond to a person's words. Instead, chaotic therapists often respond to what they see.

In chapter 5, we discussed perceptual traps, which are often effective in undermining a person's plans, particularly those that are unrealistic. These traps can also be used by therapists to lead their clients to believe important things about themselves that are actually true. For example, clients may want to believe that they are worthless or helpless. The therapist might innocently point to instances in which they were able to accomplish things, and soon they may be trapped into thinking that they are competent.

This is usually done in such a manner that the clients never suspect that a method is being used. Rather, they are simply given examples of competency, so that they can arrive at those conclusions and insights on their own. It resembles the way a con artist might get someone to conclude that they can earn a large profit by giving them proof of small profits, except that here the trap is working to the benefit of the person.

Another chaotic technique that is frequently used is to provide specific names for the vague feelings that clients are experiencing. For many people, a problem does not become "real" until it is given a label, and this can often be exploited in counseling. For instance, chaotic therapists might ask their clients, "Do you have a feeling right now that you would like to be freer?" In doing so, they have suddenly given them a name for something they have been yearning for their whole lives. Or the therapist might say, "It sounds to me like you'd be much happier living in California," and this suddenly gives them a concrete destination. These labels often remove much of the fear and uncertainty in the situation and help give the clients a sense of direction.

Chaotic therapists often try to locate and utilize mental "fissures" in their clients, where a sudden, chaotic event might lead to the collapse of an entire conceptual structure that is preventing them from having important insights. This is analogous to the way a slight blow at the right point can cause a large boulder to shatter. The therapist might intervene momentarily, weaken the structure in a critical spot, and then let nature take its course.

At the beginning of therapy, chaotic therapists often try to create the illusion that they have anticipated all of their client's responses. This is usually accomplished by skillfully utilizing the person's natural reactions to whatever occurs. At the end of therapy, however, they would try to shift power and have their clients see them as equals. Although this often destroys the magical effect they have created, it is necessary in order to set the client free.

Perhaps the best example of a chaotic approach to psychotherapy is existential therapy, which has no explicit system or formalism. Clients are encouraged to take personal responsibility for their lives, to deal with each moment as it comes, and to find meaning in the meaningless (Frankl, 1969; May, 1969). It thus makes extensive use of many of the techniques of chaotic thinking. And although it has been very influential, it has never been turned into an ordered system or institution.

## ERICKSONIAN TECHNIQUES

Milton Erickson, an innovator in the development of naturalistic approaches to therapy, employed chaotic techniques to great effect. Erickson's methods were often regarded as unconventional and even bizarre, yet they were unusually insightful and strikingly effective with many types of clients (Haley, 1973, 1985).

Typically, Erickson would try to utilize a person's natural tendencies. For instance, if a client displayed neurotic behavior, Erickson would try to use the neurosis in some constructive way. He would often use metaphors and anecdotes to communicate ideas indirectly and at multiple levels. He would create alternative realities and would complicate the situation or do unexpected things as a way of disengaging a dysfunctional plan. His clients would often report that, after talking with Erickson, new insights would emerge that suddenly provided the solutions to their problems.

One of the hallmarks of Erickson's approach was that he was often able to turn a client's disabilities into strengths. For example, a woman once came to him and complained about her in-laws, who would come to visit her three or four times a week, always unannounced. She could not bring herself to tell them to leave, and this had created so much stress in her life that she had finally developed an ulcer. Erickson suggested that her ulcer ought to be put to good use. After all, it would not be her fault if she happened to become sick the next time her in-laws came over. She quickly adopted this method, and when she wanted them to leave, all it took was a slight dyspeptic look on her face and a rubbing of her abdomen. She was thus able to utilize her ulcer and avoid a direct confrontation (Haley, 1973).

Like many chaotic therapists, Erickson had an uncanny ability to notice things that were disturbing clients and then to draw out even the most hidden secrets that were congesting them. Using metaphors and other means of indirect communication, he would often do this in such a way as to allow his clients to recognize, on their own, what these secrets were. For example, he might simply tell a client a story that contained an important lesson or theme, which the client could then relate to, and which often resulted in key insights that later emerged at unexpected moments (Haley, 1985).

Chaotic methods, such as those employed by Erickson and other therapists, typically lead to insights that often seem very real and meaningful to the person. Sometimes therapists make the mistake of trying to explain too much psychology to their clients, which usually results in second-hand conversations. By allowing clients to have insights on their own, they are often left with the feeling that those insights are genuine.

## ORDERED APPROACHES TO PSYCHOTHERAPY

Most therapists who adopt an ordered approach have specific plans in mind for working with their clients, and these often consist of explicit steps for them to follow. Once the client completes the plan, it is generally assumed that they are on the road to recovery. An ordered approach says, in effect, "We have a person who is broken and must be fixed." Most chaotic therapists would never see a client as inherently broken; they would just see a person with problems, who could benefit from gaining new insights and perspectives.

The strength of most ordered approaches is that they typically have a direct, steamroller effect. For instance, in one popular approach, rational-emotive therapy, the therapist attacks a person's negative ideas forcefully and systematically. This can have a very powerful, almost brainwashing effect on a client. A chaotic approach does not have that same sort of direct power.

Most practitioners of rational-emotive therapy believe that specific events are not responsible for how people respond, but rather that their responses are determined by their belief systems. An event is essentially a neutral thing; what matters is how one sees that event. Thus, if you can change a person's beliefs, especially their irrational beliefs, you can change how the person will act. For example, if a client said, "I want everybody to love me," a rational-emotive therapist would attack the belief, pointing out that it is irrational to think that everyone is going to love you. Because most people possess these kinds of beliefs to some degree, rational-emotive therapy can often be very helpful (e.g., Ellis & Harper, 1975; Ellis & Whiteley, 1979).

Chaotic therapists, in contrast, would almost never employ such a direct, confrontational approach, which they would likely see as devaluing the individual. For the same reason, they would generally avoid more traditional, ordered approaches like psychoanalysis and behavior modification. Instead, they would normally prefer to deal with problems in a more sensitive and personal manner and within a broader, more natural context. Also, most chaotic therapists would prefer to use methods that were improvised and that represented extensions of their own personality.

Ordered approaches often enable therapists to achieve measurable progress, especially with insecure clients, for whom the structured nature of the approach gives them something to cling to. Their drawback, however, is that weak clients who attach themselves to an ordered approach may not grow. The greatest danger for ordered therapists, therefore, is that their clients might become dependent on the system.

Self-motivated or recalcitrant clients would probably benefit more from a chaotic approach. This is because most chaotic therapists insist that people take responsibility for their own lives and not become dependent on the therapist or his or her methods. The weakness of this approach, however, is that it may give the client carte blanche to be independent before he or she is ready to assume that responsibility.

The following metaphor illustrates these contrasting limitations: The ordered therapist says to a client, "You must learn to crawl before you can learn to walk," and the client never learns to walk, because the therapist has taken away the freedom. The chaotic therapist says, in effect, "You can fly," and the client suddenly wants to jump off a building, having misconstrued the freedom.

As these examples imply, ordered and chaotic approaches to psychotherapy each have their strengths and weaknesses. One is not necessarily a better approach than the other. In general, the most appropriate approach depends on the nature of the problem, the type of client, and the natural style of the therapist.

# 7

## Survival Applications

Having considered applications of chaotic techniques in many common, everyday situations and interactions, we next turn to applications of these techniques when the very worst happens, as when disasters strike or when one's world is suddenly turned upside down. It is at such moments that chaotic thinking give one a distinct advantage, whereas the careful plans and preparations in ordered thinking may suddenly fail.

There are a number of reasons why chaotic thinking is particularly useful in many emergency and survival situations. The situations themselves are inherently chaotic, for the moment is intensified and the future is suddenly unpredictable. In addition, most survival situations call for rapid decision making and improvising. This resonates to the natural strengths of chaotic thinking.

The specific types of situations we consider in this chapter include how to survive when sudden emergencies arise, such as accidents, fires, and natural disasters; what to do when someone is trying to rob or harm one; how to respond when crises occur on the job; how to adapt when one is suddenly unemployed, undergoes a major career change, or experiences a marital breakup; how to improvise when one suddenly finds oneself in a dangerous or confining situation; or how to react when one is under intense harassment or psychological attack.

### EMERGENCY SITUATIONS

When catastrophes strike, usually the single most important thing one can do is to suspend every other concern and respond to what is actually happening at that moment. The situation is now chaotic and calls for chaotic responding. In most emergencies, it becomes essential to forget about past or future plans and to deal with the situation in the immediate present.

As mentioned previously, there is a strong tendency in ordered thinking to ponder a crisis and reflect upon how it might impact one's future. Instead of dealing with an emergency, one might be distracted by things that are now irrelevant, or dwell on the fate of plans that are no longer appropriate. In a true crisis, most plans for the future need to be suspended or disengaged.

The irony in this is that ordered thinkers often make careful contingency plans in anticipation of an emergency, as discussed in chapter 3. For instance, they might make lists of the specific things they would need to do in the event that a disaster occurred, like a hurricane or a tornado. Yet, in comparison with chaotic thinkers, they are generally less able to deal with these emergencies when they actually do occur. Despite their extensive preparations, they seldom anticipate fully the myriad of complex events and emotions that any real disaster creates.

For example, although they might make extensive preparations for a major storm, there will always be certain things that they will likely overlook. There might be a sudden need for extra light bulbs if some get broken. There might be a sudden need for additional shingles if some blow off the roof. There might be a sudden need for an emergency door should the old one get damaged. Having already convinced themselves that they were totally prepared, most ordered thinkers would be less able to respond to these unexpected needs. Instead of trying to anticipate every possible contingency, a chaotic thinker would make a few basic preparations and then improvise as necessary.

Another type of emergency is a fire in the house. Again, in anticipation of the fire, an ordered approach would usually involve making extensive contingency plans. Ordered thinkers would likely plan escape routes, put fire extinguishers in convenient locations, leave phone numbers for the fire department, or have fire drills. All of this seems perfectly fine until the fire actually occurs, whereupon one might make the mistake of assuming that one still had to follow each of these rules.

A fire is an inherently chaotic event, as is any real emergency. It changes rapidly and in unpredictable ways. Whereas it is usually a good idea to make some advanced preparations in case of a fire, it is just as important not to allow those preparations to blind one to the actual situation. The planned escape route might be blocked, or the fire extinguishers might be unreachable. One could follow an escape plan to the extent that those actions were appropriate, but should one find some avenue blocked, one would need to adapt or improvise.

When relying on ordered thinking, one tends to become confused and disoriented upon realizing that an escape plan may have failed. The rigid, structured qualities of ordered thinking, which are often its strength, can suddenly become a liability. At such times, ordered thinkers may panic, or continue to commit themselves to the plan in spite of changing circumstances. As a result, they might end up getting hurt or causing others to get hurt.

Sometimes ordered thinkers show an "anti-panic" reaction in a crisis, in which they seemingly display a complete detachment from the situation. It is as if they were observing the crisis from a distance. This may reflect a need to shield themselves from the intensity of the crisis, since they are often overwhelmed by such events.

Some ordered thinkers, however, regard a crisis as a challenge and respond by trying to organize things, take charge, and assign duties to others. This is usually helpful as long as one is experienced in dealing with that particular type of crisis. If this is not the case, however, the plans are likely to be inappropriate.

Another type of emergency situation is a riot or coup. If caught in a riot, it is important to become aware of the immediate, emerging conditions. For example, one might try to notice where people are gathering and how they seem to be feeling at any given moment. The reactions of people in riots are usually unpredictable, and one can suddenly find oneself in an explosive situation in which plans and rules that applied before are no longer valid. Although one might try to make preparatory plans for dealing with a riot, such plans must have an inherent flexibility or they will likely collapse.

Similar considerations apply in coups, where a group suddenly tries to take over the government. The leader who is being challenged by the coup can no longer say, "I am in power; I will not be overthrown," for the situation is now chaotic. As in a riot, one needs to be aware of what is happening at the moment and be ready to react immediately to any unexpected developments. There is usually no time to analyze the situation.

In these types of crises, chaotic thinkers are often able to pick up on the contextual cues that define normal behavior within the situation and can usually respond in ways that do not draw attention to themselves. Ordered thinkers tend to have more trouble doing this effectively. They often stand out in a riot and may be tempted to confront the rioters or the police on the basis of principle. And even when they take no direct action, their behavior often belies their lack of understanding of the situation, and they are likely to be seen as outsiders.

## DANGEROUS ENCOUNTERS

Another type of crisis situation is to be suddenly approached by robbers or attackers. Chaotic thinkers are generally more aware of how to avoid such confrontations; they either stay out of danger to begin with, by noticing the warning signs, or they find ways of blending in, by becoming inconspicuous. Ordered thinkers, however, might unwittingly walk through a bad part of town just to save time, not realizing how obviously they stood out. If suddenly confronted, they might argue or resist, overlooking the dangers of doing so.

Suppose, for example, that one was being robbed. An ordered response might be to try to convince the robbers that they will probably be caught, or to resist on the grounds of some moral principle—for example, that one should not allow criminals to steal from people. One might also assume that one would not be shot without a good reason, but this is never a wise assumption because robbers seldom obey these kinds of rules.

A chaotic response would be to remain silent and cooperate fully, and give the robbers one's money without protest. This accepts the reality of the moment, and is nonconfrontational. Whereas most ordered thinkers might become overwhelmed by their unexpected emotional reactions in this situation and might panic, most chaotic thinkers would tend to stay calm and would try to define the situation as a nonemergency.

Suppose you were being robbed and did not have any money. This is a particularly dangerous situation, because the robbers are likely to get angry or frustrated. To minimize this anger, you might complain to the robbers that you really hated your boss for firing you the way he did, throwing you out on the street like this and not caring whether you ever found another job again. You could mention that you would really like to run into your boss someday and get even. This conveys a message that most robbers can identify with, one that might even generate sympathy for you. It also provides an acceptable excuse for why you have no money.

Naturally, to reduce the chances of being robbed in the first place, one should try to avoid places where robberies tend to occur. However, this is not always possible. If one has to walk someplace where one knows that one might be robbed, a chaotic strategy would be to wear "street" clothes, and possibly bring along a paper bag containing a bottle. This would allow you to become a chameleon, in effect, and create the favorable illusion that there is no reason to rob you. Many ordered thinkers would avoid trying to blend in using such methods, either because they were unaware of the danger or were convinced that they could handle any problems.

Here, too, it is rather ironic that ordered thinkers often go to great lengths to prepare for such encounters. They might purchase mace, take self-defense courses, or even invest in a weapon, but then often end up doing the very things that place them at greater risk. For instance, if they were late for an appointment, they might walk down a side street regardless of the suspicious-looking characters inhabiting it. Chaotic thinkers generally make fewer preparations for these encounters, but they are usually better able to deal with them when they occur.

Suppose you were in a store that was being robbed. A chaotic impulse might be to take out your wallet and hide it, while leaving some money in your pocket, for the obvious reason that the robbers would probably ask everyone to give them their wallets. If they then asked you for your wallet, you could say that you did not bring it because you just came down for some beer, but they are welcome to take your money. This avoids having to resist the robbers, and keeps you from losing your credit cards and other items of personal value.

As another example of using chaotic methods to survive a dangerous encounter, suppose somebody broke into your house. If you were not able to get to a phone, you might turn on as many lights as you could, and blast the television or stereo. If the robber saw you and started to panic, you could simply explain that your friends were about to arrive for a party. This creates the illusion that there will be lots of people there shortly, so the robber would not have time to hurt you.

These examples illustrate the chaotic principles of intensifying the moment, utilizing natural events, increasing purposeful clutter, and doing the next best thing. They also illustrate the importance of avoiding direct confrontation and going with the flow. In chaotic thinking, one generally accepts the reality of the encounter, utilizes it if possible, complicates it if necessary, and does not worry about trying to stop it.

When a burglars enter one's house, an ordered response might be to get a gun and try to shoot them. This is seldom advisable, because most burglars either have their own guns or know how to take guns away from people. Also, a gun escalates the situation into an either–or proposition: "Either I shoot them, or they shoot me." Allowing robbers the opportunity to simply take what they want and leave avoids this type of critical confrontation.

A common precaution among many homeowners today is to install barking dog tapes that are activated whenever someone approaches. Most burglers, however, are now aware of these tapes and have learned to recognize when they are being used. A chaotic variation on this would be to post notices on your door, supposedly from the police or your landlord, warning you to control your dog, which has recently growled at and chased some of your neighbors. This would help to make the illusion more effective.

Chaotic thinkers often treat these situations as games. They know that in a dangerous encounter, things are more serious than usual, but they usually do not take them so seriously that they lose their perspective on them. Most ordered thinkers tend to do the opposite and regard such encounters too seriously. They might keep reminding themselves that things are critical, with life-and-death implications, and this often keeps them from from acting sensibly.

In dealing with dangerous encounters, it helps to distinguish between ordered and chaotic criminals. Most ordered criminals regard crime as a profession. They usually plan their crimes carefully, have a stable family life outside their work, avoid violence (to the extent that they may not even use a gun), and regard the risks as financially justified. Most chaotic criminals commit crimes impulsively, do not mind an occassional shoot-out (which intensifies the moment), and care little about the risks or the long-term consequences of their actions. They also like to add elements of complexity to their crimes in order to throw off the authorities.

One can make a similar distinction between ordered and chaotic con artists. As a rule, ordered thinkers usually make better insidemen, given their planning and organization skills, whereas chaotic thinkers usually make better ropers, given their ability to create alternative realities and to utilize a person's responses. In addition, each will usually try to depict scenarios that go against their natural traits. For instance, an ordered con artist may try to convince a mark that there is no plan at work, that the losses are simply due to bad luck. A chaotic con artist, however, may let the mark think that there is a workable plan that they can use to beat the system (e.g., Maurer, 1974).

When ordered criminals become very powerful or wealthy, they sometimes lose the distinction between reality and fantasy. They might then begin to believe that the normal rules of society no longer apply to them, and that they can do anything they want. This is when they are often caught. For example, someone who has become rich by selling drugs might risk everything by shoplifting or committing some minor crime, believing he or she can now break any law and not be prosecuted.

To discourage criminal behavior among ordered thinkers, one might try to increase the uncertainty they face, so that their plans are always more complicated and risky. For example, police have often resorted to techniques such as having policewomen pose as prostitutes, or announcing that someone has poisoned a large supply of an illegal drug. This limits the success of ordered criminals, for they can no longer predictably expand their operations, and are always having to wonder whether or not the customer or drug is legitimate.

One can also set perceptual traps to try to capture ordered criminals who are still at large. For example, one might create an official-looking notification saying that they have just won a lot of money, then send it to their last known address or to one of their relatives. The notification might instruct them to go to a certain office to collect their money, whereupon they would be arrested. Such traps often catch ordered criminals off guard, where the prospect of winning something blinds them to potential dangers.

It is also important to recognize when criminals are using chaotic techniques. For example, after taking valuable items from a house or apartment, a chaotic thief might leave some money behind, to create purposeful clutter. The victim might then wonder whether the items were taken by someone they knew, who left the money out of guilt, or whether they should report the money to the police. The thief might plan on taking only one item, leaving behind more desirable items such as a television set or a VCR, so that the police would wonder whether the reportedly stolen item was really stolen after all. The thief might also leave a portion of the stolen goods in a poor neighborhood, so that someone else would take them and possibly be caught trying to sell or pawn them. The police would then be thrown completely off track and would probably assume that a local gang was responsible.

If one suspects that people are doing illegal things, and does not wish to become directly involved, a useful chaotic technique is to create an alternative reality that encourages others to get involved. For instance, if you suspected that illegal drugs were being used in your apartment complex, and the manager was doing nothing about it, you might write to the owner, pretending to be the mother of one of the tenants, and say that you and your husband were visiting your daughter and were very disturbed to find that her neighbors were using drugs. You could explain that your daughter did not want you to say anything about this, which is why you were not revealing your name, but that you were really shocked to discover that she was living in a hash house, and that you were planning to contact the authorities and have the complex shut down if something was not done about it right away. The owner will likely contact the manager of the apartments immediately, who will then be forced to take the situation seriously.

## CRISES AT WORK

Having to deal with unexpected problems at work can sometimes be just as stressful and threatening as many of the dangerous situations just considered. A common problem is when your boss or supervisor refuses to deal with you honestly or fairly, or is overly critical of your performance. When those who think in highly ordered ways come into positions of power, they usually want to demonstrate their authority at some point, often by trying to find fault with their subordinates. If this happens, instead of trying to fight the situation, one might employ chaotic methods that promote more sensible and rational policies.

For instance, if your supervisor persisted in criticizing you severely for relatively minor mistakes, you might respond by asking for the supervisor's approval for every little thing you planned to do, saying that you wanted to make sure that you did not repeat those same mistakes again. You could also mention that there were others in the organization who seemed to be making lots of similar mistakes, and that the supervisor might want to keep an eye on them as well. Most supervisors would want to avoid these constant distractions in their daily routines and would probably stop criticizing you.

If you were always being treated as a scapegoat, the chaotic technique of creating favorable illusions might help. For instance, you might try to create illusory problems that the person would constantly have to track down or worry about, or invent various imaginary enemies who supposedly were trying to undermine the person. They would then end up chasing ghosts, so to speak, which would keep them from focusing their scapegoating tendencies on you.

Suppose your boss was always getting upset with you for not doing exactly what he expected, and the situation was becoming intolerable. For example, he might constantly reprimand you for not doing more to help the organization, even though you had actually been a reliable and responsible worker. Here are some examples of chaotic strategies that might be effective in creating useful complications in this situation and helping you to survive:

1. You might begin by pressing your boss to commit himself on some controversial issue, such as the proper role of women or minorities in the organization. You could say that you felt that it was important for strong leadership

to have clearly stated policies on such matters, so that everyone would have confidence in the strength of that leadership.

2. When your boss responded to this issue one way or the other, you might compliment him on his courage for taking a stand and then publicize his position throughout the organization, pointing out how it was really a shame that other bosses seldom showed this kind of admirable willingness to deal head-on with controversial issues.

3. You might then use this opportunity to redefine your boss's position, elaborating or expanding on it, so that it became as extreme as possible. For example, if your boss said that women should play a bigger role in the organization, you could claim that he said that women should take over the organization.

4. When your boss became upset because you have misrepresented his position, you could publically acknowledge and apologize for your error and then attribute to him the exact, opposite position, such as that all women should be banned from the organization.

Eventually, your boss is likely to see the wisdom of simply letting you do your job, instead of trying to involve you more extensively in the inner workings of the organization. These misunderstandings, however, must convey the impression that you are trying to be the most cooperative worker you can be, so that they are not perceived as being purposely disruptive.

In general, these chaotic techniques should create the favorable illusion that you are trying to help the person, which offers you some protection. Their real purpose is to escalate the situation to a crisis point, so that the person is then forced to confront and deal with the existing problems in a realistic and rational manner. This encourages the situation to move towards a state of greater harmony and cooperation.

When supervisors begin to tighten their requirements or expectations in order to have more control over their workers, they often create unanticipated freedoms for them. By regulating their activities to an excessive degree, they releave the workers of some of their obligations to be responsible for themselves. Thus, the workers acquire the freedom to be irresponsible, with the result that these managing tactics ultimately fail. This problem is considered further in chapter 10.

Whenever one is forced to be in an undesirable work situation, it usually helps to try to have fun and to utilize the situation in playful and creative ways. Instead of worrying about how one's future or career will be affected, or trying to fight the existing forces, it is usually better to accept the situation and react chaotically to it, which often then allows constructive changes to take place.

## ECONOMIC SURVIVAL

In an economic crisis, it is often essential to abandon or restructure one's former plans and to stop thinking of oneself in terms of one's previous profession or identity. It does not matter if one were a skilled technician, a lawyer, or a bank president. Economic survival usually means finding work, any work. One might still feel that one belongs in a certain type of job, but this is now in the past.

With ordered thinking, the natural reaction to major disruptions like economic upheavals is to plan even harder. An ordered thinker will often to try to control the increasing amounts of chaos by resorting to plans that are increasingly rigid and inflexible. For most chaotic thinkers, the natural tendency would be to plan even less, for these disruptive events would remind them that life is inherently unpredictable.

Surviving in hard economic times means living for the moment, concentrating on immediate and essential things, and assessing one's current resources. These are activities for which chaotic thinking is well suited. Instead of thinking about how things used to be or the uncertainties of the future, one would consider the things one absolutely needed, avoid making any long-term plans, and accept the harsh reality that what was is now forever gone.

Under such conditions, chaotic thinkers can often find creative and resourceful ways of living and eating cheaply. If they needed food, they might check out various charitable agencies (such as churches, the Salvation Army, or the United Way), see if they were eligible for food stamps, or explore the bent and broken sections at their local stores. If they needed emergency shelter, they might ask for damaged rooms at motels, stay at campgrounds or rest stops, or sleep in their car. If they needed medical attention, they might go to the local free clinic (e.g., Brown & Morgan, 1984).

Most ordered thinkers would probably regard such options as unpalatable or even revolting. They would likely exclude them from their plans, especially if they had considerable pride and had convinced themselves that they would never end up out on the street. But in a true economic crisis, such options become increasingly pragmatic.

At such times, ordered thinkers might benefit by making economic survival an ongoing challenge, rather than a burden or embarrassment. This could enable them to live from moment to moment, enduring each day, until they could set up a regular survival routine. In doing this, however, one should be prepared for constant changes and uncertainties, especially if the crisis persists for a long time. Coping with prolonged uncertainty is usually easier for chaotic thinkers, as they often thrive on the unpredictability of a crisis.

Survival can also be enhanced by exploring alternative realities. For example, one might take on a variety of different part-time jobs, to examine other types of working environments, and to explore different ways of getting essential things like food and money. The more options and opportunities one can generate during a prolonged crisis, the better one's chances to survive.

One might also begin saving various odds and ends, because everything one collects might be utilized in some creative way. For instance, when chaotic thinkers go into a store and find various items on sale, they often buy them, knowing that they can always do something useful with them later on. They might, for example, be able to sell the items to neighbors or trade them for food. This illustrates the principle of increasing purposeful clutter, which often creates unexpected opportunities and resources.

In general, whereas ordered thinking emphasizes predictability and efficiency, chaotic thinking emphasizes adaptability and resilience. For most chaotic thinkers, it is more important to accept and endure adversity than to try to make things work efficiently. This is why they are often better able to survive in extended hard times.

Dropping out of society, however, is usually easier than getting back in. When making the transition back into society, ordered thinking becomes increasingly important, for one needs to establish stability and reliability. For instance, it helps to have a stable address, hold the same job, apply for credit cards to rebuild credit, take classes at community colleges (which often looks good to employers), and join various community groups and organizations. Whereas chaotic thinking is generally more useful when situations become unstructured, ordered thinking is generally more useful when one returns to a structured existence.

## CAREER CHANGES

Although usually less drastic than the economic upheavals just considered, major career changes, even voluntary ones, can often create a surprising amount of anxiety, uncertainty, and chaos. This is especially true if one is concerned about the possibility of ruining one's future by making the change.

If one were thinking about leaving one's present job, it often helps to assess multiple skills that could be marketable. For instance, one might go to the library and read books on how to explore alternative careers (e.g., Adams, 1983; Beard & McGahey, 1983; Bolles, 1994). Also, some community colleges offer free career assessment. By becoming more aware of one's options and alternatives, one reduces much of the anxiety over having an uncertain future.

When contemplating career changes, ordered thinkers tend to preoccupy themselves with certainties and guarantees. They often want a career change that assures them of success and happiness in the end. However, any career change needs to be extremely flexible, so that if things do not work out as expected, one still has other options. For example, a secretary might decide to become a financial consultant in order to make lots of money, and so quits her present job and returns to school. She might then discover, however, that she cannot pass the necessary courses. Because she has focused all of her efforts on becoming a financial consultant, having anticipated its rewards, she might not be able to get off this path. She might then begin to think that she is now a complete failure and that there is nothing else she can do.

Even when people successfully enter a new profession, they may not anticipate all of the complications and unforeseen appurtenances that are often associated with it. For instance, a man might decide that he wants to become a doctor, and does well in medical school, but then discovers that he cannot stand the sight of blood. There will always be at least some negative aspects of any new career that cannot be seen from the outside.

A strong tendency among many ordered thinkers is to idolize a career before finding out what that career really involves. At such times, they might benefit by talking with chaotic thinkers, to explore other possibilities and to see themselves in different and often more realistic ways. As discussed in chapter 6, chaotic thinkers can often point out other options that people have not yet considered, show them specific things they could do, and help them to visualize themselves in situations that they normally cannot see. In ordered thinking, one often develops a blindness of vision down one career path, whereas chaotic thinkers can often present people with alternative paths and multiple visions.

Sometimes one cannot change careers right away and has to tolerate a less than ideal situation. In such cases, it is useful not think of oneself as being identified with one's job, which often occurs in ordered thinking. Merely working at a job does not have to define who a person is, especially if the job is embarrassing or demeaning. One's essense need not be equated with what one has to do to earn money.

Whenever one begins a new job, it is usually necessary to pick up on the informal rules and structures that already exist within that organization. This usually means suppressing one's expectations for how things ought to be run and carefully attending to what is actually happening in the new situation. This relates to the chaotic principle of letting the structure emerge. Some of these structures include the pecking order, and whom one has to see in order to get certain things done. Until one becomes familiar with these informal rules and structures, one cannot really do a new job effectively.

If one does move on to a better positon, it is usually better not to overtly antagonize former employers and colleagues, especially if one felt mistreated or underappreciated. They may be asked someday to provide an opinion, or one might need a reference. From an ordered perspective, one might tend to look upon these situations only in terms of winners and losers, as in saying, "I win by leaving this job, and you lose." A chaotic approach would be to try to leave people with a good feeling about one, even if things did not go particularly well on the job. For example, one might simply attribute one's advancement to good luck.

Ordered thinkers are usually more likely to make planned career switches than chaotic thinkers, because they are usually more concerned with developing their careers. A chaotic thinker might be perfectly content to simply remain in an inglorious job, until something happened that stimulated an impulse to leave. This might seem to contradict the notion that chaotic thinkers usually try to avoid predictable and repetitive situations, but it follows from their essentially passive nature and their focus on living in the moment. They tend not to see themselves as remaining in a rut over an extended period of time, and in fact, might not even realize how long they have been working at the same job until one explicitly called this to their attention. We consider this aspect of chaotic thinking further in chapter 8.

Finally, a forced career change, as when one is suddenly laid off, is likely to have all of the built-in anxieties of a major disaster. For many ordered thinkers, it could be the worst thing that could possibly happen. Chaotic thinkers are likely to accept an unexpected layoff more easily, because they would generally assume that unpredictable changes in the job market were simply part of a naturally chaotic world.

## MARITAL BREAKUPS

As discussed in chapter 6, marriages between ordered and chaotic thinkers often lead to problems. Many ordered thinkers might initially enjoy the sense of freedom that a chaotic spouse provides, but at some point they might start to complain that the person was too unpredictable or was not doing enough to help them develop their careers. Eventually, they might become unbearably frustrated, the chaotic spouse might then leave, and the marriage might end in divorce.

Once a marriage breaks up, realizing that the relationship is now over may be one of the hardest things a person ever has to accept, especially for someone who relies heavily on ordered thinking. Once the stability, security, and predictability of the relationship have been shattered, one is likely to encounter a chaotic situation of enormous uncertainty and stress, and may become desperate to return to the way things were.

When having to deal with marital breakups, ordered thinkers sometimes become obsessed with trying to understand all of the reasons behind them. But this usually wastes time and increases anxiety. There is a tendency to think about what might have been, how nice things used to be, and how the future plans are now ruined. The potential that the relationship had can be missed almost as much as the person. One might continue to hold onto the fantasy that the person will come back somehow, and that the relationship will be restored once again. All one needs to do is say the right thing, and the damage will be undone. These expectations, however, are seldom fulfilled.

There is also a tendency to want to remain "friends" with an ex-spouse immediately after a breakup, so as to retain a fragment of the relationship. It might be possible to reestablish a friendship someday, but at the moment a breakup occurs, this is unrealistic. In any event, this would only be possible after the expectations from the marriage had disappeared.

Dealing with marital breakups is often complicated by thinking of the other person in terms of winning or losing them. For example, the success of a plan to marry someone might lead ordered thinkers to conclude that they have "won" the person, whereas the end of a marriage might lead them to think that they have now "lost" the person. From a chaotic perspective, one often loses by winning, and wins by losing.

Viewing a marital breakup solely in terms of winners and losers can have several adverse consequences. For instance, it tends to create residual animosities. Either you will become angry, or you will have an angry ex-spouse. It also tends to divide your friends or families into opposing teams. They will either support you or support the other person. Such polarizations can prolong negative feelings about the breakup and are especially difficult for children to deal with.

If one had an angry ex-spouse, a chaotic approach could help to limit this anger or minimize its effects. One might begin by listening to what the person had to say and then try to explain that the marriage was over and that it served no purpose to be angry. Should that fail, which it probably would, one could then try to contrast the anger with a more reasonable perspective on things. This is often helpful if there are children involved, and one's ex-spouse has told them unpleasant things in order to retaliate.

For instance, to say something like, "Well, your mother is just an extravagant slut," after she had told your children that you were a tightwad, accomplishes nothing. Instead, you could explain, "Your mother and I had some disagreements over money. Perhaps she perceives me as being a little tight, and I can understand that." This will not only benefit your children, but when they repeat this to your ex-spouse, it may have some beneficial effects there as well. By responding to anger with reasonability and insight, at some point the anger will no longer be able to hold on by itself. And even if this does not work, your children will begin to perceive your ex-spouse as the one who is being unreasonable.

Sometimes ex-spouses become even angrier when you try to be calm and reasonable with them. Usually, however, this occurs when you are dealing with them directly. By being reasonable with your children, you tend to neutralize that anger, because your ex-spouse will want to avoid appearing to them to be the one who is responsible for the misunderstandings. By setting rationality as a standard, you begin to encourage rationality in others.

Another chaotic approach is to try to view the breakup and the reasons that caused it from the perspective of multiple realities. In ordered thinking, one tends to have a single vision of how the marriage broke up, which usually solidifies at some point. There may, however, be any number of reasons for the breakup that are just as plausible. By considering these various alternatives, one reduces the tendency to dwell on a single, fixed reality that is locked into the past.

The biggest danger for many chaotic thinkers in a breakup is that they might be taken advantage of. For example, their ex-spouse might tell them, "This is how we're going to divide the property," or "I'll take the house and you'll take the car." Because most chaotic thinkers are passive by nature and wish to avoid confrontations, they may simply let such things be decided for them, as long as they were able to achieve their freedom.

## SURVIVING CONFINEMENT

When confined, chaotic thinkers are usually better equipped to survive, in part because of their natural, fatalistic outlook. In general, they tend to see themselves as not having much control over what happens in their lives. As a result, as long as the confinement were not totally unstimulating or overly oppressive, they would likely accept it and simply endure.

Prison represents an interesting combination of an ordered environment in which chaos often runs rampant. One does not usually know, from moment to moment, exactly what will happen next. Violent acts can occur unpredictably and at any time, not only between prisoners and guards, but also between prisoners and prisoners, resulting in a highly unstable situation. Ordered and chaotic thinkers would usually approach the prospect of going to prison in very different ways.

Once sent to prison, most ordered thinkers would try to devise long-term plans, file appeals, set up parole hearings, and develop exercise schedules. They might even try to get some sort of education. Most chaotic thinkers would try to survive on a day by day basis and would regard prison as just another place where unexpected things can happen. In fact, they might even prefer life in prison, were it not for the unsavory company. They could be perfectly content not having any responsibilities, with meals and health care provided for them. It is usually easier for chaotic thinkers to endure adverse situations, like prison or an unpleasant job, if they know they are compelled to be there. This frees them from having to make decisions about their future.

Most chaotic thinkers would quickly pick up on the informal rules of the prison, such as how to gain favors, who to befriend, and who to avoid. It usually takes most ordered thinkers longer to learn these informal rules and the consequences of violating them. Although at some point they might be successful at creating structures within the prison setting that could help them to survive, they are usually less aware of its immediate dangers. Chaotic thinkers are more likely to quickly assimilate themselves into the prison situation, and to see the immediate advantages of it, such as getting free food and shelter, having free time to read or write books, or having an opportunity to study the criminal mind.

Ordered thinking is typically geared toward setting up plans and then confronting whatever gets in the way of those plans. Initially, going to prison is likely to be a bigger blow to most ordered thinkers, not only because they would probably feel that they did not belong there, but also because it would disrupt whatever plans they had previously made, which rarely include the possibility of going to prison. On the other hand, given sufficient time, they can often become masters of the prison organization. The prison can then become a microcosm of the world in general, which operates according to rules and plans and which can be manipulated for personal needs.

Ordered and chaotic thinkers would also probably employ different methods of trying to escape from prison. In an ordered escape attempt, one would likely make detailed plans for the escape, assign various responsibilities to others, perhaps form an escape committee, and possibly even create a fake plan to mislead the authorities. In a chaotic escape attempt, one would simply take advantage of any momentary opportunities, without making detailed plans or anticipating various contingencies.

These differences could have important implications for prison officials. In the case of an escape by an ordered thinker, it is likely to have been the result of an elaborate plan, with possible conspiracies, and thus a cause for concern. In the case of an escape by a chaotic thinker, it is likely to have been a spur-of-the-moment decision and probably less cause for concern.

Chaotic thinkers would usually notice and take advantage of small errors or patterns in the system in order to escape. For instance, they might notice that a guard paused in a certain place to rest or to have a snack, or that there was a 10-second delay between a gate clicking and the gate being locked. They would then try to utilize these patterns if the opportunity to escape suddenly arose. Their escape attempts are therefore less likely to be anticipated, because they would probably occur on impulse. On the other hand, although the escape plans of ordered thinkers can often be ingenious, they are more likely to be discovered. Prison officials might infiltrate those plans, using spies or talking with known associates. With most chaotic thinkers, even their best friends might not know about the escape attempt.

A mental hospital represents another form of prolonged confinement. As with prisons, mental hospitals usually contain a volatile mixture of structure and chaos. Many forms of mental illness exhibit strong chaotic tendencies, yet most mental hospitals are highly structured and ordered, with rigid rules and expectations. These rules function, in part, to define certain behaviors as mentally ill and to treat them as such.

These institutions often create perceptual traps, which one can easily fall into if one tries to defeat the system. One is in a "Catch-22" situation, since, by definition, one is mentally ill. Any attempt to fight this diagnosis, to convince others that one is actually sane, will likely be taken as further evidence that one is not (e.g., Cameron, 1980; Rosenhan, 1973). One therefore cannot win by fighting the situation. But one can often do the next best thing, which is to accept the situation and go with the flow.

In general, the best way to defeat any type of perceptual trap is to not care about winning. For instance, if confined to a mental hospital, one might simply admit that one was insane and needed help. Any attempt to resist or challenge the therapy would simply be interpreted as a sign that one still needed the therapy. Eventually, at an appropriate time, one could simply demonstrate one's competence, and show that the therapy had been successful. By going with the flow, one would increase the chances of getting out more quickly, especially if it seemed that one were enjoying the experience.

## SURVIVING HARASSMENT

People who take their plans too seriously may sometimes resort to threatening or harassing others, thinking that this will help to ensure that their plans will be fulfilled. When their plans fall apart, they might then try to blame those whom they thought were responsible, even though it might not have been their fault. Chaotic methods can often deal effectively with various forms of harassment, and can help to discourage various types of abusive tendencies.

One of the simplest methods is to employ passive resistance. For instance, suppose you were being harassed at work whenever your supervisor happened to be in a bad mood, or whenever things did not go as planned. Every time such an incident occurred, you might simply call in sick the next day. This would discourage the harassment without having to confront the person. It would also avoid the risk of retaliation that might occur if you tried to make formal charges.

Creating favorable illusions is another useful method. For instance, if you were being harassed by someone who was living in another city, you might send the person a flyer from an imaginary publisher, which announced a book you had just written supposedly describing many of your unpleasant experiences. This could include a picture of the book cover and several enthusiastic endorsements. Then, for the next few months, you could send the person letters from various fictional readers, asking if some of the things that were said in the book were really true. These might include questions like, "Did you really glue your girlfriend to a chair, to keep her from walking out on you?" or "Is it true that you used to feed stray cats to your dog?" The person might then feel compelled to prove that these things never really happened, and claim that you had no right to publish them. But the book is merely an illusion.

The point of doing this is to demonstrate to those intend on harassing you that there are consequences of mistreating someone that cannot always be anticipated, ignored, or mollified. In using this chaotic approach, one creates alternative realities that cannot easily be dismissed. Specific allegations concerning actual incidents can usually be challenged or rationalized away, whereas with purely imaginary events, there is nothing to fight against.

Using the same technique, one could also try to create the illusion that one was about to go on a talk show and tell the entire nation about the way the person had harassed them. For example, you might have a friend call the person, pretending to be the assistant producer for the talk show, and explain that you would be appearing in a few weeks and that the producer wanted to know if the person would like to join in to respond to your allegations. It would be explained that you were doing this not to get personal revenge, but to discourage this kind of thing from happening to others. This would intensify the problem, and possibly lead the person to recognize the potential ramifications of continuing to treat people in this manner.

As a rule, most chaotic thinkers do not take angry threats very seriously. In fact, they will often simply smile at someone who is threatening them, which usually intensifies the moment and frustrates further efforts to intimidate them. Instead of trying to retaliate or get even, they would simply respond chaotically, believing that abusive and manipulative people will eventually end up hurting themselves.

To control the desire to blame or harass others when one's plans were not working out, one might simply focus on getting past those moments in which one felt outraged. In the spirit of chaotic thinking, one could regard these feelings as being part of the present moment, but not necessarily belonging to future moments. One could then try to become involved in other plans, to avoid obsessing over the plans that failed.

## PSYCHOLOGICAL ATTACKS

Although not physically dangerous, verbal attacks, especially those that skillfully play off one's psychological weaknesses, can often be quite devastating. These attacks, too, can often be handled using chaotic methods. For instance, when chaotic thinkers are insulted, they often try to utilize the insults and create alternative realities that incorporate them in creative and insightful ways.

Suppose someone had just subjected you to intense and unwarranted personal criticism, merely to bolster his or her pride. If this were someone whom you rarely see, you could pretend that, as a result of the valid points they had made, you have decided to quit your job and move to some other part of the country, where you hoped to rid yourself of these feelings of emptiness and personal failure. You could then write ocassional letters to this person and have a friend mail them from this other location, expressing your gratitude for helping you to realize just how worthless you really were.

You could say, for example, that you have decided to work for a trucking company, because you clearly do not have the intelligence or personal skills to handle professional-level work. You could then periodically send the person photographs revealing various aspects of your new life, showing the local street people, whom you could describe as your new friends, or showing a dilapidated, run-down dump, which you could describe as your new apartment. You could say that you were learning many new skills, such as how to refinish furniture, and that this has given you a new feeling of confidence and pride. You could then send the person a photograph of the sorriest-looking piece of junk you could possibly find.

These letters would create an alternative reality that the person would have trouble accepting at first, but might then begin to explore later on. The person would likely wonder if these things were really happening, or whether you were simply making them all up. This ambiguity would add to the chaotic quality of the situation and would encourage the person to become curious and even more involved. In effect, you would have invited the person to participate in an alternative reality in which they could explore some of the possible consequences of having hurt another person's feelings.

Sometimes the alternative reality can intensified by purposely ignoring feedback from the other person. For instance, if the person tried to convince you to return to your previous job, or raised questions about the believability of your recent experiences, you might simply ignore these responses, and continue to describe your new world. This often enhances the bizarre qualities of the kinds of things you might describe.

These chaotic responses are usually more effective if the alternative realities are not tied to a specific plan. Rather, their purpose should be to involve both people as mutual players in a game that unfolds without rules or time limits, and in which each person can achieve new insights. As with many chaotic methods, they provide a mirror into which one can explore hidden aspects of one's personality and gain new realizations about one's true nature.

Another chaotic strategy is to try to turn an individual, psychological attack into an attack on an entire group of people. You might claim, for example, that the person has insulted not only you, but every person who is tall, blond, skinny, wears glasses, or believes in free speech. This would encourage others to become involved in the issue and take sides, and would force the person who made the attack to sort out exactly what it was that he or she disliked about you, but which did not pertain to others.

Sometimes people purposely insult or denigrate others as a way of trying to make them feel guilty, so that they can more easily manipulate them. This tends to be more effective when used with ordered thinkers, who generally worry about making and correcting mistakes. However, it seldom works with chaotic thinkers. They might feel guilty in the moment, but once the moment passes, so does the guilt. For most chaotic thinkers, there is no such thing as atonement, because one can never really go back and change the past. This is why they often tell people who have wronged them, "Don't apologize; just don't do it again."

# 8

## Limitations of Chaotic Cognition

We have so far focused mainly on the advantages and benefits of chaotic thinking. In this chapter, we try to put chaotic thinking into perspective, by calling attention to some of its limitations and possible drawbacks. Many of these limitations arise out of its assets, which, like any virtue, can become a liability when taken to extremes.

In doing so, we also pause to consider some of the advantages of ordered thinking. Whereas chaotic thinking is usually more helpful in situations that are unpredictable or that require rapid responding, ordered thinking is usually more appropriate in situations that have become stabilized or that need to be managed in a systematic fashion. We emphasize again that both styles have their advantages and disadvantages. Which style is more effective usually depends on the particular situation.

By and large, the weaknesses of chaotic thinking are mirrored by the strengths of ordered thinking, and vice versa. For instance, the impulsiveness of chaotic thinking can be contrasted with the calculated, controlled qualities of ordered thinking. The tendency to increase complexity in chaotic thinking can be contrasted with the tendency to simplify in ordered thinking. In this regard, ordered and chaotic thinking often balance one another, in much the same way that ordered and chaotic forces in nature often hold one another in check.

### EXCESSIVE IMPULSIVENESS

Because of their natural, impulsive tendencies, chaotic thinkers sometimes lose sight of the consequences of their thoughts and actions. Their ideas might continue to flow beyond the constraints that normally tie them to the immediate situation. If left unchecked, these impulses might become so great that they simply take over, resulting in an eventual loss of control.

At such times, chaotic thinkers may not know when to stop. Once they begin to act on their impulses, they might end up going so fast that they fail to see the dangers that lie ahead. They might become so caught up in the moment that they might do whatever they feel like doing, regardless of the consequences. Any desire might become a desperate need. Any conflict might become a fight to the death.

This impulsiveness creates a delicate balance within chaotic thinking. It normally works to one's advantage when one is taking information in from the environment and reacting to it spontaneously and naturally; then chaotic thinking is in harmony with what is happening. But there can come a point where the impulses overwhelm a chaotic thinker and become more important than being in harmony with the moment.

This seems to go against the notion that chaotic thinkers are generally more in touch with what is going on around them and what the moment requires, as discussed in previous chapters. It is true that this is normally one of the advantages of chaotic thinking. But when chaotic thinkers get caught up in their impulses, they sometimes begin to ignore this feedback altogether and lose sight of multiple realities. Their impulses might then lead them astray, and chaotic thinking might become irrational.

This runaway impulsiveness can sometimes lead to psychological problems or even criminality. For instance, if chaotic thinkers had a sudden impulse to speed through the center of town, they might go ahead and do so, unaware of or unconcerned about the consequences. This can become almost pathological at times, as when one neglects work, food, or relationships in order to focus entirely on one's impulses.

These problems, however, are generally avoided in ordered thinking. Most ordered thinkers typically weigh the consequences of their actions and consider how those actions will affect their future. They are therefore usually better able to hold their impulses in check. Indeed, one of the criticisms of ordered thinking is that it is not impulsive enough. Most ordered thinkers try to avoid any possibility of being out of control, and any sudden impulses they might feel are normally held in check by their commitment to achieving their goals. Yet, if they lose sight of these goals and begin to believe too strongly in their past accomplishments, then they, too, can sometimes behave impulsively and irrationally.

At their best, chaotic thinkers fit into the moment and the total environmental context perfectly, and things flow smoothly around them. When their impulses are out of control, however, they can be like a whirling dervish or a tornado. Instead of increasing harmony, they tend to create random chaos and disharmony.

At such times, they might not realize the effects their impulsiveness is having on others. For example, a man might wake up one day and suddenly decide that he no longer wants to be married, leave without warning, and call his wife from somewhere thousands of miles away, explaining, "It just didn't work out." Many chaotic thinkers do not have sufficient reflective power on the past or the future to see what kind of damage this might cause.

Another example of excessive impulsiveness in chaotic thinking is when one accepts a small reward in the present instead of waiting for a larger reward in the future. Again, this can happen when chaotic thinkers act on their impulses without considering future consequences and implications. Normally, chaotic thinkers are aware of how things are proportioned in the moment, but they often do not consider the trade-off between long-term and short-term gains.

Ordered thinkers, too, sometimes sabotage long-term rewards, but usually for different reasons. As mentioned in previous chapters, they tend to get into confrontations over relatively minor issues and turn them into must-win battles, which can jeopardize jobs, marriages, or long-range plans. Also, when ordered thinkers act impulsively, it is usually because they are suddenly presented with a convenient opportunity to execute their plans. As we have seen, this makes them more suspectible to perceptual traps. Impulsiveness in chaotic thinking usually stems from a need for stimulation, rather than for achievement or easy profit.

There are other contrasts in the way ordered and chaotic thinkers typically deal with their needs and impulses. Chaotic thinkers often deny themselves the things they desire, until they become irresistable, whereupon those desires are converted to impulses, which might then be acted upon spontaneously and without forethought. When ordered thinkers desire things, those desires are often converted to plans. As a result, their desires are usually expressed in the more controlled manner of allowing their plans to unfold.

Sometimes their impulsiveness can make chaotic thinkers seem as if they were doing things for no good reason, even when there might have been a clear purpose behind their actions. For example, they might begin jumping in a field and waving their hands in the air, which might lead others to think that they were crazy, when they were simply trying to catch lightening bugs, having suddenly become fascinated with them.

Excessive impulsiveness has several other limitations. Chaotic thinkers might continue to place themselves back into aversive situations, such as a bad job or relationship, even after having realized just how aversive those situations are. This tendency results from their impulsiveness combined with a need to intensify the moment. Because a situation that was aversive yesterday might not be so today, they become intrigued with finding out.

Chaotic thinkers might also agree to make long-term commitments impulsively, such as suddenly deciding to marry someone, whereas ordered thinkers are usually much more careful about making such commitments. They are more likely to think through the practical problems that are associated with the commitment, whereas chaotic thinkers might neglect to even consider these problems. Chaotic thinkers might therefore find themselves trapped by a commitment that they had made on impulse. Even if this happens, however, they would usually find ways to retain their freedom.

We have mentioned that chaotic thinkers often act according to the notion that it is better to go nowhere fast. This helps to sharpen one's intuitions and avoids having to always doubt or second-guess oneself. The problem with going nowhere fast, however, is that you might sometimes end up where you do not want to be. By going too fast at times, chaotic thinkers risk becoming out of control and detached from the exigencies of the moment.

## INCONSISTENCY OVER TIME

By its very nature, chaotic thinking tends to be poorly structured and spontaneous, whereas ordered thinking tends to be highly structured and governed by long-term plans and principles. As discussed in chapter 4, specific thoughts and actions are seldom repeated in chaotic thinking, even in the same situation. Ordered thinkers usually set up strong habits and patterns that they repeat over and over. But for most chaotic thinkers, every moment is unique. Chaotic thinking can therefore appear strikingly inconsistent over time.

As discussed previously, most chaotic thinkers strive to intensify the moment. Their ideas can seem refreshing and insightful during that moment, but in retrospect may seem less impressive or even contradictory. Chaotic thinking might thus appear superficial or capricious at times. For example, chaotic thinkers might say or do what seems right at the moment, irrespective of what they said or did previously. This tends to confuse or frustrate those who are looking for consistency. They are likely to mention, "That isn't what you said yesterday," or "That isn't what you were doing last week," whereupon chaotic thinkers might respond, "But it is the right thing for right now."

From their own perspective, most chaotic thinkers would likely see themselves as entirely consistent at any moment, given the total context of the situation. But when they are evaluated over time, particularly by ordered thinkers, they can appear inconsistent and unreliable. Ordered thinkers are usually more reliable and consistent in the long run, but they can fail to respond to the needs of the moment. In a sense, chaotic thinkers are often out of place in the past or future, whereas ordered thinkers are often out of place within the present.

Because of their focus on the present, many chaotic thinkers underutilize information about repetitive patterns in another person's behavior. They may not recognize when a person was doing the same thing time and time again, especially if they were attending to the person's present needs. They are therefore more susceptible to being taken advantage of by those who might appear hurt or helpless, and who continue to repeat the same stories or excuses. For example, a person might convince a chaotic thinker that he or she was lonely and needed someone to talk to, then make the very same complaint day after day.

Whenever they lack stimulation, chaotic thinkers tend to fall into temporary, regular patterns and habits, which can in fact seem quite predictable in the short run. This reflects their inherent passivity. These patterns quickly disappear, however, if the situation suddenly changes or a crisis develops. Ordered thinkers may be less predictable in the short run, because they often behave according to plans that may be known only to themselves. But if the situation changes, they may continue with those plans and can thus appear rigid and unyielding over time.

The apparent inconsistency of chaotic thinking is also related to the lack of pride. Despite the problems it often creates, pride helps promote a concern for consistent, quality work. Because of pride, ordered thinkers usually want to make things last—whether this pertains to their possessions, their businesses, or their relationships—whereas most chaotic thinkers generally care little about permanence. Their ideas and creations, therefore, often lack enduring qualities.

Another reason chaotic thinking might seem inconsistent at times is that it emphasizes multiple realities. From a chaotic perspective, any situation can be viewed in a multiplicity of ways, and hence there are always many possible responses from which to choose. When chaotic thinkers respond in different ways to the same situation over time, they are exploring these multiple, alternative realities.

Many of these inconsistencies disappear, however, once one sees the underlying theme or purpose in a chaotic thinker's behavior. For example, a chaotic thinker might say to someone, "You really need to try to get more freedom in your life," then later tell that person, "Actually, you need to be less free." The person might be bothered by this contradiction, until the chaotic thinker explains that what was meant was that the person should be more free in exploring career options, but less free in expressing anger. Ordered thinkers are often good at pointing out these apparent inconsistencies to chaotic thinkers, which can then inspire them to make finer and clearer distinctions.

It might sometimes appear that chaotic thinkers are rationalizing their inconsistencies when someone tries to pin them down as to exactly what they mean. They might then respond by raising other issues and considerations, which merely seem to complicate matters. But most chaotic thinkers would not consider this as a form of rationalization. Instead, they would see it as an attempt to find deeper, more harmonious explanations for the apparent inconsistencies. If pressed, they may simply say, "I know this seems inconsistent, but that's the way things are."

Rationalization in ordered thinking, in contrast, often reflects an unwillingness to accept inconsistency. If one's plans fail, this may be attributed to a specific reason, such as an unexpected event or the failure of someone else to do his or her part. In their desire to be consistent, ordered thinkers often adopt relatively simple and stable themes and then generate complex arguments or rationalizations from them. Chaotic thinkers usually try to make simple points that stem from complex themes, which often change over time.

Most ordered thinkers stay in touch with their previous thoughts and ideas, which allows them to refine, correct, and integrate those ideas over time. This contributes to their concern with achieving perfection, as discussed in chapter 6. Most chaotic thinkers seldom worry about perfection or consistency but are usually more concerned with exploring new possibilities or restoring harmony to the moment. In fact, they might easily forget an idea they just had, once the moment changes and there are new things to think about.

In essence, chaotic thinking often walks the fine line between brilliance and incoherence, profundity and contradiction. Chaotic thinkers can seem astonishingly insightful one moment and totally confusing the next. They can have wonderful ideas today and then drift off into apparent irrelevancies tomorrow. Ordered thinking is usually more consistent, but it also tends to be less stimulating and enlightening.

## LACK OF LONG-TERM GOALS

Although often indispensible when dealing with a sudden crisis, chaotic thinking generally lacks long-term visions and goals. Because most chaotic thinkers do not structure their lives around specific goals and accomplishments, they tend to be seen as lacking ambition or purpose. Unlike most ordered thinkers, they usually seem to have no specific destiny other than to deal with the exigencies of the moment. To ask most chaotic thinkers what they will be doing 5 years from now would be pointless, because from their standpoint there are far too many options and alternative possibilities to predict what might happen in the distant future.

This lack of commitment to future goals makes chaotic thinking vulnerable to distraction. For instance, even though he or she might have a paper to write by a certain deadline, a chaotic thinker might become so fascinated watching a squirrel climb a tree that he or she could spend the rest of the day doing nothing else. It is not deliberately trying to put the paper off, but rather that he or she had simply become so involved in that moment that the goal of writing the paper no longer mattered. Almost anything that comes into a chaotic thinker's path and begins to fascinate them can occupy their attention in this way and consume it.

In a society where having long-term plans and goals is rewarded, chaotic thinkers often become discouraged, because they begin to perceive themselves as failures. They might look back on their lives and suddenly feel that they have accomplished very little and have nothing to look forward to. Ordered thinkers, on the other hand, can usually take some pride in the success of their plans and look forward to anticipated, future rewards.

A potential danger in lacking long-term goals is that one is then more susceptible to having others define those goals for one. For instance, chaotic thinkers might end up marrying someone whom they were not in love with, because they were constantly being told by others that marriage is the right thing to do. They might enter a career they did not really like, because a counselor convinced them that they would probably be good at it. Because they usually do not see themselves as having any particular direction, they often let others provide that direction. A by-product of this is that they may then feel no loyalty to the marriage or to the career; having drifted into them, they may be just as likely to drift out of them.

This is less of a risk with ordered thinkers, who usually tie their commitments to their long-term goals. However, they can sometimes become blinded by those goals. For example, having gotten into a bad marriage, one might feel a responsibility to stay in it, even if one were totally incompatible with one's spouse. Having gotten into a bad job, one might feel obligated to stick with it, even if it turned out to be something he or she could not stand.

Committing oneself too strongly to future goals, and ignoring the needs of the moment, can undermine the expected benefits of those goals. For example, a father might forget his child's birthday party because he had a deadline to meet in several weeks, which would increase his chances of getting a promotion. Such incidents might eventually begin to jeopardize his long-term plans for the family. On the other hand, chaotic thinkers can become so involved in family events that they completely forget about deadlines and long-term responsibilities at work, which can then create other kinds of problems.

Most ordered thinkers generally resist being defined or characterized by others, whereas chaotic thinkers are often searching for definition and might eagerly latch onto the suggestions that others make. They thus run the risk of allowing others to classify them with little or no justification, as when someone says that they are lazy or oversensitive. These definitions and characterizations, however, may only last within the moment, and chaotic thinkers might then accept entirely different ones later on.

As we have mentioned, chaotic methods are usually least effective when employed in connection with a specific plan, where they then lose much of their spontaneity. They are usually more effective when used to stimulate change, encourage rationality, and promote new understandings. Although chaotic thinking can help to unstructure long-term plans and make them more flexible, it is usually of limited value in formulating such plans or working towards future, external goals.

When responding to the needs of the moment, chaotic thinkers may appear to have certain long-range plans and goals in mind, but this is generally not the case. Their intention is usually to try to keep the situation open, so that effective changes and insights can occur. For instance, a chaotic thinker who has been harassed at work for missing deadlines might put up a sign that says, "Please be patient. I have a learning disability." This would have the immediate goal of getting people to stop complaining, but its deeper purpose would be to keep things open and unstructured.

In retrospect, it sometimes seems as if chaotic thinkers had planned a series of specific maneuvers and had anticipated each of their effects. Actually, their choices for what methods to use next vary from moment to moment, depending on what happens, and are thus generally unplanned. Most of their actions are spontaneous and adaptive, and encourage new and unexpected developments. Their style, in fact, resembles the "problem finding" approach of many artists, whose improvised creations might seem to have resulted from a specific design or plan, but which actually emerged from nondirected, open explorations (e.g., Getzels & Csikszent-mihalyi, 1976).

There is a sense, however, in which chaotic thinkers can be said to have long-term goals. Many of them set very broad goals for self-improvement, which they then work towards as part of their everyday activities. This reflects their concern with promoting personal growth, which was discussed in chapter 6. For most chaotic thinkers, these personal goals usually matter much more than professional goals.

## LACK OF ACHIEVEMENT

Chaotic thinkers are typically not great achievers. They usually have few long-term aspirations and take little pride in their accomplishments. They might think about things that they would like to achieve, but then never focus on actually achieving them. The one major exception is in crisis situations, where chaotic thinkers can often rise to positions of leadership and can often accomplish a great deal for as long as the emergency lasts.

Ordered thinkers, in contrast, tend to be very good achievers. Their accomplishments are often the direct result of their highly organized and carefully thought-out plans. They often take great pride in even the smallest achievements and successes. On the other hand, if chaotic thinkers were to discover a way of changing lead into gold, they would probably conclude that anyone could have done it.

Most chaotic thinkers tend to view all of their accomplishments as momentary and insignificant. This can cause them to have a low sense of self-worth. Because they usually lack the pride and determination of ordered thinkers, they often prefer to abandon a project rather than accept responsibility for having succeeded at it. Because wonderful and fascinating things are happening all the time, for most chaotic thinkers the whole notion of wanting to achieve something seems rather pointless.

In fact, many chaotic thinkers have trouble accepting the idea that they could ever really succeed at anything. For example, they might drop out of school just before graduating or give up on an assignment just before completing it. They might avoid promotions at their jobs, or long-term engagements. They tend to worry that if they achieve something, additional expectations might be imposed on them. Ordered thinkers usually look forward to these achievements as signs that they are accomplishing things. They tend to become more inspired as they near their goals.

A related limitation is that chaotic thinkers tend to trivialize their mistakes. They usually do not see a mistake with the same sort of exquisite pain that many ordered thinkers do. In ordered thinking, a mistake can almost become a burning coal, whereas in chaotic thinking it is usually no big deal. Consequently, chaotic thinkers often repeat the same mistakes. They may also violate the same rules again and again, regarding them as nonessential guidelines. Although this often contributes to their creativity, it can also cause problems over time.

To improve their sense of accomplishment and self-worth, chaotic thinkers could try to regard even minor activities and achievements as worthwhile. For example, if they enjoyed cycling or skateboarding, they could tell themselves that they have just given a truly excellent performance, instead of letting someone else define the activity as a waste of time. This could help them begin to take steps towards achieving larger goals.

Although ordered thinkers often fail to take into account life's complexities and uncertainties, their tendency to simplify things and ignore distractions helps them achieve their goals. Chaotic thinkers often fail to accomplish things because they become too involved in distractions. Ordered thinkers might notice an interesting distraction and decide to come back to it later, after their current plans were completed. For many chaotic thinkers, the intensity of the moment can take over, and they might follow the distraction in spite of whatever else they had intended to do.

Most of the achievements of chaotic thinkers fall into the category of "internal" achievements, in that they tend to work towards discovering new ideas and expanding their insights. Whereas most ordered thinkers might regard getting a good job as an important accomplishment, most chaotic thinkers would be more likely to regard having read a great book as an important accomplishment. Their sense of achievement is thus directed inwards, towards improving themselves.

Because chaotic thinkers often do not value external accomplishments and goals, they tend to minimize the plans and projects of others. For example, they might inadvertantly denigrate a person's plans by not being very impressed. In reacting this way, they are usually applying the chaotic principle that there are multiple realities and possibilities, and thus no single idea or accomplishment is particularly special. But this can hurt a person's pride, especially if the person had put a lot of time and effort into developing the ideas.

Ordered thinkers sometimes find the childlike qualities of chaotic thinkers disturbing, because these qualities do not show proper respect for their sense of accomplishment. Almost everything a chaotic thinker does appears to be fun, and this violates the ordered thinker's work ethic. For this reason, chaotic thinkers are often told by ordered thinkers to "grow up." In such cases, however, this usually means, "Meet my expectations."

In chapter 1, we mentioned that although chaotic insights can have a profound impact upon the moment, they tend not to be remembered unless recorded by others.

One reason is that most chaotic thinkers are so focused on the moment that they do not think that what they do has any real importance beyond that moment. Another reason is that they generally lack the pride and ambition of ordered thinkers, who are more inclined to want to leave a permanent record of their achievements.

## LACK OF MOTIVATION

Given their passive nature, chaotic thinkers often feel no sense of urgency and may thus be seen as lacking motivation. Initially, they often display a kind of inertia, a reluctance to get moving and to fall in with the pace of others. But once they get started, they can work at high levels of intensity, especially when they become very much attracted to something. These periods of intense activity, however, are nearly always in response to an external event and are rarely initiated by chaotic thinkers themselves.

For most chaotic thinkers, the motivating force must be supplied externally, whereupon they can exhibit tremendous energy and involvement, as when responding to a crisis or sudden provocation. But in the absence of these motivating factors, most chaotic thinkers tend to lead a relatively idle life. For example, if one's marriage was comfortable but not inspiring, and there were no strong reasons to leave, he or she would probably just stay in the marriage. If a job was going nowhere, but was relatively comfortable and created no real aggravation, he or she would probably stay with it.

Without some outside source of stimulation to motivate them, most chaotic thinkers simply endure. From their vantage point, as long as there is passion and interest in what they are doing, they see no need to initiate major changes. In contrast, because ordered thinkers tend to worry about their past mistakes or about how they might improve their careers, they are usually motivated to take charge and initiate changes.

Ordered thinkers often push chaotic thinkers to get motivated and accomplish things, perhaps by insisting that they need to contribute more to society. Because most chaotic thinkers are less inclined to want to achieve things, they are sometimes regarded as "slackers". However, it is not so much that they are inherently lazy, but that their activities often appear passive or inconsequential, as in the case of the street musician or the person who spends each day roller skating.

Their awareness of a multitude of possible options also reduces their motivation, for they see little reason to act on any of these options unless a crisis were at hand. Another reason chaotic thinkers are usually not motivated to make things happen is that they often see randomness and uncertainty as having positive effects. Just as random events sometimes make things worse, they can also make things better. From their perspective, it is usually better to have an open, uncertain future than a closed, predictable future.

Whereas ordered thinkers might dither in crises, chaotic thinkers tend to dither in everyday life. They might spend the entire day pondering the most basic of decisions. In fact, they often make their decisions impulsively to avoid this endless indecisiveness. As one might say, it is better to go nowhere fast than to be stuck in neutral. This is also why chaotic thinkers are often drawn to crisis situations, which intensify the moment and can force them to take decisive action.

Chaotic thinkers sometimes irritate others by their passivity, as when they refuse to confront a problem. Whereas ordered thinkers often feel that one must always be in command of one's fate, most chaotic thinkers simply prefer to let a situation unfold and then adapt to it, believing that if you take deliberate action to change a situation, things might get worse instead of better.

Ordered thinkers typically drive themselves, and this is clearly one of the strengths of ordered thinking. It takes almost nothing to motivate them; most are self-starters with strong goals and ambitions. As we have seen, however, chaotic thinkers can drain away this energy and slow ordered thinking down, especially when ordered thinkers try to impose their plans to an unrealistic extent. By the same token, chaotic thinkers tend to build up energy around ordered thinkers, because the ordered thinkers keep pushing them and they keep reacting.

If chaotic thinkers become terribly bored, however, the boredom can provide a powerful stimulus for them to initiate significant changes. Most chaotic thinkers like novelty, and in situations where there is always a certain amount of it, they can remain contented for years, even if those situations do not provide high levels of stimulation. But if a job or task becomes endlessly repetitive, or if a marriage becomes unbearably boring, they will eventually want to leave. For many ordered thinkers, a repetitive job or boring marriage would probably be a very acceptable arrangement, as long as it was secure and predictable.

At some point, however, even highly ordered thinkers might get the urge to leave a secure situation, especially after realizing that their predictable routines have left them with an empty and meaningless life. They might then feel that they have to look elsewhere to find that meaningfulness. But they usually cannot sustain these explorations indefinitely and may soon return to the predictability of their structured world.

Chaotic thinkers may stay in one place for years without ever feeling the need to escape. In a sense, this actually frees them to be more chaotic, in that it keeps them from becoming overwhelmed by the many other things that are going on in their daily lives. It is also why they often prefer to stay in ruts, as long as some stimulation remains. These everyday routines can help to keep the chaos from flowing totally out of control. But even when they go about these routines, most chaotic thinkers are discovering new and meaningful things all the time.

One distinctive motivating force that exists in chaotic thinking is the need to set people free. Having a sense of freedom is important for most chaotic thinkers, and if they sense that others are being denied that freedom, they often are compelled to act. They might then openly defy an authority figure or rebel against the establishment, rather than passively accepting the situation.

## EXCESSIVE FATALISM

Sooner or later, most chaotic thinkers adopt a fatalistic outlook on life. Whereas ordered thinkers often see themselves as being in charge of their lives, chaotic thinkers see themselves as always reacting to things that they have no control over. They therefore see little point in trying to influence fate, believing that whatever happens, happens. As a result of this fatalism, chaotic thinkers usually attribute their accomplishments to luck rather than to skill or effort.

By convincing themselves that they can control their fate, most ordered thinkers acquire strong, positive attitudes and become confident in the power and effectiveness of their plans. Most chaotic thinkers, however, see a world filled with multiple realities, new uncertainties, and unexpected complexities, which defy efforts to control it. They thus tend to see themselves as unimportant players in the general scheme of things.

This fatalism is almost paradoxical, in that chaotic thinkers often fight to the bitter end even if there is no hope of winning. The thought of winning or losing usually makes no difference. Ordered thinkers might be inclined to give up in a contest if they appeared to be losing; chaotic thinkers could become so totally involved in the moment that they might continue fighting regardless of the prospects for victory. Instead of sapping their energy, their fatalism often drives them to struggle harder, for it matters not that they may be defeated. Thus, although it can limit their ambition and motivation, fatalism often helps chaotic thinkers to overcome adversity.

Another consequence of their fatalism is that it often frees chaotic thinkers from having to worry about the future. When confined or stuck in an unpleasant situation, they would simply try to endure. When the moment becomes intensified, they might reach a point where they simply say, "Forget control," and just let fate dictate what will happen next. Also, their fatalism frees them from second-guessing themselves. For instance, if they lost their jobs after doing something chaotic, they would probably assume that this would have happened in any event.

The structured idealism of ordered thinking can help one to persevere as long as the plans are working. But when those plans start to fail, one can experience a rupture between the past and the future and may even come to believe that one no longer has a future. At this point, one might be at greater risk for becoming depressed or even suicidal, especially if one is unable to resolve the inconsistencies between what one expected and what actually happened. This is less of a risk for most chaotic thinkers, who would adopt a fatalistic outlook and have relatively few expectations.

Although the fatalism of chaotic thinking avoids many of the anxieties associated with an uncertain future, it can sometimes lead to recklessness, especially when combined with excessive impulsiveness. Chaotic thinkers might drive unnecessarily fast, use dangerous tools without taking proper precautions, or refuse to go to the doctor when they are sick. Either they will live or they will die. This combination of impulsiveness and fatalism eventually causes them to lose control of the moment, and often results in accidents. When ordered thinkers have accidents, it is usually for a different reason. Although they tend to stay in control, they are usually less aware of sudden, unexpected dangers, especially if they are overly preoccupied with their plans.

Because of their fatalism, chaotic thinkers sometimes just give up and have fun in situations in which it might still have been possible to take charge and salvage things. Hence, they might end up sabotaging their prospects for success. For instance, when taking a difficult exam, they might decide to come up with creative, amusing answers, although it might still have been possible to pass the exam. Sometimes taking an excessively frivolous approach to a task can be just as self-defeating as taking the task too seriously.

The chaotic thinker's fatalism is not the same as pessimism. Things could also get better; it is just that they usually feel they have little control over what happens. Ordered thinkers might save for a rainy day, but because of their idealism think that the rainy day will never come. Chaotic thinkers might spend for a sunny day, assuming that good things are just as likely to happen as bad things.

Although ordered thinkers are rather idealistic about most things in their lives, especially their plans and aspirations, they tend to be somewhat fatalistic about human nature. On the other hand, although chaotic thinkers tend to be fatalistic about most things, they are rather idealistic about human nature. They may not like an organization or a country but will often believe in its people. Ordered thinkers might believe wholeheartedly in an organization or country but not like most of the people in it.

## EXCESSIVE TRUST

Chaotic thinkers tend to be very genuine, open, and revealing, and prefer to see other people the same way. They often project trust and loyalty onto others and usually do not presume deception or malicious intent. Consequently, they are often too willing to trust people and may not take proper precautions against being exploited or victimized.

Ordered thinkers, by and large, tend to be less trusting. They are more inclined to see others as having ulterior motives and to assume that people are trying to manipulate them. As a result, they often take excessive precautions to shield themselves, which, as discussed in chapter 6, can sometimes lead to problems in interpersonal relations and communication.

In a sense, ordered thinking is like Teflon, whereas chaotic thinking is more like Velcro. Chaotic thinkers tend to accept people very easily and quickly assimilate their ideas, but then may find it hard to avoid them. Ordered thinkers are usually more effective at keeping people away, or rejecting their ideas, but then few people ever cling to them.

Because of their trusting nature, chaotic thinkers often bring out genuine qualities in people. By being genuinely warm to others, they usually elicit a warm response. When people meet a highly ordered thinker, they often sense that the person does not trust them, and this tends to evoke mutual suspicion. By implicitly trusting others, chaotic thinkers usually convey mutual trust. They seldom assume that people are simply out to take advantage of them.

Like any virtue, however, excessive trust can be a weakness. It is good to have basic faith in human beings, but there are times when one should be suspicious and on guard. By the same token, having a little mistrust of people may be a good thing, but being unable to trust anyone is not.

## OVERSENSITIVITY

Because chaotic thinkers are usually sensitive to the needs and feelings of others, they tend to feel responsible for things that are not really their fault. In their relationships, for instance, they might feel bad when they cannot love someone, even though there is no reason why they should. They might take the blame when someone's plans do not work out, even if they were not the cause of the failure. Whereas ordered thinkers may be tempted to blame others when things go wrong, chaotic thinkers are often the willing recipients of that blame.

As a result of being highly sensitive, most chaotic thinkers do not take criticism very well. They often take it personally, whereas an ordered thinker's pride usually allows them to deflect or ignore criticism. On the other hand, unlike many ordered thinkers, chaotic thinkers tend not to take insults personally. They usually try to interpret insults from the standpoint of multiple realities, and explore what the person is really trying to say. Ordered thinkers might respond to criticism indignantly, assuming that the person did not understand their work or ideas. However, an insult usually has a much greater impact on them, for it challenges their pride and can sometimes lead to intense anger and confrontation.

When criticized, chaotic thinkers often hear not just the criticism, but all of its ramifications. This is especially true when the criticism is exaggerated or overstated. Ordered thinkers often show the opposite tendency, so it is sometimes necessary to overstate matters in order to call attention to some issue or problem with their plans. When chaotic thinkers deliver criticism to ordered thinkers, they tend to understate it, and the message is usually ignored. Their sensitivity usually causes them to frame the message too softly, and it has little impact. When direct, intense criticism is given to chaotic thinkers, however, the effect can be devastating.

Although criticism might depress a chaotic thinker temporarily, the depression usually does not last. Some new distraction always comes along, and the criticism is soon forgotten. Ordered thinkers, however, might remember an insult for many years. Because of their sensitivity, chaotic thinkers might seem more emotionally affected at first, but their moods usually pass. Ordered thinkers can be more susceptible to long-term moods involving anger or depression, which can lead to problems such as physical violence or even suicide.

When pushed too far, ordered thinkers might explode, expressing rage and even violent behavior, whereas chaotic thinkers tend to implode, becoming so dissociated from the situation that they might not react at all. In such cases, ordered thinkers might lose their grasp on their plans and undermine their long-term goals, whereas chaotic thinkers might lose their grasp on the moment and undermine their sensitivity.

In general, ordered thinking encourages pruning, whereas chaotic thinking encourages growth. Each can lead to problems when taken to extremes. When you prune too much, you get a desert. When you do not prune enough, you get a jungle. Ordered thinkers often cut and trim their ideas until they are devoid of meaning, whereas chaotic thinkers often allow their ideas to grow unchecked, until they become overwhelmingly complex and meaningful. One is limited more from lacking sensitivity; the other, from being overly sensitive.

## BECOMING LOST IN THE MOMENT

As we have mentioned, chaotic thinkers often become completely absorbed in momentary, distracting thoughts or ideas. This has the advantage that it promotes personal involvement, but it also has the disadvantage that it can inhibit all other activities. For example, they might become so intrigued by something they have just seen that they have trouble thinking about anything else. Ordered thinkers, with their commitment to long-term plans and goals, are less likely to become totally absorbed in any given moment. Thus, whereas ordered thinkers often get lost in time and lose track of the moment, chaotic thinkers often get lost in the moment and lose track of time.

For instance, if a chaotic thinker were walking to the store and happened to see a friendly dog, he or she might spend hours petting and playing with the dog, becoming so absorbed that all other responsibilities and concerns would be suspended. Ordered thinkers would probably not even notice the dog, and would focus on getting to the store, finding the things they needed, and returning home as planned. This tendency for chaotic thinkers to become lost in the moment whenever an interesting or distracting event occurs can make them seem irresponsible.

Sometimes chaotic thinkers make temporary, creative repairs that work in the moment, but then forget to make more permanent repairs later on, having become distracted and absorbed in other things. For example, they might repair a broken fan belt by using a leather belt they had been wearing, which would solve the problem temporarily, but then neglect to replace it with a new one, which would eventually cause the car to break down again.

Even when they are totally involved in the moment, many chaotic thinkers are curiously indifferent to what might happen next. Ordered thinkers, in contrast, are seldom totally involved in the moment but are often passionately concerned about how things will turn out. For example, if attacked, chaotic thinkers would probably focus totally on the fight, regardless of their chances for winning. Ordered thinkers would probably care deeply about winning the fight, but they might let their concentration slip in the excitement and chaos of the moment.

This relates back to the idea of intensifying the moment, which most chaotic thinkers do instinctively. Attacks are normally intense enough, but they often intensify them further. They will sometimes charge an enemy who is charging them, like a Berzerker. Although this can be self-destructive, it can also effectively disrupt many attacks.

There is an important distinction between the way most chaotic thinkers become absorbed in things and the goal-oriented obsessions of many ordered thinkers. Chaotic thinkers, for example, often continue to play a game long after the outcome has been decided. They might become so totally absorbed in the enjoyment of the game that they want to keep on playing, even when there seems to be little point in doing so. Ordered thinkers often become obsessed with playing a game, but only for the purpose of winning. Once the secret of how to win is discovered, the obsession may disappear.

Ordered thinkers can sometimes provide comfort to chaotic thinkers who have become lost in the moment and feel that their world is slipping away. The narrow focus and idealism of most ordered thinkers can be reassuring at such times. Their self-assurance can convey confidence, even when that confidence is unwarranted. Ordered thinkers are thus often reassuring but may not be very sensitive, whereas chaotic thinkers are often sensitive but may not be very reassuring.

Even though they risk becoming lost in the moment, most chaotic thinkers enjoy their passionate involvement in life. They tend to see ordered thinkers as watching life from the sidelines, letting it go by, because they are unwilling to become involved in the moment. Most ordered thinkers, on the other hand, see chaotic thinkers as squandering their lives because they are unwilling to plan for the future.

## FAILING TO FIT INTO SOCIETY

Those who rely on chaotic thinking often have trouble fitting into the established roles of modern society. As a rule, most chaotic thinkers prefer societies in which people can simply be themselves and can relate to one another in open and sincere ways. They therefore do not easily fit into societies that emphasize structured lifestyles, social status, or professional success.

In ordered societies, people are usually regarded according to their positions in hierarchical categories. If one is seen as being in a superior position, one is often idolized. If one is seen as being in an inferior position, one is often dehumanized. Chaotic thinkers normally have little tolerance for the impersonal aspects of social roles and categories and tend not to respect them. This can result in their being denied the normal rewards that modern society provides.

Most ordered thinkers are skilled at adapting themselves to the particular roles they are supposed in play, which allows them to advance within society. They may even define themselves in terms of these roles. Chaotic thinkers may enter into many different roles when exploring alternative realities, but they rarely lose their sense of who they are, because they tend not to take any of these roles very seriously.

Ordered thinkers usually like to involve others in their roles, to validate them in the eyes of society. They prefer to surround themselves with people who can appreciate their accomplishments and who can help them achieve further success. Most chaotic thinkers are content to involve themselves and have less need for social validation. As a result, they often get left behind in an ordered society.

Ordered thinkers who have strong social ambitions might seem chaotic at times. They might know a great many people and move rapidly from conversation to conversation, but these conversations are seldom meaningful or insightful. Rather, they usually function as strategies in plans to advance socially. Most chaotic thinkers try to have meaningful conversations with people, even when this violates the roles they are supposed to play.

For example, they usually tell people how they feel about something right away. In doing so, however, they often fail to take into account how others might react. Their honesty and candidness can sometimes be shocking, especially when these fall outside the normal boundaries of expected behavior. Ordered thinkers are usually more guarded and selective in what they reveal and thus are less likely to unnerve others or jeopardize their roles.

And yet, if you asked most ordered thinkers how they personally felt about something, they might not be able to tell you. This is because they often do not trust their intuitions. Instead, they typically define their feelings in terms of what they believe they should be feeling in that situation. For instance, they might label a feeling as "right" or "wrong," in terms of the roles they were supposed to play, instead of accepting and exploring that feeling. For the same reason, ordered thinkers often know what they want, and can make plans for getting what they want, but they often cannot explain why they want what they want.

Chaotic thinkers can usually tell you exactly what it is they want or like, because they are usually more in touch with their feelings. However, they might become so involved in what they were feeling that they would neglect to make specific plans to follow up on those feelings. For example, they might fail to make long-term commitments, establish permanent relationships, or pursue a career. They thus tend to fall within the cracks of society.

As we stated at the beginning of the chapter, the limitations of chaotic thinking often stem from its assets. The same qualities that enable chaotic thinkers to respond to crises and generate creative, improvised solutions to problems can become liabilities at other times. This needs to be considered when seeking to incorporate chaotic qualities into one's own thinking style, as is discussed in chapter 9. Impulsiveness can be liberating, but it can also be self-destructive. Sensitivity to multiple possibilities can be enlightening, but it can also be distracting. Avoiding commitments to long-range plans can be adaptive, but it can also be short-sighted.

# 9

## Stylistic Convergence

Although we have emphasized many of the advantages of chaotic thinking through-out this book, we reiterate that chaotic thinking is not necessarily superior or preferable to ordered thinking. Each has its advantages and disadvantages, and each can assist the other. We next consider some ways for bringing these two styles of thinking closer together and explore some of the benefits and possible risks of this convergence.

A major reason for wanting to bring these two styles closer together is that neither extreme ordered nor extreme chaotic thinking are very desirable. In a healthy society, ordered and chaotic thinking are usually tempered by one another. Chaotic thinkers often help keep the plans of ordered thinkers from structuring and regulating things to an excessive degree, whereas ordered thinkers often help keep the creative impulses of chaotic thinkers from diverging in too many directions.

### APPRECIATING THE OPPOSITE STYLE

By learning more about the opposite style, ordered and chaotic thinkers stand to benefit in a number of ways. First, they could better appreciate their fundamental differences. Ordered thinkers are often intolerant of chaotic thinkers, regarding them as frivolous and undisciplined. Similarly, chaotic thinkers often regard ordered thinkers as excessively idealistic and tend to make fun of the seriousness with which they pursue their plans. From either perspective, the first step in learning to appreciate the opposite style is to not be so critical of it.

At the same time, it is important not to idolize the opposite style, for it, too, has its imperfections. By looking only at the strengths of something, one tends to overlook its weaknesses. Being aware of the shortcomings as well as the virtues of the other style can help one to accept one's own, natural style more fully.

To return to an earlier example, a successful business executive might look out his or her window at people surfing on the ocean below and think, "That must be the life. To go out there every day, have no worries, maybe a little part-time job, just enough to pay for surfing and having fun." Meanwhile, on the beach, the surfer might look up at the business executive's window, thinking, "Those are people who make things happen. They are achieving things and making lots of money. I'm not going anywhere; all I have is this crummy surfboard." Each begins to see the other's world as idealized, without realizing that the other person might be doing the very same thing.

A related example is when scientists begin to idolize the lifestyle of artists, and vice versa. Scientists might look at artists and see free-flowing emotionality, impulsiveness, and creativity, and wish they were more emotional, impulsive, and creative. Artists might look at scientists and see rational, well-organized people who are pursuing goals and achieving things, and wish they were more ordered, more driven, and had more goals to achieve. These idealized visions can often interfere with seeing the opposite style in a more complete and realistic way.

This can sometimes lead to jealousy. For instance, ordered thinkers might become envious of chaotic thinkers because they always appear to be having fun. They might then convince themselves that chaotic thinkers are merely lazy. To appreciate chaotic thinking, it is important to realize that chaotic thinkers are simply doing things in a different way. They cannot be measured by goals, by units of achievement, by things of that nature, because their productivity comes from a different set of considerations. Chaotic thinkers usually produce not to make money or meet deadlines, but because the work is stimulating. And if a job ceases to be stimulating, they usually begin doing other things.

Most ordered thinkers have a hard time with the easy, natural creativity that chaotic thinkers often display. This is because they tend to see everything in terms of their work ethic. They can put years into the development of a single idea, whereas chaotic thinkers can seemingly come up with many creative ideas from out of the blue. Ordered thinkers might thus see this as betraying the very foundations on which their own ideas are based.

Chaotic thinkers, in turn, tend to view ordered thinkers as rather dreary and not much fun. They might even think of them as potentially violent. However, this shows little appreciation for the tension that ordered thinkers often place themselves under, which helps to drive them towards their goals. This tension creates a certain anger at times, which can be easily misconstrued. To better appreciate ordered thinking, it is important to realize that this tension, and the anger that sometimes accompanies it, are what often enables ordered thinkers to accomplish things and to become successful.

Sometimes chaotic thinkers downplay the very things that ordered thinkers believe they should be most honored for—namely, their success and accomplishments. A chaotic thinker is likely to say, "Sure, you rebuilt that entire car, but it would have been easier to take it to a repair shop." Ordered thinkers, having taken pride in this effort, usually become angry at such comments. They will likely feel that they have been denigrated, even though that was not really the chaotic thinker's intention.

Instead of becoming envious or critical of the opposite style, both styles of thinkers could become more aware of their own strengths and value them. For example, among ordered thinkers, there is much to be said for having the ability to generate a good plan and to see it through. They need not lower the value of their plans and ideas just because it might have taken a lot of time and effort to develop them. Similarly, among chaotic thinkers, there is much to be said for attending to the needs of the moment and resolving crises, even if this never leads to long-term plans and goals.

Ordered and chaotic thinkers simply think in different ways, not necessarily better ways. Learning to appreciate this can help bring about constructive changes in many of the attitudes that pervade modern society. For instance, in our present educational system, which is heavily ordered, there is a tendency to ostracize chaotic thinkers, to want to run them off the road to higher education. This would be less of a problem if there were a greater recognition that chaotic thinkers can have strengths and abilities that are just as valuable to our culture, our society, and our future as those of ordered thinkers.

## EXPLORING THE OTHER SIDE

Most ordered thinkers try to avoid chaos, whereas most chaotic thinkers try to avoid order. Each may feel that they will jeopardize their strengths by exploring the other side. However, these fears are usually unfounded. Ordered thinkers seldom need to worry about losing their ordering tendencies, because they order things naturally. By the same token, chaotic thinkers seldom need to worry about losing their spontaneity, because they are spontaneous naturally.

When beginning to explore chaotic thinking, it would help ordered thinkers to suppress their tendency to always look for an ordered way of doing something. One cannot learn about what chaotic thinking is really like by devising a plan to be chaotic; it is a contradiction in terms. Rather, it is better to be as spontaneous and unstructured as possible, and to be aware of what is happening at each particular moment. For example, instead of placing oneself on a schedule, as in saying, "I will be chaotic for three hours this evening and then move on," one could just go somewhere, without a plan, and simply try to be more aware of things by watching and listening to whatever happens. Instead of judging or controlling situations, one could let those situations unfold naturally.

When looking at a landscape or a painting, it might help to try to see it from different points of view and explore it from different perspectives. Certain works of art encourage this, such as collages that simultaneously show many different aspects of the same event. When reading a book, one might explore different interpretations of what is happening in the story. These explorations can often help ordered thinkers get in touch with how a chaotic thinker interprets the world from the standpoint of multiple realities.

In learning to see things from multiple perspectives, it also helps to read about a wide variety of subjects. This should be done informally, whenever possible. For example, one could go to a library and simply look over various books to see which ones might capture one's attention. Instead of making a specific plan to read books on particular subjects, one could select those that just happened to strike one as interesting.

When talking with other people, one might try to express one's ideas using metaphors, to avoid relying on direct, literal descriptions or interpretations. This often helps open up conversations and make them less predictable, and allows for new and unexpected insights. Instead of planning the metaphors in advance, one might improvise them according to the flow of the conversation. One could also try to regard what people are saying as metaphors and explore novel ways of interpreting them.

If one were an ordered thinker, one could practice not carrying through every plan to a successful conclusion. For instance, when playing games with people, one might allow them to take back moves occasionally, even when one could have capitalized on their errors and achieved an easy victory. This would not only help one take the game less seriously, it would also allow one to explore new and interesting developments in the game that might not have happened if the game had suddenly been terminated.

Ordered thinkers are often so focused on winning that they overlook these opportunities. By not taking one's plans so seriously, one is often better able to consider alternatives, explore new possibilities, and deal with unexpected developments and crises. This also helps to reduce the panic or denial that often accompanies a major disruption in one's life, when all one's plans seem to have failed.

A common tendency among ordered thinkers is to apply a fixed value to their prior actions and decisions. For instance, a past achievement might always be thought of as a great accomplishment or a past mistake might always be thought of as a terrible blunder. Chaotic thinkers, on the other hand, typically change the value of their previous judgments and accomplishments. Just because a decision was right yesterday does not mean that it is right today. To achieve greater flexibility, ordered thinkers could adopt this approach and begin to think of ways in which their past accomplishments were not so virtuous, and their past failures were not so bad.

Another suggestion would be to take a vacation and do nothing. For example, one might find a beach and just walk along it every day. Instead of planning a certain distance for this, or placing it on a schedule, one could just walk out and come back. This would help one become more unfocused and better appreciate the chaotic thinker's preference for living in the moment.

These explorations could help give ordered thinkers a better sense for what chaotic thinking is like and allow them to begin to incorporate the principles of chaotic thinking into their natural thinking style. In addition, they could provide ordered thinkers with better insights into how to interact more effectively with chaotic thinkers. For instance, they could become more effective in getting chaotic thinkers to agree to do certain things.

Normally, ordered thinkers would propose an idea as part of a plan, with particular structures and schedules. With most chaotic thinkers, however, it is usually better to simply point out the desirable features of the idea and appeal to their impulsiveness. For example, if you wanted a chaotic thinker to go with you to the park, instead of proposing it as part of a general plan, you could mention how nice the trees are at the park and how it would be a good day to go there because there would not be many people.

Another way of convincing chaotic thinkers to go along with an idea is to have them participate in an alternative reality that you have suddenly created for them. For example, you could give them an enticing description of an imaginative fantasy that they could become involved with right away. This helps intensify the moment and encourages chaotic thinkers to act on their impulses. Ordered thinkers sometimes make the mistake of trying to talk a chaotic thinker into doing something at some later time, which takes the idea out of the moment.

By exploring chaotic thinking, ordered thinkers could begin to overcome many of the limitations of an ordered style. As discussed in previous chapters, although ordered thinkers are generally more prepared in life, they are also more likely to need those preparations. They often get into difficulties because they become out of touch with the immediate situation. This can lead them to construct plans that are increasingly inappropriate.

For example, as discussed in chapter 6, when ordered thinkers have problems in a relationship, they often respond by introducing more plans and structures into it, which is just what one should avoid doing. If someone complained that they were not being allowed enough freedom in the relationship, ordered thinkers might respond by further dividing up their time into smaller units, freeing some of them up while still retaining the larger plans and structures. They might think that the person simply wanted a block of time to do other things, whereas the person was actually saying that they wanted the right to unstructure the relationship.

In any situation that produces unexpected problems, ordered thinkers often react by delving deeper into their plans. By doing so, however, they further detach themselves from the needs of the moment. By exploring chaotic thinking, they could begin to recognize when this tendency to overplan was happening and thus avoid falling into these traps.

If you were a chaotic thinker and wanted to explore ordered thinking, you might start by making lists of things to do and putting yourself on simple schedules. You could impose minor deadlines and then make every effort to stick to them. You could begin to prioritize the events in your life, and commit yourself to things you might want or need to do, however small. For instance, you could tell yourself, "I will do the dishes today at 5:00," and then do them at that time. You could then begin to experience what it is like for ordered thinkers to live according to plans.

It tends to be somewhat easier for chaotic thinkers to explore ordered thinking than vice versa, because modern society has been structured to favor, value, and promote the latter. One generally has much easier access to ordered ways of doing things. In trying to learn about chaotic thinking, an ordered thinker might say, "I don't get the point of why I should go out on the beach for five or six hours and just wander around." In asking what the point is, they would miss the point. A chaotic thinker, however, could more easily understand why ordered thinkers need to have goals, plans, and explanations, because these tend to be valued in our society.

Another benefit of exploring the opposite style is that it can help make sense out of many of the seemingly pointless things that ordered and chaotic thinkers often do. For example, instead of getting angry at someone's playful impulsiveness, one could realize that the person's behavior is probably typical of chaotic thinkers. Instead of making fun of a person's rigid adherence to a plan, one could realize that the person is probably just doing what ordered thinkers typically do. This puts one in a better position to understand and accept the behavior, as opposed to simply becoming perplexed or frustrated by it.

In general, most ordered thinkers would benefit by openly embracing chaotic thinking, instead of always trying to avoid or reject it. Denying chaos completely can lead to irrationality. Likewise, most chaotic thinkers would benefit by allowing some structure into their lives. To deny any structure whatsoever can also lead to irrationality. When ordered thinkers seem to be in complete and total control of their lives, with all uncertainties carefully removed, they sometimes risk giving in to the most bizarre, chaotic impulses. Similarly, when chaotic thinkers seem to have escaped from all order and structure, they sometimes risk engaging in pointless, ordered compulsions and rituals.

In extreme ordered thinking, careful planning might be replaced by impulsiveness and indecisiveness, whereas in extreme chaotic thinking, impulsiveness and spontaneity might be replaced by irrational planning. When one suppresses or denies elements of the opposite style within oneself, those tendencies can suddenly be unleashed, as when a highly ordered general begins to make all battle decisions impulsively, or when a highly chaotic artist begins to impose bizarre structures on all of his or her works.

When ordered thinkers retain a sense of perspective, they are usually aware of the approriateness of their plans and goals. They then have the ability to stay on the right track. When chaotic thinkers retain a sense of perspective, they are usually aware of the consequences of their impulses. They then have the ability to walk along the razor's edge. However, when this sense of perspective is lost, when the strengths of either style become untempered by those of the opposite style, it can often lead to problems.

With ordered thinkers, this can begin to happen when their plans are no longer balanced by the realistic considerations of the moment. For instance, one might begin talking about becoming president of a major corporation despite not having a high school education. For many chaotic thinkers, these problems can stem from wanting to avoid contact with the order in the world. They might give up on the possibility of ever holding a steady job and are then seen as a burden to society.

Refusing to experience the other side can thus leave one with a narrow outlook on life. In some cases, it can also lead to tragic consequences. A drifter standing on the street corner who has mastered the art of chaotic thinking, but who is broke and has no place to live, is about as sorry a sight as Ebenezer Scrooge, who has lots of money and security but a dearth of meaningful, emotional attachments. It is only when Scrooge is forced to explore the chaotic side that he becomes aware of other perspectives on his life, and it is only when the drifter is forced to explore a structured existence that he or she can begin to think in terms of future goals and achievements.

For both ordered and chaotic thinkers, it is important to recognize that life itself is comprised of these two forces. There will always be some people who are afraid of chaos or life's uncertainties, or who are afraid of order and the structuring forces in the universe. But these fears can often be overcome by putting oneself in touch with the opposite style. When ordered thinkers begin to experience small changes, they can often learn to tolerate larger changes and discover how to deal with them. When chaotic thinkers begin to take on small responsibilities, they can often learn how to deal with larger responsibilities.

As we have tried to show, there are a variety of ways in which one can explore and benefit from the opposite style. Ordered thinkers can learn to attend to the cues of the moment, temporarily disengage their plans, entertain novel alternatives or perspectives, and replace a concern for winning with permission to have fun. Chaotic thinkers can learn to impose plans occasionally, think more about the future, organize their schedules, and become more focused on achieving certain goals.

## EXPANDING ONE'S PERSPECTIVE

By exploring the other style, one also gains deeper insights into oneself and begins to expand one's own perspective. One learns what it is like to experience things from a radically different point of view. This allows one to appreciate reality in a more coherent way, because one begins to see the world as both ordered and chaotic, instead of as one or the other.

Usually, these explorations can be carried out without having to abandon the strengths of one's natural thinking style and without the risk of losing one's identity. In fact, it would be rare for a person to completely switch from being one type of thinker to the other, as we elaborate on later in the chapter. For instance, if one were a highly ordered thinker, it would be unlikely that one could ever become a true chaotic thinker simply by learning about and practicing chaotic techniques. However, one might gain useful insights into how chaotic thinking works and could begin to overcome many of the limitations of ordered thinking. The reverse would true for most chaotic thinkers.

In this regard, we should distinguish between using chaotic techniques occasionally or when necessary and employing them as a way of life. Ordered thinkers who only use these techniques now and then would probably have trouble making the kinds of rapid, spontaneous decisions necessary to maintain chaotic thinking over time. For this reason, when one decides to experience chaotic thinking, it is important to actually practice spontaneity, not just to make a conscious decision to try to be more spontaneous. One could then begin to explore the rapid shifts and alternative realities of chaotic thinking more effectively, even if one never became as proficient at using these techniques as naturally chaotic thinkers. It is by acquiring this sense of awareness for what the other style is really like that one begins to expand one's own perspective.

We also need to distinguish between people who are trapped in the wrong style, having been brought up that way, and those who may simply feel unfulfilled. In the former case, when they begin to explore the other style, they may end up making major shifts in their lives and will be very comfortable doing so. In the latter case, where they are already comfortable being ordered or chaotic thinkers, they will tend to make relatively minor changes, which can then enhance their natural style.

In expanding one's perspective, one can begin to discover where one fits in with respect to the major contrasts between ordered and chaotic thinking, and can become more aware of those aspects of each style that exist within oneself. One is then in a better position to discover one's true talents and potentials. In fact, one may often find out that there is really no point in trying to switch completely over to the opposite style, however attractive it might have once seemed.

Consider, for example, the surfer who has begun to move into a more structured existence. He might return to school and get a regular job, but then at some point realize that this ordered lifestyle is not for him and revert back to his totally chaotic existence. He may not have changed, but he now has a better sense for his true nature. Likewise, consider the business executive who has decided to quit his job and spend every day at the beach. He might quickly discover that the daily uncertainties of life on the beach are too unsettling, and realize that he belongs back in a regular, predictable job.

## LIVING IN BOTH WORLDS

Ideally, one could achieve a more integrated thinking style by drawing on and combining the elements of both ordered and chaotic thinking. There are some risks in doing so, but for the most part trying to integrate the two styles can be beneficial.

Consider, for example, the problem of learning how to fly an airplane. Trying to do so using a purely chaotic strategy, in which one responds impulsively to the immediate conditions of flight and relies on trial and error, could be disastrous, as could trying to use a purely ordered strategy, in which one only studies the formal principles of flight and has no practical experience in actually flying a plane. One could spend years reading books on flight but still be lost in a cockpit. It would be better to try to integrate the two approaches.

Similarly, consider the aeronautical engineer who has never made difficult maneuvers in a plane, versus the barnstormer who has no idea how to design one. A truly good designer of planes would be someone who has not only studied the principles of flight mechanics and aerodynamic design, but who has also actually been in a plane and knows what it feels like to make those maneuvers. This person would know what could and could not be done in a plane, and which laws or rules must be followed. By combining these perspectives, the person would have a much better vision of what a plane could and should do than someone who had approached the problem from only one perspective or the other.

As another example, consider the chemist who studies only the formal properties of chemical reactions, versus someone who has had enormous experience actually mixing chemicals together and seeing what happens. One would want to try to integrate both of these perspectives in developing new chemicals and predicting how they would react.

There are, in fact, many ways of trying to achieve a balance between ordered and chaotic thinking. For example, most ordered thinkers regard tools as having a specific purpose and tend to take them too seriously, whereas most chaotic thinkers tend not to take them seriously enough and fail to give them proper respect. Whereas ordered thinkers usually want to use the right tool for the right task, chaotic thinkers often use whatever tool is handy, apart from its intended purpose, such as trying to use a screwdriver as a crowbar. A balanced perspective would say, in effect, that in many situations any tool will do, but that there are certain situations in which one would only want to use certain tools.

Part of achieving this integration is learning to recognize when a particular thinking style is most appropriate. This is another reason why it is helpful to actually practice the techniques of the opposite style. Most situations lend themselves more naturally to one style or the other; by combining the two styles, one gains the capacity to deal with a wider variety of situations.

In general, one could work toward achieving long-range goals while appreciating and attending to the needs of the moment. If one were an ordered thinker, one might consider postponing or restructuring one's original plans if the context of the moment suddenly changed, without worrying that the plans were now ruined. One could also strive to make one's principles and ideals more metaphorical. If one were a chaotic thinker, one might consider responding to the needs of the moment by thinking about possible plans for the future, without worrying about becoming inhibited by them. One could also strive to temper impulsiveness with foresight.

When incorporating elements of the opposite style, it is important to know when a natural balance has been achieved. For example, ordered thinkers could tell that they have included just enough chaos into their lives when they began to feel mildly uncomfortable with the increased clutter, but were not yet overwhelmed by it. Similarly, chaotic thinkers could tell that they have included just enough order when they began to feel mildly discomfited, but were not yet overly restricted. They might feel a bit uneasy about having additional responsibilities, but not to the point where they suddenly had a desperate desire to run away.

Sometimes special circumstances arise that encourage a more integrated thinking style. Ordered thinkers might suddenly develop major disabilities that forced them to live on a day-to-day basis such that their previous long-term plans and aspirations were no longer appropriate. Chaotic thinkers might suddenly acquire new and inescapable responsibilities that required them to plan for the future. Such circumstances usually require more than just casual explorations of the other style.

Some people fall naturally in the middle, in between the two extremes. They have a tremendous gift, for they would be able to move freely within both worlds. They could perhaps live a more integrated life than anyone, having a natural ability to both appreciate and coordinate the two styles and accept the conflicting impulses within themselves. Their plans would be open and flexible. They could combine a commitment to work with a desire to have fun. They could focus on the moment or reflect on the past and future as the situation demanded.

Their weakness, however, is that they would never be fully accepted within either world. Most chaotic thinkers would regard them as too ordered, whereas most ordered thinkers would regard them as too chaotic. They would be caught between two cultures, so to speak (Snow, 1964). And although they would benefit from the strengths of both styles, they might also suffer from each of their weaknesses. They might be impulsive when it would undermine their plans. They might be ordered when it would inhibit their creativity. It would often seem as if they were working against themselves. On their best days, they might be beautifully integrated, but on their worst days they might be tripping over their own feet.

## PROMOTING CREATIVE REALISM

The highest forms of creative achievement usually involve a combination of ordered and chaotic qualities. Consider, for example, a great scientist such as Einstein, who brings meaning to the order of the universe, or a great artist such as Leonardo da Vinci, who brings order to meaningful things in nature. Such achievements exemplify what has been termed *creative realism* (Finke, 1995), which often results from combining the structure and endurance of ordered thinking and the creative potential and meaningfulness of chaotic thinking.

All great artistic and scientific advances fulfill the criteria of both endurance and meaningfulness. A scientific work that is highly structured, but which fails to intensify the moment, is likely to be seen as unnecessary or irrelevant. On the other hand, an artistic creation that captures the essence of the moment, but which lacks enduring structure, will likely be forgotten once the moment passes.

Consider, for instance, the idea of "fire" as an art form. A colorful flame can be a beautiful thing in the moment, but it does not endure. Many artists have moved toward just this sort of extreme chaotic expression, leaving nothing for posterity. The art merely exists in the moment, as in "performance art," and then disappears (e.g., Goldberg, 1988). At the opposite extreme, one can have art that is devoid of any obvious meaning, where what supposedly matters is the structured system or philosophy that is behind the creation (e.g., Wolfe, 1979). Here, too, creative realism is lacking, but for different reasons.

A chaotic artist might claim that the true value of art is its transitory nature; the fact that it fails to endure is exactly the point. Similarly, an ordered scientist might claim that a narrow experiment that is highly structured and is directed towards future goals is what science should be all about. These represent the extremes of chaotic and ordered thinking, where the whole point of something is either that it is transitory but meaningful, or meaningless but structured and enduring. In trying to achieve creative realism, one strives to create enduring structures that are also meaningful.

Ordered thinkers usually express their creativity by taking existing themes and varying them in original ways, whereas chaotic thinkers usually express their creativity by drawing on multiple realities and changing the themes. For example, many modern movies use simple variations on a few basic themes, which represents ordered attempts at creative expression. Every so often, however, a chaotic movie comes along that does something completely novel, that takes the art of filmmaking a step beyond. Yet such films take big risks, and many do not survive. Films that exhibit creative realism remain structurally connected to earlier, proven themes, but they also introduce meaningful extensions of them. This often results in new, emergent themes that withstand the test of time.

To enhance creative realism, one could therefore try to introduce themes and ideas that intensify the moment, but which are structurally connected to those that have worked in the past. One would avoid sticking too closely to previous forms and structures but would not fully abandon them, either. This approach draws on the strengths of both ordered and chaotic thinking.

Some special problems can arise with ordered thinkers who are highly creative. They might want to produce on a regular basis, but this may work against their creative impulses. Their pride might make them more vulnerable to the perils of creative risk-taking, as compared with chaotic thinkers. They might also have a harder time seeing the divergent qualities of their work, which could suggest new avenues for exploration. All of these things would inherently work against them.

Their advantage, however, is that they would often be able to bring an ordered, enduring quality to their creations.

Artists who are ordered thinkers might wish to generate unstructured, creative works but be constantly restrained by their principles and structuring tendencies. For instance, they might want to improvise but feel that they must do so only within a particular structure or system. Chaotic artists tend to have the opposite problem; they often have trouble finding a concrete structure or format in which to express what they want to express.

There is another difficulty that creative, ordered thinkers might face. After a while, they might begin to convince themselves that their ideas were more significant or meaningful than they actually were, simply because those ideas were highly structured. Creative realism might then be prevented, because they would no longer measure themselves against their usual standards. Instead, they might become increasingly trapped within their pride and detached from the normal constraints and limits of their profession.

## AVOIDING STYLISTIC CORRUPTION

There is always the danger that showing someone the other side can have deleterious consequences. For example, ordered thinkers might forsake their principles or ambitions when shown the virtues of chaotic thinking, and chaotic thinkers might not be able to control their newfound ambitions when shown the virtues of ordered thinking. Each must therefore be on guard against being corrupted by the strengths of the opposite style.

For instance, a common problem arises when ordered thinkers begin to plan chaotic responses after having become enamored with chaotic thinking and wanting to imitate it. They often make the mistake of not recognizing that chaotic thinking is fundamentally spontaneous and opportunistic, and that one cannot really plan a chaotic reaction. Attempts to plan chaotic responses almost always fail, as when an ordered thinker says, "I'm not going to care about the future any more; I'm just going to do whatever I feel like." Similar problems can arise when a chaotic thinker might suddenly decide, "I'm going to stop worrying about what other people need and concentrate on getting what I want." To step totally outside the constraints of one's natural style is usually risky.

These constraints serve an important purpose. Obviously, nature does not want to have forces that are so free that they consume everything else. Ordered thinkers who lose their perspective on the future, and suddenly feel that they are free to do anything they want at any given moment, or chaotic thinkers who become filled with ambition, and suddenly feel that there are no limits on what they can achieve, can each contribute to the further disintegration between the two styles. To pursue ambition without constraint can be dangerous thing for both ordered and chaotic thinkers.

One can minimize these risks by exploring the other side only after having acquired sufficient self-esteem within one's own, natural style. When this self-esteem is lacking, these explorations could result in the loss of perspective and lead to extreme forms of behavior. For instance, a chaotic thinker could end up becoming a self-proclaimed messiah, and an ordered thinker could end up becoming a dictator or the leader of a cult.

This requires some clarification. First, consider what might happen with ordered thinking. Normally, the pride of ordered thinkers is tied to their actual achievements. When this connection is lost, however, they can become mesmerized by their own greatness, as in the case of Custer or Napoleon. This is why introducing chaotic techniques that suddenly force ordered thinkers into the moment can be risky. Without further achievements to validate their pride, they can become victims of inflated power and self-worth.

Ordinarily, an ordered thinker is like a locomotive, always pushing forward. When you suddenly remove the tracks, however, the wheels begin to spin, the pressure builds, and there is no place else to go. This often happens when an ordered thinker abandons the future, and becomes a revolutionary, as in the case of Robespierre: a highly ordered thinker who, during the French Revolution, began executing people in the name of the state (Thompson, 1962).

There are actually two phases to this process. Initially, as their pride increases, ordered thinkers might focus on their past accomplishments and begin to lose sight of their future goals. The second stage occurs when they no longer think of their future at all and acquire a complete, absolute self-righteousness that transcends personal glorification. They might then come to believe that they represent or embody an entire organization or state.

An example of the latter would be Hitler. Whereas Napoleon began to believe he was greater than the state, Hitler made the state an emblem of who he was, much like Stalin. At some point, when ordered thinkers disintegrate, and have power, they often become identified with the state. Both Hitler and Stalin had enormous pride, but not in the same sense as Napoleon or Custer. Their ultimate desire was for the state to be great, as opposed to seeking individual glorification. Thus, as this disintegration progresses, one starts out with an inflated personal ego, and then a transcendent ego takes over, at which point the person and the state may become synonymous.

Chaotic thinkers, in contrast, rarely become obsessed by political or military power when corrupted but are likely to display a more isolated type of fanaticism. When ordered thinkers lose their constraints, they often still have enough organizing power to take control. When chaotic thinkers lose their constraints, however, they usually become antithetical to the powers that be. They are more likely to become spiritual or revolutionary cranks in the street, or someone like Rasputin, the mad monk, who became highly ambitious but without an ordered plan (Oakley, 1989).

These ambitions are at a much more personal level for the chaotic thinker. Rasputin was not interested in ruling Russia; he wanted to have a divine influence over people. For many chaotic thinkers, at the first level of disintegration there is the desire to have absolute freedom from all societal restraint. They often then become surrounded by followers who also want this freedom. At the next level, chaotic thinkers might begin to think of themselves as deities, because they are no longer bounded by any constraints. Like a god, they are acutely aware of multiple realities, of everything that is happening in the moment, and therefore become omniscient. This is in contrast to what can happen when ordered thinkers lose their constraints and end up regarding themselves as omnipotent.

We can thus begin to understand the contrast between people who try to establish a theocracy or a dictatorship and become fused with their visions of the state, and people who end up being worshipped as a god or a messiah and become fused with their visions of themselves. These represent the opposite extremes to which ordered and chaotic thinking can deteriorate when their natural constraints are removed.

There are certain things that ordered and chaotic thinkers could do to avoid falling into these traps. Ordered thinkers, for example, could watch their pride. When this begins to grow unbounded, it is a sign that they are in trouble. Their pride should always be measured against their next achievement, not their past victories. As long as they retain this perspective, they are likely to remain on solid ground.

Chaotic thinkers, on the other hand, need to stay in touch with their fatalism. As long as they see themselves as merely a part of their environment, they are fine. But the moment they begin to see themselves as the center, around which everything else must revolve, they are in trouble. Their awareness of multiple realities, which normally causes them to see themselves as playing a relatively minor role in the total scheme of things, can instead lead them to become the center of attention. This can be avoided by reminding themselves that they are only small players, which would help them to retain their perspective.

## ORDERED AND CHAOTIC DRIFT

Even when one can successfully incorporate the strengths of the opposite style, there is a tendency to eventually drift back to relying upon one's own natural strengths. Ordered thinkers who are initially drawn to the freedom and meaning-fulness of chaotic thinking might soon return to a completely ordered way of life, especially if chaotic thinkers are no longer around to inspire them. The liberating but uncertain possibilities that they began to explore can then seem less and less attractive. Similarly, chaotic thinkers who are initially drawn to the control and sense of accomplishment that ordered thinkers convey, and who begin adding some structure to their lives, may eventually drift back to their natural, chaotic style, especially if ordered thinkers are no longer around to provide proper incentive.

Consider, first of all, the tendency to drift back to an ordered style. Ordered thinkers who begin to explore chaotic techniques may eventually have trouble using them in the open, unstructured manner in which they were intended. This is particularly true if they try to incorporate those techniques into their existing plans or use them to achieve specific goals. They are then likely to resort back to a purely ordered approach, especially if they become impatient or frustrated.

Oftentimes, ordered thinkers who have begun to explore chaotic thinking will think about a past situation or problem and then consider the various chaotic techniques that they should have used. This tendency to think about chaotic techniques in retrospect, and to reflect upon what should have been done, promotes a return to an ordered approach. A genuine chaotic response is spontaneous and fits the moment perfectly; once that moment has passed, it can never be recreated.

Similarly, chaotic thinkers can begin to have trouble staying with an ordered approach. They might naturally oppose the structure that they have begun to impose on themselves, and may eventually reject that structure, in much the same the way that the human body might reject a transplanted organ. Eventually, they might come to realize that they will never be as good as ordered thinkers at coming up with plans for the future and will then drift back to their purely chaotic existence.

And yet, even when one drifts back to one's natural style, one often ends up having a deeper sense for one's own true strengths, as discussed previously. One can then actualize one's strengths in a more balanced and realistic way, which comes from having seen things from an entirely different perspective. One can then begin to expand the horizons of one's own nature.

For instance, even when ordered thinkers drift back to a completely ordered style, they often preserve the insights that chaotic thinkers have inspired in them, and may then employ their natural ordering tendencies to develop those insights in practical and organized ways. Similarly, chaotic thinkers often use some of the qualities of ordered thinking that they have absorbed to enable themselves to be more independent, as when they work towards getting a part-time job so that they can then free up the rest of their time to do other things.

## INTERACTIONS AMONG CHAOTIC THINKERS

Much of this book has been focused on the ways in which ordered and chaotic thinkers interact with one another and has examined many of the problems and misunderstandings that can arise from these interactions. We have also considered many of the benefits of bringing the two styles together. However, we have not yet addressed to any extent the way in which chaotic thinkers typically interact among themselves.

Interactions among chaotic thinkers tend to be fraternal, egalitarian, and relatively free of hierarchies and pecking orders. Leadership in a group of chaotic thinkers is usually awarded to whomever happens to be leading. They rarely question why things are being done; either you go along with what happens or you don't. As Ken Kesey once put it, you're either on the bus or off the bus.

When chaotic thinkers get together, there is often an expanded sense of intellectual freedom. They are usually able to generate new ideas and explore novel possibilities without having to think about their consequences or worry about having to meet someone else's expectations. The unrestricted, chaotic interplay of thoughts and ideas often gives rise to emergent structures that might not have occurred in isolation. There is also a strong sense of "shareability" among ideas when chaotic thinkers get together, in which no one person possesses an entire concept, but where the concept can then emerge as a collective insight (e.g., Freyd, 1983).

Sometimes, however, inertness is the result when chaotic thinkers interact. Indecisiveness can prevail, and then nothing happens. It is like looking into opposing mirrors, where the images and symbols are reflected back and forth and become part of an infinite cycle. Unless there is a strong focusing point or event, interactions among chaotic thinkers can sometimes diverge along paths that never seem to end.

In contrast, interactions among ordered thinkers tend to be much more focused, structured, and hierarchical. Positions of leadership are usually made explicit and are determined in systematic ways. When interacting among themselves, ordered thinkers usually have a sense for their rank or position within the group. Most of the time, everyone is expected to play his or her role or do his or her part.

Ordered interactions can be extremely efficient, especially when everyone is involved in the same plan. However, problems can often arise when plans clash and there are no specific rules or guidelines for resolving the conflict. In such cases, one usually finds a lack of tolerance for different agendas or points of view, in contrast to the noncritical openness that tends to characterize interactions among chaotic thinkers.

# 10

## Chaotic Implications

We conclude by exploring some implications of chaotic cognition in various other fields. These include its potential ramifications for cognitive psychology, personality theory, science and technical research, business and organizational psychology, government, and education. We also consider some of its implications for ecology and ecological systems.

First, however, we wish to restate certain themes that were introduced at the beginning of the book. In making a general distinction between ordered and chaotic thinking, we emphasize that this is not the only way to divide up the world. We believe the main value of this dichotomy is that it can provide useful insights into many current psychological and sociological problems and can lead to a better appreciation of the fundamental differences between ordered and chaotic thinkers.

Second, our intention has been to provide a broad, theoretical analysis of these contrasting styles and to identify general properties of chaotic thinking, without attempting to develop a formal, mathematical theory or model. Efforts to extend the formalisms of modern chaos theory to psychology and related fields are well underway (e.g., Abrahams & Gilgen, 1994; Goerner, 1994; Lewin, 1992; McCown et al., in press; Waldrop, 1992). We believe that the present analysis will complement those efforts and point to areas in chaotic thinking that may be best suited for the application of more formal methods.

Also, we emphasize that the use of the various chaotic techniques we have described in previous chapters should be based on an understanding of the principles of chaotic thinking together with an appreciation for their limitations. When one first hears about chaotic methods, there is the temptation to try to use them to accomplish particular goals. However, as we have argued, their primary purpose should be to promote new insights and rational behavior, or to restore harmony to a situation that has become intolerably structured or disruptive. Rarely are these techniques used to achieve specific ends or elicit specific reactions, as their natural effect is to increase uncertainty and to create opportunities for exploration and discovery.

We reiterate that the approach we have taken in this book is somewhat atypical. For instance, we have tried to explore chaotic thinking within a very broad context and from multiple perspectives, rather than by focusing on specific aspects of it or by taking a single perspective. Also, we have attempted to make many of our points by referring to familiar, everyday examples and situations, as opposed to relying exclusively on empirical methods or programmatic research. This is, in fact, very much in the spirit of chaotic thinking, in that we have attempted to draw on a diverse range of sources and ideas and to consider how the emerging principles might touch upon many different issues and subjects.

## COGNITIVE SCIENCE

The distinction we have made between ordered and chaotic thinking reflects the traditional contrast between top-down and bottom-up approaches in cognitive science. Top-down approaches have emphasized the role that cognitive structures play in organizing, simplifying, and making sense out of the complexities of the world (e.g., Anderson, 1983; Neisser, 1967), and thus typify ordered thinking. Bottom-up approaches have emphasized the importance of allowing meaning and insight to emerge from the natural structure of the incoming information (e.g., Bowers et al., 1990; Gibson, 1966), and thus typify chaotic thinking. With top-down approaches, it is generally assumed that one's expectations and beliefs can influence what one perceives or experiences, which reflects an ordered viewpoint. With bottom-up approaches, it is generally assumed that intuitions often arise without awareness or control of the underlying processes, which reflects a chaotic viewpoint.

A similar contrast can be made between early- and late-selection models of attention (Anderson, 1990; Reed, 1982). In early-selection models, it is assumed that one is largely in control of what information is initially filtered out or selected for further processing. In late-selection models, it is assumed that one has relatively little control over the initial selection process. The former is more indicative of the controlling, selective nature of ordered thinking, whereas the latter is more indicative of the passive, reactive nature of chaotic thinking.

As discussed in previous chapters, there are two general approaches to creative thinking. With an ordered approach, one usually begins by identifying a specific problem or need and then crafts a form or structure to fit that need. Thus, form follows function. With a chaotic approach, one often begins by exploring playful combinations of elements, which can then yield emergent forms and structures and which can often create new problems or needs. Thus, function follows form. The creative process can therefore be approached from either an ordered or chaotic perspective (Finke, Ward, & Smith, 1992).

There are other aspects of cognitive science that illustrate the difference between ordered and chaotic approaches. In the study of memory, for instance, researchers have long recommended various methods, based on ordered strategies, for improving the recall of information. For example, in the memory technique known as the method of loci, a person constructs a mental image of a well-known pathway and then associates the items to be recalled with familiar landmarks along the pathway (Lea, 1975; Yates, 1966). This provides a structured procedure for retrieving the needed information. Another ordered strategy for recalling information is to logically reconstruct a past event according to how it must have occurred (e.g., Lindsay & Norman, 1977). However, when normal retrieval pathways are blocked, or when direct or logical strategies fail, chaotic retrieval strategies can often be employed. These strategies emphasize defocusing one's attention, exploring divergent associations, and allowing the retrieval process to incubate (e.g., Smith, 1995).

The alternative realities that chaotic thinkers often create can lead to confusion about what is real and what is imaginary. This bears on the study of *reality monitoring* (Johnson & Raye, 1981), which explores the way people distinguish actual and imagined events. Chaotic thinkers would probably be less successful at reality monitoring than ordered thinkers, because they tend to be more spontaneous and are more likely to involve themselves in fantasies and counterfactual possibilities.

Are the mental structures underlying ordered and chaotic thinking fundamentally different? One possibility is that most ordered thinkers may have mental representations that exhibit a strong hierarchical organization (e.g., Atkinson & Shiffrin, 1968), whereas most chaotic thinkers may have representations that are connected in a much looser, more interactive fashion, allowing them to explore associations that cut across traditional conceptual boundaries (e.g., Martindale, 1991; McClelland & Rumelhart, 1981, 1986). Another possibility is that chaotic thinkers might exhibit less hemispherical specialization than ordered thinkers, which is characteristic of the more creative and undifferentiated thinking of children (e.g., Springer & Deutsch, 1981).

Ordered thinkers probably have a greater capacity to mentally replay past events, conversations, melodies, or how their plans unfolded— in general, anything that has a strong, time-dependent quality. This is why they are often good at detecting temporal inconsistencies. Chaotic thinkers are usually better at recalling specific details about a person or subtle things that occurred within the moment, for they are more likely to recognize their meaning or significance. However, they may have trouble remembering exactly what a person said or the particular sequence of events that took place.

Ordered thinkers may also have a greater tendency to mentally project events into the future, as when they anticipate how a conversation might go, how a song might continue, or how their plans might unfold. They may thus exhibit greater amounts of *representational momentum,* which refers to the tendency for events to be remembered as having continued farther along their implied directions than they actually did (Freyd, 1987; Freyd & Finke, 1984). For example, ordered thinkers might mistakenly think that a plan had already reached a certain level of success, merely because it was strongly headed in that direction. Chaotic thinkers, on the other hand, may show less representational momentum, because they would not be as strongly inclined to anticipate future events.

In general, chaotic thinking would tend to promote inductive reasoning (Holland, Holyoak, Nisbett, & Thagard, 1986), whereas ordered thinking would tend to promote deductive reasoning. Chaotic thinkers are usually better at inferring deeper meanings and implications from simple facts (as depicted, for example, by the methods of Sherlock Holmes), whereas ordered thinkers are usually better at deducting consequences using a set of rules or conditions (as exemplified by many bureaucrats, policemen, military officers, and lawyers). Whereas ordered thinking is usually more convergent, chaotic thinking is usually more divergent.

## PERSONALITY AND COGNITIVE STYLES

The study of chaotic cognition also has general implications for research on personality and cognitive styles. We begin by considering the so-called "Big Five" personality dimensions (Costa & McCrae, 1988; John, 1990; Goldberg, 1990), and speculate on how ordered and chaotic thinking might bear on each of these:

1. *Extraversion–Introversion.* This first dimension is probably independent of the distinction between ordered and chaotic thinking. Ordered and chaotic thinkers may be either extraverted or introverted, depending on how their natural tendencies are expressed (Eysenck & Eysenck, 1985). For example, most extraverted ordered thinkers would be outgoing in ways that conformed to the existing structures and hierarchies in society, like a person who actively organizes social or sporting events. They might also exhibit a flamboyant personal style and proudly announce their plans to the world. Introverted ordered thinkers, in contrast, would tend to be loners and keep their plans to themselves. Extraverted chaotic thinkers would often seem more childlike, guileless, out of control, and willing to take big risks than introverted chaotic thinkers, who would tend to be more reflective and perhaps somewhat less impulsive.

2. *Agreeableness.* Chaotic thinkers tend to be more approachable, more accepting, and generally more likeable, whereas ordered thinkers tend to be less approachable and more contentious. We would therefore expect that chaotic thinkers would tend to score higher on measures of agreeableness.

3. *Conscientiousness.* This dimension is clearly related to one of the central distinctions between ordered and chaotic thinking. Most ordered thinkers want to

be in control of whatever they do and to be in charge of their lives at all times. They are usually committed to working in a steady and regular manner and to being punctual. Most chaotic thinkers have less control over their impulses and are often spontaneous, unpredictable, and less reliable in their work habits. They would therefore tend to score lower on measures of conscientiousness.

4. *Stability.* Stability is probably less related to the fundamental differences between ordered and chaotic thinking, and has more to do with how well the natural tendencies of the two types of thinkers match their environments. Ordered thinkers, for example, might become insecure if living or working conditions became uncertain or unpredictable, and if they were unable to effectively control what happens. Similarly, chaotic thinkers might become insecure if they were stuck in highly ordered situations or were made to feel that they were not fitting into their expected roles in society.

Chaotic thinkers would probably be regarded as less stable than ordered thinkers, especially if one examines their behavior over extended periods of time. As we have discussed, one of the limitations of chaotic thinking is that it is generally less consistent than ordered thinking. It may therefore seem that chaotic thinkers are unstable, when in fact they are merely behaving in natural, unpredictable ways.

5. *Openness to Experience.* The relation between openness to experience and chaotic thinking was discussed previously in chapter 4. Chaotic thinkers are generally more open to new experiences and exploring their possibilities. They tend to be more open-minded and willing to take chances. Most ordered thinkers, in contrast, prefer having experiences that are predictable or that conform to their plans and expectations.

Thus, with regard to the Big Five dimensions, three of the dimensions seem clearly related to the distinction between ordered and chaotic thinking, whereas two seem relatively independent of this distinction. Chaotic thinkers are likely to be more agreeable, less in control of their impulses, and more open to new experiences than ordered thinkers, whereas either type of thinker could be extraverted, introverted, stable, or unstable.

There are other personality dimensions and constructs that seem related to the ordered–chaotic distinction. For instance, chaotic thinkers would probably score more highly on measures of *absorption* (Tellegen & Atkinson, 1974), which refers to the tendency to become deeply involved in imaginative and self-altering experiences. As we have discussed, chaotic thinkers often become intensely involved in the moment, especially when exploring alternative realities and their implications.

Another distinction that may be related to the contrast between ordered and chaotic thinking is that of field dependence versus field independence (Witkin, 1981). Field-independent people are probably more likely to be ordered thinkers, because they are usually better able to focus on the specific features of a situation apart from its overall context. Field-dependent people are usually more tied to the total context of a situation, and are thus more likely to be chaotic thinkers.

One also should consider the possibility that certain behaviors that are classified as personality disorders may be based on misunderstandings about the opposite thinking style. Consider, for instance, people who are diagnosed as having Attention Deficit Hyperactivity Disorder (ADHD). The major characteristic of this syndrome is that the person has difficulty avoiding distractions and keeping their attention focused on a particular task (e.g., Weiss, 1993). This syndrome might be confused with the inherent distractibility of chaotic thinking. Thus, chaotic thinkers might be misdiagnosed as having ADHD, merely because those making the diagnosis might not fully understand the nature of chaotic thinking and might see it as a disorder only from the perspective of ordered thinking.

Obviously, there are many possible dimensions of personality and cognitive style. How, then, does one decide which dimensions are most fundamental? One way is to conduct factor analytical studies, which has been the standard approach. But beyond purely statistical evidence, a fundamental dimension should be manifested in terms of basic misunderstandings among people. Consider, for example, all of the ways that ordered and chaotic thinkers misunderstand one another, as we have considered in this book. Similarly, consider how extraverted and introverted people typically misunderstand one another and often come to think that there is something wrong with the opposite style.

Where do the various contrasting traits in ordered and chaotic thinking come from? One possibility is that most ordered thinkers are inclined to become specialists, whereas most chaotic thinkers are inclined to become generalists. As specialists, ordered thinkers know everything about something, which contributes to their efficiency and pride. As generalists, chaotic thinkers know something about everything, which contributes to their flexibility and openness.

Because most ordered thinkers strive to master subjects, they are usually controlled, rather than impulsive, and see single paths in life. Most chaotic thinkers see multiple possibilities and choices, which frees them to be impulsive. The comparatively narrow focus of most ordered thinkers leads them to search for perfect ideals, hence their thinking is often idealistic. Most chaotic thinkers do not believe in such ideals, hence their thinking is often fatalistic.

One of the reasons why chaotic thinkers tend to be more passive and allow structures to emerge, whereas ordered thinkers tend to project structure and order onto the external world, is probably that they are more at peace within themselves. Ordered thinkers may be more unsettled internally, and thus feel the need to organize and simplify the world around them.

Are people born to be predominantly ordered or chaotic thinkers? As mentioned in the previous chapter, it would seem likely that, at least to some extent, one would be predisposed toward becoming a particular type of thinker. However, the environmental context would almost certainly play a role. For instance, a natural chaotic thinker who was raised in a highly ordered environment would probably exhibit

more moderate chaotic traits than one who was raised in a highly chaotic environment. Similarly, a natural ordered thinker who was raised in a highly chaotic
environment would probably exhibit more moderate ordered traits.

## TRADITIONAL SEX ROLES

In our society, ordered and chaotic thinking have been identified, traditionally, with
male and female roles. This may be due in part to cultural factors and in part to
stylistic predispositions. Men often appear to be more controlled and organized,
more concerned about the future, and more likely to become upset when their plans
do not succeed; women often appear to be more spontaneous and impulsive, more
focused on the present, and better able to put things into perspective.

We would not claim, however, that men are inherently ordered, or that women
are inherently chaotic, although there may be general tendencies in these directions.
Indeed, there are many examples of men who are chaotic thinkers and women who
are ordered thinkers. One of the values of learning about chaotic cognition is to
help those who fall outside of these traditional roles to achieve a deeper understanding and acceptance of their behavior. They are more likely to stand out as
being deviant in society and might begin to suspect that there must be something
wrong with them. This tendency can be reduced by recognizing that one is simply
a chaotic thinker among ordered thinkers, or vice versa. In addition, many difficulties in communication that have been attributed to differences between the sexes
(e.g., Glass, 1992) may actually be due to differences between ordered and chaotic
thinkers.

A similar situation arises when chaotic thinkers find themselves in professions
in which ordered thinking dominates, such as the military, scientific research, or
law enforcement, or when ordered thinkers find themselves in professions in which
chaotic thinking dominates, such as acting, art, or social work. Most professions
tend to favor one type of thinking or the other, but there is no reason for this to
exclude potentially important contributions from the other style. By accepting and
even encouraging these contributions, common misunderstandings within these
professions can be minimized.

## BUSINESS AND ORGANIZATIONAL PSYCHOLOGY

In the world of business, we have begun to see a shift towards increasingly
unstructured approaches. Open systems of management are now gaining acceptance, in which information can flow freely among different levels of the organization, in which leadership within units is shared, and in which team performance
is valued over individual performance (Dunnette & Hough, 1990; Katz, 1978; Katz,
Kahn, & Adams, 1980). We have also seen an increase in the popularity of total
quality management, in which the system as a whole is evaluated (Deming, 1982).

These changes represent a movement away from traditional, highly ordered approaches to running an organization and a growing acceptance of more chaotic approaches.

In applying chaotic strategies in the business world, there are two general principles to consider: First, an exclusively ordered approach to business eventually leads to chaos. Sooner or later, a large company that relies on ordered and inflexible policies will lose its share of the market, their profits will fall, and the company will likely collapse. Second, an exclusively chaotic approach to business eventually leads to order. For example, innovators who start out breaking all of the standard rules are ultimately forced to conform to at least some traditional business policies; otherwise their innovations may not survive.

When organizations try to fit people into specific, well-defined roles, like the cogs and wheels of a large machine, it causes problems, especially for workers who are chaotic thinkers. Most chaotic thinkers prefer take a more organic approach and look at the particular strengths and talents of each individual. However, this often works against the overall structure of the system or the expectations of supervisors.

An ordered approach to business emphasizes efficiency. But this is usually in relation to efficient machines and systems, not human welfare. From a chaotic point of view, having harmonious human relations can be more important for the ultimate success of a business than using time effectively or maximizing worker output.

Chaotic thinkers often ask what an organization is really accomplishing at any given moment. For example, the organization might start out with the implicit goal of benefitting people, but then end up sacrificing people so that it can survive. This usually results in the organization becoming little more than an empty shell. Problems can therefore occur when those in charge of an organization fail to realize that it has outlived its usefulness.

In highly ordered organizations, there is a tendency to think that all troubles are due to image problems or bad press. One then tends to focus on improving appearances, rather than actually getting to the heart of the problems. Consider, for example, the way many businesses and federal agencies now encourage their employees to smile, rather than dealing directly with the real reasons for poor morale and bad attitudes. This is another drawback of overrelying on an ordered approach.

There is also the problem of always taking an ordered, assembly-line approach to dealing with customers. Many businesses now seem more intent on imposing their rules and policies than on trying to accommodate potential customers. These policies might help the business run more efficiently in principle, but they can prevent effective interactions with consumers.

As a rule, chaotic thinkers typically have good working relations with people, but they often neglect the bottom line of making a profit. Ordered thinkers typically have a good sense for how to increase profit, but they tend to have poor relations with their customers and employees. Also, they tend to make efficiency itself the goal and thus overlook the real purpose of the job or business.

Many companies are reluctant to hire chaotic thinkers because they are regarded as unmanageable. However, hiring only those who are easy to manage limits the creative input into a business and can reduce its ability to adapt to changing conditions. There is also a tendency in many businesses to get rid of "slackers," such as by eliminating job security. However, this usually results in only being able to hire substandard workers who are willing to take a less secure job.

Many businesses might consider hiring chaotic thinkers as general innovators or troubleshooters. They are often able to deal immediately with unexpected crises and problems and can often sense when important changes are needed. In addition, they often come up with creative ideas for products that have the potential for widespread appeal. Ordered thinkers, in turn, could function as "conceptual engineers," taking the ideas of chaotic thinkers and refining or operationalizing them.

If you were an ordered thinker who ran a business, and you were having problems with your employees, you might wish to hire chaotic thinkers to deal with the workers and to have the kinds of effective interactions that you desired. Similarly, in negotiations, you might benefit by using chaotic mediators. One could still profit, if not from employing chaotic thinking directly, by at least knowing when it can be used by those who are skilled at it.

Chaotic thinkers, in turn, could use ordered planners or managers to assist them. For example, chaotic artists could benefit from having managers who could arrange regular showings of their paintings, set up deadlines for completing their works, and in general help them organize their lives so that they could be more effective, more directed, and more successful.

## SCIENCE AND TECHNICAL RESEARCH

The operating principle that has governed much scientific research is that of "linearity"— the notion that science should advance in straightforward, predictable stages, and should constantly display measurable progress (e.g., Skinner, 1953). This philosophy reflects a strong bias towards ordered thinking, for it emphasizes predictability and consistency. Yet many scientific advances have come from essentially chaotic approaches. In fact, chaotic thinkers have often bridged the gap between highly technical work and playful exploration.

For instance, it is striking that so many important scientific discoveries have emerged from imaginary premises or alternative realities, as opposed to being formally deduced from prior facts and assumptions. Some examples are Einstein's theory of relativity and Kekule's discovery of the structure of organic molecules. These types of discoveries are often regarded as miracles of science, in that they seem to defy the standard explanations for how science is supposed to work (e.g., Shepard, 1978). In general, discoveries that are based on chaotic thinking often seem mysterious and unexplainable from an ordered perspective.

With a purely ordered approach, it would be assumed that things like art, literature, or everyday experience should have no real bearing on scientific thinking.

Most ordered thinkers tend to see science as a separate entity with it own set of rules and methods. Other fields should therefore have little impact on the essential workings of science. How could looking at a painting, reading a novel, or watching clouds in the sky possibly have any connection to scientific principles or problems? Most chaotic thinkers, however, would see science as connected to everything else, including art and fantasy.

Science has traditionally neglected chaotic thinking, regarding it as undisciplined and largely irrelevant. Yet, it could hold the key to understanding how nature really works. By skillfully applying the principles of chaotic thinking, scientists could potentially overcome many common obstacles to scientific progress and enhance their ability to make new discoveries.

For example, one of the reasons why many scientists initially had trouble accepting the quantum theory was that it was essentially a chaotic theory. The notions of inherent unpredictability, emergent qualities (where position and momentum emerged as precise values only after being measured), and the wavelike properties of matter are in essence chaotic concepts. Those scientists who were committed to the strongly deterministic view that nature should in principle be predictable were thus unable to accept the basic assumptions and implications of the quantum theory.

Because ordered thinkers tend to think in terms of "yes/no," "right/wrong" categories, they sometimes try to suppress new ideas that conflict with their previous assumptions and beliefs. Whereas they tend to see contradictions in those cases, most chaotic thinkers would try to see an organic connectiveness. Instead of saying "Yes or no," they would tend to say "Yes *and* no." Chaotic thinking can thus often utilize apparent contradictions in science and help one to see the deeper principles that might be operating.

Scientists who are ordered thinkers are often devastated when their experiments do not turn out as expected. If they obtain odd results, they are likely to regard the tests as flawed and may throw away the results rather than attempt to utilize them. This commonly happens when their experiments are designed to support a specific hypothesis. Chaotic thinkers, in contrast, would almost prefer to be wrong, because it would intensify the moment and open up alternative possibilities. The tendency in ordered thinking to avoid being wrong or making mistakes at all costs can limit scientific progress.

By not committing oneself to a single, expected outcome, one also reduces the tendency to distort scientific research. An increasing problem in modern science is the tendency to falsify results or discount data in order to confirm one's beliefs or expectations (e.g., Gardner, 1981). This problem often arises because scientists are under considerable pressure to generate successful predictions and validate their theories. But unexpected results can often indicate that something important has been overlooked.

In the spirit of chaotic thinking, scientists could benefit by regarding research failures as invitations to discover unexpected possibilities. They could thus avoid the tendency to think that the only measure of success is whether or not they have confirmed their predictions or expectations. Instead, they could use their failures to explore what others have not yet explored and thereby take advantage of "botched" experiments. A good example of this is the Hubble telescope. Having to deal with its flawed mirror led to advances in how to remove distortions from data. Instead of blowing up the telescope, scientists utilized the problem to learn something new.

Some specific recommendations for how scientists might apply the principles of chaotic thinking in their research are: (a) They might try to introduce new complexities into their experiments, to increase purposeful clutter if those experiments did not seem to be working out as expected; (b) they could utilize chaotic events whenever these occurred in the course of an experiment; (c) they might do the next best thing, rather than the most obvious thing, in planning a research study; or (d) they might spend more time reading general newspapers and magazines, to learn about remotely related issues and topics that might provide useful insights into current scientific problems.

Another way to enhance scientific discovery is to explore multiple realities. Typically, most scientists try to interpret the results of a study within a narrow range of possibilities and assume that there is always a single, "best" explanation for any finding. It is often more revealing, however, to consider multiple ways of interpreting results, including highly unlikely explanations. Even if these are then rejected, they can often help to clarify a problem and suggest more likely explanations.

Ordered thinkers tend to put their egos on the line in their research and become overly concerned about being right. However, much that is learned in science comes from tests that go awry, from studies that did not turn out as expected. More information can usually be gathered from these situations than from those which merely reinforce what one already knew. By always wanting to be right, one limits the usefulness of this information. Instead of gaining real insights, one simply confirms what one assumed all along. This can result in confirmation bias, which, as discussed in chapter 2, can often lead scientists to follow misleading paths.

One can minimize these problems by trying to have more fun when conducting research. Ordered thinkers tend to take their research too seriously, which can lead to bad science. For this reason, it might help to lighten up the research atmosphere and to become less concerned or worried about the success of one's ideas and theories. At scientific conferences, for instance, one might try to promote a more playful atmosphere by using various chaotic techniques. This could help loosen up the conferences, which tend to be rather dry, staid events, and would help break up old mindsets. It would also let people know that one has a sense of proportion about one's work.

Scientists could also be encouraged to attend science fiction conventions, to promote cross-fertilization of ideas and to explore alternative realities. There is a tendency to dismiss science fiction as being the product of fanciful misunderstandings or perversions of traditional science, yet it can often stimulate new insights and alternative ways of thinking about important scientific problems.

Because ordered thinkers often hold positions of power in most scientific fields, it becomes important to present new or controversial ideas in as nonthreatening a way as possible. To do this, one might apply the chaotic principle of going with the flow, by trying to show how the new idea ties in with and gives deeper meaning to existing ideas that others have proposed. One could then expand upon these connections to intensify the moment and encourage the scientific community to explore the alternative realities that the idea engenders.

In general, chaotic thinking could help destructure scientific fields and stimulate creative insights by calling attention to alternative approaches and possibilities that might not have been considered otherwise. It could also help to initiate paradigm shifts in those fields in which conventional and highly structured theories have predominated (Kuhn, 1970; Thagard, 1992), by serving as a catalyst for new perspectives.

## GOVERNMENT AND STRUCTURED SOCIETIES

The principles of chaotic cognition can also provide insights into the comparative strengths and weaknesses of various forms of government and social systems. Consider, for example, the contrast among totalitarianism, anarchy, and democracy. Totalitarianism represents the ultimate ordered system, in which structure is imposed absolutely. Anarchy represents the ultimate chaotic system, in which the only structure is that which emerges from the chaos. Democracy represents a blending of both ordered and chaotic systems. There is the judiciary, which is ordered, the legislature, which is chaotic, and the executive, which tries to integrate the two.

Whenever there is excessive chaos in society, people begin to seek structure, even totalitarian structure, as a way of relieving the tension. This structure, however, is often imposed at the expense of freedom and civil liberties. Consider the Russian Revolution, where the communists managed to seize the moment and eventually created a highly structured state, or the French Revolution, which led to the dictatorial rise of Napoleon. In both cases, order was imposed onto chaos, but at the cost of eliminating individual freedom (Skocpol, 1979).

The recent collapse of the Soviet system is another example of the limitations of creating an excessively ordered society. The Soviet system was highly centralized and well-organized, with its 5-year plans for the future, but it eventually collapsed. A major reason was that those plans did not adapt well to local conditions or changes. They were not flexible and could not respond to unexpected developments in the Soviet society. When one ignores chaos, one eventually gives in to it, and this is just as true for ordered governments as for ordered thinkers.

In governments that are highly ordered, there is a tendency to bend reality to fit the plans, rather than changing the plans to fit reality. This can cause a government to pretend that emerging problems do not exist, instead of accepting and responding to those problems. The government can then become fragile, and the slightest chaotic impulse might shatter it. In contrast, in governments that are highly chaotic, the lack of order and structure can result in so much flexibility that the governments simply fade over time.

Consider the contrast between the Greek civilization, which was highly chaotic, and the Roman civilization, which was highly ordered. The Roman Empire eventually fell to chaos, whereas the Greek civilization eroded because it was never sufficiently organized. Unlike the Greeks, the Romans had a highly structured political and military system, which was heavily grounded in rules and principles. They would never have employed a Trojan horse, for example. Yet this created inflexibility and inhibited adaptive changes in response to changing times. The Greeks, on the other hand, effectively repelled invasions, but once the crises were over, idleness prevailed.

One reason why democratic governments seem to endure is that they achieve a balance between the organizing principles of an ordered system and the adaptability of a chaotic system. The chaotic elements within the government result in new, emergent structures and insights, whereas the ordered elements provide for effective, long-term planning.

In any stable society, there is a natural balance between culture and counterculture, between self-interest and altruism, between workers and slackers. Each checks the excesses of the other. If you eliminate slackers, it is like eliminating the grass the holds the soil. They help support those who fall out of the system. Ordered thinkers often want to rid society of its slackers, but you cannot keep removing those who fall behind the pace, for eventually you would have nothing left.

## EDUCATIONAL IMPLICATIONS

The principles of chaotic thinking may someday lead to significant changes in society's approach to education, which continues to favor ordered thinking. As we discussed in previous chapters, chaotic thinkers have usually had enormous difficulty fitting into our educational system, and have often been pushed out of it. They usually find structured approaches to education excessively constraining and unnatural and end up either rejecting them or being rejected by them.

At various times, there have been attempts to move away from traditional, structured approaches to education, but these have seldom had a lasting impact. For example, John Dewey, who for many years had championed the need for educational reforms, emphasized the importance of providing students with unstructured opportunities for learning and discovery and of making education a more democratic process. These ideas were explored on an experimental basis, but were seldom incorporated into the standard educational curriculum, which has remained highly structured and formalized (Paringer, 1990; Rich, 1981).

One of the problems with highly structured educational systems is that they do not allow students to become deeply involved in their subjects. Rather, they tend to encourage relatively superficial explorations of facts and ideas, like sampling appetizers. To really understand and appreciate a subject, one needs to become immersed in it, without boundaries or schedules. This is especially important with gifted children, many of whom are likely to be chaotic thinkers (Klein & Tannenbaum, 1992; Pendarvis, Howley, & Howley, 1990).

We are now witnessing some of the drawbacks of taking an assembly-line approach to education and the impact this is having on both students and teachers. In many of our colleges and universities, those who support alternative or nontraditional points of view are slowly being pushed out of the system, and this threatens the richness and diversity of academic life. Time management methods are now being foisted upon teachers in an attempt to improve their efficiency. Conceptual conformity is now encouraged, and conceptual deviance is suppressed. These developments have begun to move education from merely being more efficient to becoming almost sterilized.

In an exclusively ordered approach to education, there is a tendency to try to define what people should think, feel, or appreciate. For example, consider the common practice of telling students what they are supposed to feel when reading Shakespeare, listening to Mozart, or looking at a Leonardo da Vinci painting. Instead of allowing them to react in natural, and possibly unconventional ways, our educational system has taken the ordered viewpoint that students are supposed to have correct and predictable reactions to things. In fact, this is often seen as one of the goals of education.

Our present system also emphasizes that education is important for obtaining professional rewards later in life. Yet this may be more of a social value than a real virtue. Rather than focusing on long-term rewards, such as getting a better job or having a better future, it might be better if we taught our students that education was its own reward. The enjoyment of learning should be just as important as any long-term professional goals. When we attend only to the latter, we often denigrate education, making it seem like bad-tasting medicine that one has to swallow in order to succeed later on. By focusing more on the immediate rewards of education, we could come to value it in other, more satisfying ways.

What could be done to promote chaotic thinking in our schools? One possibility would be to hire more teachers who have broad backgrounds and experiences, not just those who have been narrowly trained within structured academic programs. Teachers who rely on ordered thinking tend to focus on the detailed structure of courses and curricula, the bureaucratic aspects of the profession, and the politics that are at work within the system. This often interferes with being effective at teaching and promoting good scholarship. Chaotic thinkers often make good teachers, not only because they tend to be open and stimulating and can bring multiple perspectives to bear on many issues and topics, but also because they tend to be less preoccupied with the political or bureaucratic features of the system.

We also could change some of the criteria we presently use to evaluate and promote teachers. For instance, we could emphasize more the impact they have on students, or the creative qualities of their ideas, and less their organizational or bureaucratic skills. Good teachers often risk losing their jobs if they are perceived as not fitting into the structure of the system, especially if they are seen as taking unconventional approaches to learning. On the other hand, mediocre teachers can often advance within the profession simply by being efficient organizers or being skilled at creating the right impressions.

This does not mean that we need to abandon our current educational practices, but merely encourage chaotic spontaneity within them. The existing structures need to be loosened up, not eliminated. As in governments, both ordered and chaotic elements are needed in order to balance structure and change. In an ideal educational environment, ordered and chaotic thinkers would coexist and benefit from each other's strengths.

## ECOLOGICAL IMPLICATIONS

Throughout this book, we have regarded ordered and chaotic thinking as distinct styles that have developed with contrasting strengths and weaknesses. We believe that these two styles reflect the interplay between ordered and chaotic situations throughout nature. Some lifeforms are better adapted for stable, enduring situations; others are better adapted for transient, changing situations. Because nature itself can vary in how much order or chaos is present at any time, this dichotomy allows for greater overall adaptability.

Consider, for example, lions versus crocodiles. Lions take an active, ordered approach to hunting. They plan their attacks, carefully stalk their prey, and then execute their kills with precise, calculated timing. Crocodiles take a more reactive, chaotic approach. They lie and wait, set perceptual traps, and utilize any opportunities that the moment provides. Both play useful roles in nature and have existed together for ages.

As a rule, chaotic behavior is exhibited more often by animals that are in danger of being pursued. They change direction in unpredictable ways, are intensely aware of what is happening at all times, and tend to be highly reactive. They might employ passive resistance, as when playing dead. They might intensify the moment, as when suddenly charging back at a pursuer. In nature as in human societies, it is often the powerless who employ chaotic methods.

The notion of "survival of the fittest" applies equally well to ordered and chaotic thinkers. In one sense, being forceful or powerful increases the chances of survival, and this is the advantage of ordered thinking. In another sense, being adaptable or flexible increases the chances of survival, and this is the advantage of chaotic thinking. Thus, survival of the fittest can work both ways, in relation to the ordered and chaotic aspects of nature.

Chaotic processes might also operate at basic genetic levels to promote the rapid evolution of new forms. For instance, the concept of *punctuated equilibrium* in modern evolutionary theory can be regarded in terms of chaotic events that promote rapid change and emergent genetic structure, which are then followed by relatively stable periods (Gould, 1982; Gould & Eldridge, 1993). Similarly, the concept of *emergenesis* has begun to explain how exceptional talents can sometimes emerge from parents having ordinary traits (Lykken, McGue, & Tellegen, 1992).

Chaotic thinkers are usually more likely to adopt an ecological point of view than ordered thinkers. They often see ordered thinkers as laying down asphalt over grassy fields, taking what is natural and trying to civilize it, structure it, control it, and improve on it in the name of idealism and progress. They tend to see them as always trying to increase the efficiency of nature, not realizing that nature's inefficiencies often exist for good reasons. It might be tempting to try to improve on a lake, or make the landscape less chaotic, but these attempts to structure nature often result in unanticipated problems and complications. Although it is often desirable or even necessary to gain some control over nature, chaotic thinkers remind us that this needs to be kept in perspective.

## CHAOTIC CONCLUSIONS

The main danger we now face is having a society that continues to be dominated by just one thinking style. A stongly ordered society has little adaptability and tends to fall apart when rapid changes occur. The more rigid it becomes, the more easily it can then be shattered. On the other hand, in a society that has no order, order must eventually be imposed, otherwise that society cannot truly develop or endure. It is thus essential that we accept and embrace both ordered and chaotic thinking.

Chaotic thinkers often start new movements in many fields, seizing the moment and responding to impending changes. This has frequently happened, for example, in art, religion, politics, and even science. These chaotic movements typically promote widespread enlightenment, such as that which occurred during the romantic period (Garraty & Gay, 1972). However, ordered thinkers are usually the ones who organize those movements and provide the structures that maintain them over time. They give stability and endurance to the chaotic insights. Again, this reflects the natural, symbiotic relation between the two thinking styles.

Perhaps the most immediate benefit of promoting a mutual acceptance of ordered and chaotic thinking is that it can help people to discover that being in uncertain situations need not be terrifying, and that being in structured situations need not be inhibiting. We can learn to adapt to unexpected changes without having to abandon our planning and organizing skills. Similarly, we can learn that our ability to enjoy the moment need not disappear if we commit ourselves to planning for the future.

# References

Abrahams, F. D., & Gilgen, A. R. (Eds.). (1994). *Chaos theory in psychology*. Westport, CT: Greenwood.

Adams, J. L. (1974). *Conceptual blockbusting*. Stanford, CA: Stanford Alumni Association.

Adams, J. M. (1983). *Career change: A planning book*. New York: McGraw-Hill.

Anderson, J. R. (1983). *The architecture of cognition*. Cambridge, MA: Harvard University Press.

Anderson, J. R. (1990). *Cognitive psychology and its implications*. New York: Freeman.

Atkinson, R. C., & Shiffrin, R. M. (1968). Human memory: A proposed system and its control processes. In K. W. Spence & J. T. Spence (Eds.), *The psychology of learning and motivation: Advances in research and theory* (Vol. 2, pp. 89–195). New York: Academic.

Babcock, C. R. (1988). *Essential Freud*. New York: Blackwell.

Bailey, F. L. (1971). *The defense never rests*. New York: Stein and Day.

Bailey, F. L. (1982). *To be a trial lawyer*. Marshfield, MA: Telshare.

Bartlett, F. C. (1932). *Remembering*. Cambridge: Cambridge University Press.

Beard, M. L., & McGahey, M. J. (1983). *Alternative careers for teachers*. New York: Arco.

Bolen, J. S. (1979). *The Tao of psychology: Synchronicity and the self*. San Francisco: Harper & Row.

Bolles, R. N. (1994). *What color is your parachute?: A practical manual for job-hunters and career changers*. Berkeley, CA: Ten Speed Press.

Bower, G. H. (1970). Organizational factors in memory. *Cognitive Psychology, 1*, 18–46.

Bowers, K. S., Regehr, G., Balthazard, C., & Parker, K. (1990). Intuition in the context of discovery. *Cognitive Psychology, 22*, 72–109.

Boyer, W. H. (1984). *America's future: Transition to the 21st century*. New York: Praeger.

Brome, V. (1978). *Jung*. New York: Antheneum.

Brown, J. M. (1977). *Ghandi and civil disobedience: The Mahatma in Indian politics, 1928–34*. Cambridge: Cambridge University Press.

Brown, T., & Morgan, B. (1984). *Tom Brown's field guide to city and suburban survival*. New York: Berkeley.

Bryans, P. (1984). *Organizational theory: Core business program*. New York: Facts on File Inc.

Butz, M. R. (1993). Practical applications from chaos theory to the psychotherapeutic process, a basic consideration of dynamics. *Psychological Reports, 73*, 543–554.

Cameron, D. (1980). *How to survive being committed to a mental hospital: A true story*. New York: Vantage.

Chaliand, G. (1982). *Guerrilla strategies: An historical anthology from the Long March to Afghanistan*. Berkeley: University of California Press.

Clark, R. W. (1971). *Einstein: The life and times*. New York: World Publishing Company.

Cooper, R. G. (1986). *Winning at new products*. Reading, MA: Addison-Wesley.

Costa, P. T., & McCrae, R. R. (1988). From catalogue to classfication: Murray's needs and the five-factor model. *Journal of Personality and Social Psychology, 55*, 258–265.

Cousins, N. (1979). *Anatomy of an illness as perceived by the patient.* New York: Norton.

Craik, F. I. M., & Lockhart, R. S. (1972). Levels of processing: A framework for memory research. *Journal of Verbal Learning and Verbal Behavior, 11*, 671–684.

Craik. F. I. M., & Tulving, E. (1975). Depth of processing and the retention of words in episodic memory. *Journal of Experimental Psychology: General, 104*, 268–294.

Curtis, R. C. (1989). *Self-defeating behaviors: Experimental research, clinical impressions, and practical implications.* New York: Plenum.

de Bono. E. (1975). *New think: The use of lateral thinking in the generation of new ideas.* New York: Basic Books.

Deming, W. E. (1982). *Quality, productivity, and competitive position.* Cambridge, MA: MIT Press.

Doyle, A. C. (1930). *The complete Sherlock Holmes.* Garden City, NY: Doubleday.

Dunnette. M. D., & Hough, L. M. (1990). *Handbook of industrial and organizational psychology.* Palo Alto, CA: Consulting Psychologists Press.

Edwards, B. (1986). *Drawing on the artist within: A guide to innovation, invention, imagination, and creativity.* New York: Simon & Schuster.

Egan. G. (1986). *The skilled helper: A systematic approach to effective helping.* Monterey, CA: Brooks/Cole.

Ekman, P. (1982). *Emotion in the human face.* Cambridge: Cambridge University Press.

Elbow, P. (1981). *Writing without teachers.* London: Oxford University Press.

Elkind. D. (1988). *The hurried child: Growing up too fast too soon.* Reading, MA: Addison-Wesley.

Ellenberger, H. F. (1970). *The discovery of the unconscious: The history and evolution of dynamic psychiatry.* New York: Basic Books.

Ellis, A., & Harper, R. A. (1975). *A new guide to rational living.* Hollywood, CA: Wilshire.

Ellis, A., & Whiteley, J. M. (1979). *Theory and empirical foundations of rational-emotive therapy.* Monterey, CA: Brooks/Cole.

Eysenck, H. J., & Eysenck, M. W. (1985). *Personality and individual differences: A natural science approach.* New York: Plenum.

Fagan, J. (1970). *Gestalt therapy now: Theory, techniques, applications.* Palo Alto, CA: Science and Behavior Books.

Falwell. G. F. (1974). *The counselor's handbook.* New York: Intext Educational Publishers.

Fink, S. (1986). *Crisis management: Planning for the inevitable.* New York: American Management Association.

Finke, R. A. (1989). *Principles of mental imagery.* Cambridge, MA: MIT Press.

Finke, R. A. (1990). *Creative imagery: Discoveries and inventions in visualization.* Hillsdale, NJ: Lawrence Erlbaum Associates.

Finke, R. A. (1995). Creative realism. In S. M. Smith, T. B. Ward, & R. A. Finke (Eds.), *The creative cognition approach* (pp. 303–326). Cambridge, MA: MIT Press.

Finke, R. A., Ward, T. B., & Smith, S. M. (1992). *Creative cognition: Theory, research, and applications.* Cambridge, MA: MIT Press.

Fiske, S. T., & Taylor, S. E. (1984). *Social cognition.* New York: Random House.

Forbes. E. (1967). *Thayer's life of Beethoven.* Princeton, NJ: Princeton University Press.

Frank, P. (1947). *Einstein: His life and times.* New York: Knopf.

Frankl, V. E. (1969). *The doctor and the soul.* New York: Bantam.

Freeman, A. M. (1993). *Cognitive therapy of suicidal behavior: Manual for treatment.* New York: Springer.

French, A. P. (Ed.). (1979). *Einstein: A centenary volume.* Cambridge, MA: Harvard University Press.

Freyd, J. J. (1983). Shareability: The social psychology of epistemology. *Cognitive Science, 7*, 191–210.

Freyd, J. J. (1987). Dynamic mental representations. *Psychological Review, 94*, 427–438.

Freyd, J. J., & Finke, R. A. (1984). Representational momentum. *Journal of Experimental Psychology: Learning, Memory, and Cognition, 10*, 126–132.

Fuoss, D. E., & Troppmann, R. (1981). *Effective coaching: A psychological approach.* New York: Wiley.

Gardner, M. (1981). *Science: Good, bad, and bogus.* Buffalo, NY: Prometheus.

Garraty, J. A., & Gay, P. (Eds.). (1972). *The Columbia history of the world.* New York: Harper & Row.

Gartner, A., & Riessman, F. (1984). *The self-help revolution.* New York: Human Sciences Press.

Gentner, D., & Stevens, A. L. (1983). *Mental models.* Hillsdale, NJ: Lawrence Erlbaum Associates.

Getzels, J. W., & Csikszentmihalyi, M. (1976). *The creative vision: A longitudinal study of problem finding in art.* New York: Wiley.

Ghandi, M. (1951). *Non-violent resistance.* New York: Schocken Books.

Ghiselin, B. (1952). *The creative process.* Berkeley, CA: University of California Press.

Gibson, J. J. (1966). *The senses considered as perceptual systems.* Boston: Houghton Mifflin.

Gibson, J. J. (1979). *The ecological approach to visual perception.* Boston: Houghton Mifflin.

Gick, M. L., & Holyoak, K. J. (1980). Analogical problem solving. *Cognitive Psychology, 12,* 306–355.

Glass, L. (1992). *He says, she says: Closing the communication gap between the sexes.* New York: Putnam.

Gleick, J. (1987). *Chaos: Making of a new science.* New York: Viking.

Glucksberg, S., & Keyser, B. (1990). Understanding metaphorical comparisons: Beyond similarity. *Psychological Review, 97,* 3–18.

Goerner, S. J. (1994). *Chaos and the evolving ecological universe.* New York: Gordon and Breach.

Goldberg, L. R. (1990). An alternative "description of personality": The big-five factor structure. *Journal of Personality and Social Psychology, 59,* 1216–1229.

Goldberg, R. (1988). *Performance art: From futurism to the present.* New York: Abrams.

Gooding, M. (Ed.). (1993). *Surrealist games.* Boston: Shambala/Redstone.

Gordon, W. (1961). *Synectics: The development of creative capacity.* New York: Harper & Row.

Gould, S. J. (1982). Darwinism and the expansion of evolutionary theory. *Science, 216,* 380–387.

Gould, S. J., & Eldredge, N. (1993). Punctuated equilibrium comes of age. *Nature, 366,* 223–227.

Grey, L. (1994). *How to win a local election: A complete step-by-step guide.* New York: Evans.

Guilford, J. P. (1968). *Intelligence, creativity, and their educational implications.* San Diego: Knapp.

Haley, J. (1973). *Uncommon therapy: The psychiatric techniques of Milton H. Erickson, M.D.* New York: Norton.

Haley, J. (1985). *Conversations with Milton H. Erickson, M.D.* New York: Triangle Press.

Hayano, D. M. (1982). *Poker faces: The life and work of professional card players.* Berkeley: University of California Press.

Hayes, J. R. (1981). *The complete problem solver.* Philadelphia: Franklin Institute Press.

Hilgard, E. R. (1977). *Divided consciousness: Multiple controls in human thought and action.* New York: Wiley-Interscience.

Hofer, E. (1951). *The true believer.* New York: Harper & Row.

Holland, J. H., Holyoak, K. J., Nisbett, R. E., & Thagard, P. R. (1986). *Induction: Processes of inference, learning, and discovery.* Cambridge, MA: MIT Press.

Holtzman, R., & Levin, L. (1973). *Holtzman's basketball: Winning strategies and tactics.* New York: Macmillan.

Holyoak, K. J., & Thagard, P. (1995). *Mental leaps: Analogy in creative thought.* Cambridge, MA: MIT Press.

Ivey, A. E., Ivey, M. B., & Simek-Downing, L. (1987). *Counseling and psychotherapy: Integrating skills, theory, and practice.* Englewood Cliffs, NJ: Prentice-Hall.

James, W. (1907). *Pragmatism.* New York: Longmans, Green, & Co.

Janis, I. L. (1972). *Victims of groupthink.* Boston: Houghton Mifflin.

John, O. P. (1990). The "Big Five" factor taxonomy: Dimensions of personality in the natural language and in questionnaires. In L. A. Pervin (Ed.), *Handbook of personality: Theory and research* (pp. 66–100). New York: Guilford Press.

Johnson, J. A. (1994). *Introduction to the foundations of American education.* Boston: Allyn and Bacon.

Johnson. M. K., & Raye, C. L. (1981). Reality monitoring. *Psychological Review, 88,* 67–85.

Joyce. J. (1939). *Finnegan's wake.* New York: Viking.

Jung, C. G. (1964). *Man and his symbols.* Garden City, NY: Doubleday.

Jung, C. G. (1971). *Psychological types.* Princeton: Princeton University Press.

Kafka, F. (1937). *The trial.* New York: Knopf.

Kafka, F. (1954). *The castle.* New York: Knopf.

Katz, D. (1978). *The social psychology of organizations.* New York: Wiley.

Katz, D., Kahn, R. L., & Adams, J. S. (1980). *The study of organizations.* San Fransicso: Jossey-Bass.

Keefe. C.. Harte, T. B., & Norton, L. E. (1982). *Introduction to debate.* New York: Macmillan.

Keirsey, D., & Bates, M. (1984). *Please understand me: Character and temperament types.* Del Mar, CA: Prometheus.

Kerouac. J. (1957). *On the road.* New York: Buccaneer Books.

Klein, P. S., & Tannenbaum, A. J. (1992). *To be young and gifted.* Norwood, NJ: Ablex.

Koestler, A. (1964). *The act of creation.* New York: Macmillan.

Kohler. W. (1947). *Gestalt psychology.* New York: Mentor/Liveright.

Kosslyn. S. M. (1980). *Image and mind.* Cambridge, MA: Harvard University Press.

Kuhn, T. S. (1970). *The structure of scientific revolutions.* Chicago: University of Chicago Press.

Langer, E. J. (1989). *Mindfulness.* New York: Addison-Wesley.

Laqueur, W. (1976). *Guerrilla: A historical and critical study.* Boston: Little, Brown.

Lea, G. (1975). Chronometric analysis of the method of loci. *Journal of Experimental Psychology: Human Perception and Performance, 1,* 95–104.

Leader, Z. (1991). *Writer's block.* Baltimore: Johns Hopkins University Press.

Lee, R. E., & Lee, K. K. (1989). *Arguing persuasively.* New York: Longman.

Lehman, D. (1991). *Signs of the times: Deconstruction and the fall of Paul de Man.* New York: Poseidon.

Levine, M. (1987). *Effective problem solving.* Englewood Cliffs, NJ: Prentice-Hall.

Lewin, R. (1992). *Complexity: Life at the edge of chaos.* New York: Macmillan.

Lindsay, P. H., & Norman, D. A. (1977). *Human information processing.* New York: Academic Press.

Loftus, E. F. (1979). *Eyewitness testimony.* Cambridge, MA: Harvard University Press.

Lykken, D. T., McGue, M., & Tellegen, A. (1992). Emergenesis: Genetic traits that may not run in families. *American Psychologist, 47,* 1565–1577.

Malone, M. (1977). *Psychetypes.* New York: Dutton.

Mandell, M. I. (1984). *Advertising.* Englewood Cliffs, NJ: Prentice-Hall.

Martindale, C. (1991). *Cognitive psychology: A neural-network approach.* Pacific Grove, CA: Brooks/Cole.

Maurer, D. (1974). *The American confidence man.* Springfield, IL: Charles Thomas.

May, R. (1969). *Existential psychology.* New York: Random House.

McClelland, J. L., & Rumelhart, D. E. (1981). An interactive model of context effects in letter perception: I. An account of basic findings. *Psychological Review, 88,* 375–407.

McClelland, J. L., & Rumelhart, D. E. (1986). *Parallel distributed processing: Explorations in the microstructure of cognition.* Cambridge, MA: MIT Press.

McCown, W., Johnson, J., & Shure, M. (in press). *The impulsive client: Theory, research, and practice.* Washington, DC: American Psychological Association.

McKirahan, R. D. (1978). *Plato and Socrates: A comprehensive biography.* New York: Garland.

McLeod, J., & Cropley, A. (1989). *Fostering academic excellence.* New York: Pergamon.

Mednick. S. A. (1962). The associative basis of the creative process. *Psychological Review, 69,* 220–232.

Mehrabian, A. (1972). *Nonverbal communication.* Hawthorne, NY: Aldine-Atherton.

Melder, K. E. (1992). *Hail to the condidate: Presidential campaigns from banners to broadcasts.* Washington, DC: Smithsonian Institution Press.

Mesthene, E. G. (1970). *Technological change: Its impact on man and society.* Cambridge, MA: Cambridge University Press.

Miller. G. A., Galanter, E., & Pribram, K. H. (1960). *Plans and the structure of behavior.* New York: Holt, Rinehart, and Winston.

Mischel. W. (1986). *Introduction to personality.* New York: Holt, Rinehart, and Winston.

Monaghan. J. (1959). *Custer: The life of General George Armstrong Custer.* Boston: Little, Brown.

Myers, I. (1962). *The Myers–Briggs type indicator.* Palo Alto, CA: Consulting Psychologists Press.

Neisser. U. (1967). *Cognitive psychology.* Englewood Cliffs, NJ: Prentice-Hall.

Nierenberg, G. I. (1973). *Fundamentals of negotiating.* New York: Hawthorn.

Nisbett, R. E., & Ross, L. (1980). *Human inference: Strategies and shortcomings of social judgment.* Englewood Cliffs, NJ: Prentice-Hall.

Oakley. J. (1989). *Rasputin: Rascal master.* New York: St. Martin's Press.

Ortony, A. (1979). Beyond literal similarity. *Psychological Review, 86,* 161–180.

Osborn. A. (1953). *Applied imagination.* New York: Charles Scribner's Sons.

Paringer. W. A. (1990). *John Dewey and the paradox of liberal reform.* Albany, NY: State University of New York Press.

Parsons, R. D., & Wicks, R. J. (1983). *Passive-aggressiveness, theory and practice.* New York: Brunner/Mazel.

Pendarvis. E. D., Howley, A., & Howley, C. B. (1990). *The abilities of gifted children.* Englewood Cliffs, NJ: Prentice-Hall.

Perkins, D. N. (1981). *The mind's best work.* Cambridge, MA: Harvard University Press.

Perls, F. (1969). *Gestalt psychology verbatim.* Lafayette, CA: Real People Press.

Peters, T. (1992). *Liberation management: Necessary disorganization for the nanosecond nineties.* New York: Knopf.

Pirsig, R. (1974). *Zen and the art of motorcycle maintenance.* New York: Bantam.

Popper, K. R. (1959). *The logic of scientific discovery.* New York: Basic Books.

Prigogine, I., & Stengers, I. (1984). *Order out of chaos: Man's new dialogue with nature.* New York: Bantam.

Pylyshyn, Z. W. (1973). What the mind's eye tells the mind's brain: A critque of mental imagery. *Psychological Bulletin, 80,* 1–24.

Rachman, S. (1980). *Obsessions and compulsions.* Englewood Cliffs, NJ: Prentice-Hall.

Raiffa, H. (1982). *The art and science of negotiation.* Cambridge, MA: Harvard University Press.

Rand, A. (1968). *The fountainhead.* Indianapolis: Bobbs-Merrill.

Reed, S. K. (1982). *Cognition: Theory and applications.* Monterey, CA: Brooks/Cole.

Rich, J. M. (1981). *Innovations in education: Reformers and their critics.* Boston: Allyn and Bacon.

Rock, I. (1983). *The logic of perception.* Cambridge, MA: MIT Press.

Rogers, C. R. (1951). *Client-centered therapy.* Boston: Houghton Mifflin.

Rosch. E., & Mervis, C. B. (1975). Family resemblances: Studies in the internal structure of categories. *Cognitive Psychology, 7,* 573–605.

Rosenhan, D. L. (1973). On being sane in insane places. *Science, 179,* 250–258.

Royal, R. F., & Schutt, S. R. (1976). *The gentle art of interviewing and interrogation: A professional manual and guide.* Englewood Cliffs, NJ: Prentice-Hall.

Rubin, J. Z., & Brown, B. R. (1975). *The social psychology of bargaining and negotiation.* New York: Academic Press.

Sandage. C. H., Fryburger, V. R., & Rotzoll, K. B. (1983). *Advertising theory and practice.* Homewood, IL: Irwin.

Sandrow, N. (1972). *Surrealism: Theater, arts, ideas.* New York: Harper & Row.

Schank. R. C., & Abelson, R. (1977). *Scripts, plans, goals, and understanding.* Hillsdale, NJ: Lawrence Erlbaum Associates.

Schooler, J. W., & Melcher, J. (1995). The ineffability of insight. In S. M. Smith, T. B. Ward, & R. A. Finke (Eds.), *The creative cognition approach* (pp. 97–133). Cambridge, MA: MIT Press.

Shapiro, D. (1981). *Autonomy and rigid character.* New York: Basic Books.

Shepard, R. N. (1978). Externalization of mental images and the act of creation. In B. S. Randhawa & W. E. Coffman (Eds.), *Visual learning, thinking, and communication* (pp. 133–189). New York: Academic Press.

Simpson, D. W. (1981). *Winning elections: A handbook in participatory politics.* Chicago: Swallow Press.

Skinner, B. F. (1953). *Science and human behavior.* New York: Macmillan.

Skocpol, T. (1979). *States and social revolutions: A comparative analysis of France, Russia, and China.* Cambridge: Cambridge University Press.

Smith, E. E., & Medin, D. L. (1981). *Categories and concepts.* Cambridge, MA: Harvard University Press.

Smith, R. L. (1980). *Ecology and field biology.* New York: Harper & Row.

Smith, S. M. (1995). Fixation, incubation, and insight in memory and creative thinking. In S. M. Smith, T. B. Ward, & R. A. Finke (Eds.), *The creative cognition approach* (pp. 135–156). Cambridge, MA: MIT Press.

Smith, S. M., & Blankenship, S. E. (1991). Incubation and the persistence of fixation in problem solving. *American Journal of Psychology, 104,* 61–87.

Smith, S. M., Ward, T. B., & Schumacher, J. S. (1993). Constraining effects of examples in a creative generation task. *Memory and Cognition, 21,* 837–845.

Snow, C. P. (1964). *The two cultures.* Cambridge: Cambridge University Press.

Springer, S. P., & Deutsch, G. (1981). *Left brain, right brain.* San Francisco: Freeman.

Stebbing, L. S. (1959). *Thinking to some purpose.* Baltimore: Penguin Books.

Sternberg, R. J., & Davidson, J. E. (Eds.). (1995). *The nature of insight.* Cambridge, MA: MIT Press.

Tellegen, A., & Atkinson, G. (1974). Openness to absorption and self-altering experiences ("absorption"), a trait related to hypnotic susceptibility. *Journal of Abnormal Psychology, 83,* 268–277.

Thagard, P. (1992). *Conceptual revolutions.* Princeton, NJ: Princeton University Press.

Theroux, P. (1982). *The mosquito coast.* Boston: Houghton Mifflin.

Thompson, H. S. (1982). *Fear and loathing in Las Vegas: A savage journey to the heart of the American dream.* New York: Warner Books.

Thompson, J. M. (1962). *Robespierre and the French revolution.* New York: Collier.

Toffler, A. (1970). *Future shock.* New York: Random House.

Tourangeau, R., & Rips, L. (1991). Interpreting and appreciating metaphors. *Journal of Memory and Language, 30,* 452–472.

University Associates. (1980). *Behavioral science and the manager's role.* San Diego, CA: Author.

Urban, G. L., & Hauser, J. R. (1993). *Design and marketing of new products.* Englewood Cliffs, NJ: Prentice-Hall.

Van Doren, C. (1991). *A history of knowledge: Past, present, and future.* New York: Ballantine Books.

Waldrop, M. M. (1992). *Complexity: The emerging science at the edge of order.* New York: Simon and Schuster.

Ward, T. B. (in press). Structured imagination: The role of conceptual structure in exemplar generation. *Cognitive Psychology.*

Wason, P. C., & Johnson-Laird, P. N. (1972). *Psychology of reasoning: Structure and content.* Cambridge, MA: Harvard University Press.

Weiss, G. (1993). *Hyperactive children grown up: ADHD in children, adolescents, and adults.* New York: Guilford.

West, A. (1992). *Innovation strategy.* New York: Prentice-Hall.

Wickelgren, W. A. (1974). *How to solve problems.* San Francisco: Freeman.

Witkin, H. A. (1981). *Cognitive styles, essence and origins: Field dependence and field independence.* New York: International Universities Press.

Wolfe, T. (1968). *The electric Kool-Aid acid test.* New York: Bantam.

Wolfe, T. (1979). *The painted word.* New York: Bantam.

Yates, F. A. (1966). *The art of memory.* Chicago: University of Chicago Press.

# Author Index

# Subject Index

networks in, 6
ordered approaches to, 3, 6, 17, 64, 185–187
organization of, 64, 185–186
parallel processing in, 6
plans in, 6, 64
Cognitive science, 185–187
Cognitive styles, 1, 17–19, 187–190, 198–199
Communication, *see also* Conversation
    body language in, 64, 114–116
    failures in, 61, 114–116, 162, 172, 190
    improving, 61–62, 69–70, 114–116
    metaphors in, 37, 85, 129, 171
    point of view in, 61–62, 114, 116
    sensitivity in, 64
Complexity, *See* Chaotic techniques, increasing
    complexity; Chaotic thinking, complexity
    of; Games, complexity of
Compromise, 81, 105
Compulsive behavior, 26–27, 173
Confidence games, *see also* Crimes; Games.
    chaotic strategies in, 93, 128, 136–137
    ordered strategies in, 93, 136–137
    perceptual traps in, 93, 128
Confinement, *see also* Prison
    chaotic strategies for surviving, 145–146
    ordered strategies for surviving, 41, 145–146
Confirmation bias, 95, 194
Conscientiousness, 187–188
Context, *see* Chaotic thinking, context in; Ordered
    thinking, context in
Convergent thinking, 187
Conversations, *see also* Communication
    controlling, 32, 67, 77, 114, 127
    disrupting, 29, 77, 114
    emergent patterns in, 11, 25, 32, 126–127
    meaning in, 57, 64, 127, 166
    metaphors in, 85
    rules for, 115, 127
    structuring, 32, 41, 67, 114–115, 186
    unstructuring, 25, 29, 56, 116, 127
Corporations, *see also* Business; Organizations
    bankruptcy in, 16, 191
    competition among, 98
    flexibility in, 16, 51, 83, 191
    management of, 4, 30, 83
    structure in, 13, 191–192
Counseling, *see* Psychotherapy
Coups, *see* Riots
Creative Realism, *see also* Creativity
    achieving, 177–179
    in art, 177–179
    endurance in, 178–179

in films, 178
meaning in, 177–179
order in, 177–179
in science, 177–178
Creativity, *see also* Chaotic thinkers, creativity of;
    Creative Realism; Ordered thinkers, crea-
    tivity of
combinational play in, 48–49, 183, 185
enhancing, 2, 29–31, 44, 46–48, 58–59, 62, 68,
    73–75, 82, 85–86, 94, 108, 117, 139,
    148, 158, 177–179, 192, 195, 198
form vs. function in, 49, 185–186
inhibiting, 46–48, 96, 108, 168, 177, 192
intentional, 49, 162
spontaneous, 13, 18, 46, 140, 164, 167, 169
structured, 49, 178–179, 185
theories of, 17, 49
unstructured, 33, 178, 186
Crimes, *see also* Confidence games; Criminals
avoiding, 134–135
discouraging, 134–138
perceptual traps in, 137
punishing, 102
solving, 33, 55, 62–63, 70, 95
Criminals, *see also* Crimes
chaotic, 136–137, 151
establishing guilt of, 55
ordered, 136–137
overconfidence in, 137
Crises, *see also* Emergencies
at work, 138–139
avoiding, 134
creating, 46, 54–55, 59, 62, 84, 139
dealing with, 1, 3–5, 9, 18, 23–24, 34, 38,
    44–46, 62, 68, 85, 132–134, 138–141,
    154–155, 157, 159–160, 167,
    170–171, 192, 196
economic, 45, 139–141
emotional qualities of, 4, 15, 45–46, 54, 62,
    133–135
health, 46, 162
surviving, 17, 44–46, 139–141
unpredictibility of, 7, 15, 45, 140
Cultural revolution, 7

**D**

Daredevils, 27
Daydreaming, 67
Debate, *see also* Negotiation
avoiding, 37, 76, 123
chaotic strategies for, 99–101
logic of, 99–101